Women's Autobiography

Women's Autobiography

Essays in Criticism

Edited with an Introduction by

ESTELLE C. JELINEK

Bloomington
INDIANA UNIVERSITY PRESS
London

To my students—for their support, their innovative thinking, and, above all, their enthusiasm

First Midland Book Edition 1980
Copyright © 1980 by Indiana University Press

Manufactured in the United States of America
Library of Congress Cataloging in Publication Data
Main entry under title:
Women's autobiography.
Includes bibliographical references.
1. Autobiography—Women authors—Addresses, essays, lectures. I. Jelinek, Estelle C.
CT25.W6   810'.9'9287   79–2600
ISBN 0–253–19193–9   1 2 3 4 5 84 83 82 81 80
0–253–20241–8 pbk.

Acknowledgments

"Towards a Theory of Form in Feminist Autobiography: Kate Millett's *Flying* and *Sita*; Maxine Hong Kingston's *The Woman Warrior*" by Suzanne Juhasz first appeared in a slightly different version in *International Journal of Women's Studies*, vol. 2, no. 1, 1979. Copyright © Eden Press Women's Publications, Inc., Montreal. By permission.

"Anaïs Nin's *Diary* in Context" by Lynn Z. Bloom and Orlee Holder originally appeared in *Mosaic: A Journal for the Comparative Study of Literature and Ideas*, published by The University of Manitoba Press, vol. XI, no. 2 (January 1978), pp. 191–202. By permission.

"The Lady's Not for Spurning: Kate Millett and the Critics" by Annette Kolodny was first printed in *Contemporary Literature*, vol. 17, no. 4, pp. 541–62. Copyright © 1976 by the Board of Regents of the University of Wisconsin System. By permission.

CONTENTS

Smith apply the thinking of Jacques Lacan to Hellman's memoirs, arguing that their "latent content" makes the memoir as self-revelatory and, therefore, as legitimate a form as autobiography proper. Using an archetypal approach, Demetrakopoulos lauds the matrilinearism in four modern autobiographies, the result of a new self-consciousness among women in the last decade.

Some of the critics who emphasize the formal aspects of the genre touch on the differences they find between men's and women's autobiographies. In my introductory essay, I explore the differences between the sexes in terms of both the content and the style of the autobiographies. Assuming that women's autobiographies share certain distinct characteristics, Bloom and Holder contend that diaries, especially Nin's, in exhibiting these characteristics, deserve a critical place in the women's autobiographical tradition. Finally, Juhasz and Kolodny describe some of the innovative forms women are creating to fit their new awareness of themselves, rejecting the structures men have devised as inappropriate to the "process" type of lives women lead.

In choosing these essays, my overall intention was to gather critiques that viewed autobiographies primarily as literary works. Therefore, in addition to representing a sampling of the new flux of criticism being written today on women's autobiography, these essays fill gaps in the history and development of the genre itself and draw attention to the neglected contributions by women to the autobiographical mode. While some of the essays reflect the critics' feminist sympathies, the anthology as a whole supports no particular philosophy, and all the essays are written in the spirit of academic objectivity, describing rather than prescribing. As one can see from the table of contents, most of the critics working on women's autobiography are women. The large proportion of essays concerned with interpreting the self-image expressed in the autobiographies and with defining the new forms by women reflects the different interest and, even, vision of female critics today compared with traditional autobiographical criticism.

It has been gratifying to read all the essays sent to me and to discover that the critics are drawing similar conclusions about the form and content of women's autobiography, substantiating our contention that there is a literary tradition in which women write autobiography that is different from that by men. Even the few papers that were submitted on Continental autobiographers described similar characteristics, for example, the tendency of women to write in discontinuous forms and to emphasize the personal over the professional. I think it will be as enlightening to the contributors as it will be to the readers of this collection to compare the overlapping conclusions and to discover possible explanations for what may have only been described. Also, I hope that critics and readers alike will see from these representative essays that women's autobiographical criticism is a substantial literary discipline and one which has done much to give legitimacy and status to many excellent and innovative autobiographies by women that have been ignored or excluded from the critical canon. I hope this collection will encourage and inspire other students of women's autobiography to contribute their own criticism to this renaissance in the study of the genre of autobiography.

Estelle C. Jelinek

PREFACE

The idea for this collection came to me in 1976 when I was writing my dissertation on the tradition of women's autobiography. I found practically no criticism on women's autobiographies, except for that on Gertrude Stein's, and so had no way of comparing ideas with other critics to see if they were coming to the same or different conclusions as I had, working alone. I wrote that dissertation without the benefit of any feedback but vowed to encourage such criticism by compiling this collection so that those working in the field could communicate with one another and individual articles would not be lost in journals in disparate places but seen as a whole and as a distinct school of criticism.

The contents of this collection—fourteen essays (I could easily have included many more if the exigencies of publishing had permitted)— represent a cross-section of the criticism being written today on women's autobiographies. The authors treated also represent those most often read in courses in women's autobiography and in genre courses, as well as outside the university. All the essays treat autobiographies by English-speaking women, with far more by American autobiographers than British. Most of the essays treat individual writers, but several cover a number of autobiographies during a given historical period. Four of the essays deal with autobiographies before the twentieth century, ten cover predominantly the twentieth. Of the latter, the greatest interest is in those life studies published during the last decade. The critiques of autobiographies before the nineteenth century discuss writers who had no professions as such, and some of the essays that deal with the nineteenth and early twentieth centuries treat female autobiographers who were active in politics or other non-literary occupations, but most of the autobiographers analyzed here are creative writers.

Eight of the essays are concerned with describing or interpreting the contents of the autobiographies, the emphasis being on the self-image of the autobiographers, and six concentrate on more formal aspects. The contemporary autobiographies are the ones usually subjected to formal analysis; thus the essays in the collection are arranged more or less chronologically as well as according to substantive and formal intentions. Of those which deal with the writers' self-image, the methodologies include the historical, the sociological, the psychological, and the ethnic.

Pomerleau probes secular autobiographies of this emerging genre during the seventeenth and eighteenth centuries in England and describes the women's growing dissatisfaction with their dependent status. Without opportunities in professions, many women turned to religion as a means of escape from the confinement of their defined roles, and Edkins describes how in America such women chose a religious life to gain acceptance by the community while at the same time acquiring some degree of independence. Winston and Spacks cover autobiographers in both England and America from the late nineteenth century to the mid-twentieth, but come to different conclusions about the self-image of women during this time. Spacks attributes the low self-image she finds in five autobiographies by politically successful women to an unconscious repression of self. Winston, critiquing different autobiographies than Spacks, sees a progression from a low self-image before 1920 to a high one after the second quarter of the century as social changes gave a more affirmative nod to professional women. Both Myers' interpretation of Martineau's autobiography and my essay on Stanton's assume a high self-image in the autobiographer, both attributing any toning down of self-image to a conscious autobiographical intention. Blackburn's analysis of the self-image of contemporary black autobiographers demonstrates the use of the genre to investigate and affirm a black female identity.

In the latter essays which concentrate on formal aspects of the genre, the approaches include the rhetorical, the poststructuralist, and the Jungian. Using a formalistic or New Critical approach, Breslin analyzes the aesthetic problems of Stein's "no-identity" autobiography and explores her manipulation and defiance of the genre. Billson and

1.

Introduction:
Women's Autobiography
and the Male Tradition

ESTELLE C. JELINEK

It has only been since World War II, when the formal analysis of all branches of literature flourished, that autobiography began receiving consideration as a literary genre worthy of serious critical study. The earlier history of autobiographical criticism was characterized by its concentration exclusively on content and on the morality of the autobiographers themselves. One pioneering study before the First World War was Georg Misch's *History of Autobiography in Antiquity* (1907), in which he traced the growth of the concept of individuality from the self-presentations of Egyptian inscriptions through Greek love lyrics and Roman orations to its culmination, according to Misch, in Augustine's *Confessions*. In another early work, *Autobiography: A Critical and Comparative Study* (1909), Anna Burr concentrated on French memoirs and British Quaker journals of the seventeenth and eighteenth centuries, which, for the most part, she rated according to the seriousness, sincerity, and high moral character of their authors.

Not until the 1930s, with the publication of a large number of autobiographies, was there a revival of interest in their critical analysis. However, in the Misch-Burr tradition, critics discussed only the subject matter of the autobiographies and made moral judgments about their authors. They rarely saw any stylistic distinction between autobiography and biography—considering both the story of a person's life. Edgar Johnson best sums up this thirties view in his definition of biography: it includes "not only formal biography, but all kinds of autobiography—letters, journals, reminiscences—for all biography is ultimately founded in a kind of autobiography."[1] The publication after the Second World War of two bibliographies of autobiography, William Matthews' *British Autobiography: An Annotated Bibliography of British Autobiographies Published or Written Before 1951* (1955) and Louis Kaplan's *A Bibliography of American Autobiographies* (1961), provided valuable source material for many new critical works, which investigated the form of the genre but which focused primarily on classical or British and Continental autobiographies. Scholarship on American autobiography has come into its own only recently with the publication of a number of articles and books on the subject, but a full-scale formal study of American autobiography has yet to be written.

In addition, in none of these works is it even noted that there are many important autobiographies by women, and with the exception of Gertrude Stein's *Autobiography of Alice B. Toklas*, only a few are given even passing mention. For example, of the major studies on the genre, Wayne Shumaker's classic *English Autobiography* (1954) covers all the famous autobiographies—too numerous to list here—from Augustine through Yeats, with separate chapters on Mill, Trollope, and George Moore. While Shumaker's study pays respectable attention to several eighteenth-century female autobiographers, in his survey of the period up to the Second World War, he treats briefly only three nineteenth-century women—Margaret Oliphant, Harriet Martineau, and Annie Besant. Though in *Design and Truth in Autobiography* (1960) Roy Pascal discusses Teresa's *Life* in the context of classical and early post-Christian autobiographies, for the modern period he examines all the major male autobiographies and includes the twentieth-century life studies by Freud, Trotsky, Yeats, O'Casey, Collingwood, Gosse, Churchill, and Gandhi, but refers only in passing to the autobiographies by Martineau and Beatrice Webb. Robert Sayre concentrates entirely on Franklin, Adams, and James in *The Examined Self* (1965), and James Olney's *Metaphors of Self* (1972) devotes whole chapters to Montaigne, Fox, Darwin, Newman, and Eliot with not a single reference to a woman's autobiography.

Of the oft-quoted articles on the subject, Stephen Spender's discusses the autobiographies of Augustine, Rousseau, and Henry Miller; Georges Gusdorf's, those by Augustine, Cellini, Montaigne, Cardinal de Retz, Goethe, Chateaubriand, Newman, and Mill; and Stephen Shapiro's, those by Rousseau, Goethe, Gibbon, Collingwood, Freud, Darwin, and Trotsky, among many other British and Continental autobiographers, and from America—Franklin, Adams, and Henry Miller. In none of these three articles is a single woman's autobiography mentioned. Both Barrett John Mandel and James Cox refer to Stein, with Mandel examining Augustine, Rousseau, Goethe, Cowper, Wordsworth, George Bellamy, and Franklin, Twain, and Adams; and with Cox concentrating on Franklin, Thoreau, Whitman, and Adams. Francis Hart touches on Nin's dairies, but his analyses center on Gibbon, Wordsworth, George Moore, Gosse, O'Casey, Wells, T. E. Lawrence, Basil Willey, C. Day Lewis, Goethe, Gide, Sartre, and Malraux, plus a number of Americans—Hemingway, Nabokov, Dahlberg, Mailer, Claude Brown, Richard Wright, Podhoretz, and Cleaver.[2]

Even when women's autobiographies are given some scant attention in studies, social bias against the condition or the delineation of their lives seems to predominate over critical objectivity. Shumaker credits three eighteenth-century courtesan autobiographers—Laetitia Pilkington, Teresia Constantia Phillips, and Frances Anne Vane—with major innovations in the genre, yet disparages them for their moral conduct. Calling their *vies scandaleuses* "frigidly sentimental chronicles," he concludes that the

> effect of these autobiographical romances, coming on the heels of
> *Pamela* and *Clarissa*, may have been important to the development
> of a subjective emphasis. . . . If autobiography was to conquer areas
> of more subtle meaning, the reading public had to be shown that
> writers could do with their own real lives what Richardson had done
> with his fictive one. . . . Since before the publication of these three
> amorous confessions secular lives regularly ignored the feelings,
> whereas afterward they often did not, there is at least a possibility
> that three *dishonest and libertine women* did autobiography a lasting
> service. (pp. 23–24; italics mine)

Recent reviews of two autobiographical works, one Buckminster Fuller's *Synergetics* (1975), the other Kate Millett's *Flying* (1974), demonstrate the continuation of this bias to our present decade. O. B. Hardison, Jr., critiquing Fuller's work, writes,

> It is alternately brilliant and obscure, opaque and shot through with moments of poetry. What becomes clear with patience is that the virtues and the liabilities are one. . . .
>
> .   .   .   .
>
> Primary dissociation occurs in language. Words carry with themselves a vast clutter of attitudes, myths, errors, and sloppy approximations that have nothing to do with what we recognize, on reflection, as reality. Hence Fuller's Style. It is not an accident. It is as carefully and self-consciously formed as the style of James Joyce, and its purpose is similar to the purpose of poetry: to tell the truth, neither more nor less, as far as possible. Properly understood it is not English but an artificial language with—let it be admitted—all of the liabilities associated with the first version of any complex invention.[3]

With hardly a change of wording, this review could have been describing *Flying*, but typical of the ruthless attacks on that work are Louise Montague Athearn's remarks, which annihilate the intention and style of *Flying* in one devastating condemnation.

> . . . a book? No. It is the personal outpouring of a disturbed lady— albeit genius—whose eclectic life is of more interest to her than to the reader. There is no story line, no plot, no continuity. Her writing is a frantic stringing together of words without any thought for the ordinary arrangement of noun and verb. It is hard reading. . . . It is utter confusion.[4]

One critic's response to this comparison of the differing receptions to Fuller's and Millett's works was, "if both Millett and Fuller write experimental prose, but Fuller's is accepted by the general public while Millett's is not, could this be because neither Millett's work nor her life is seen as significant enough to tolerate her eccentricity?"[5]

"Insignificant," indeed, expresses the predominant attitude of most critics toward women's lives. To illustrate this difference in attitude, imagine how a sampling of women's autobiographies might be described by merely changing their authors' gender. It is not surprising that the description of Stein's *Autobiography of Alice B. Toklas* would differ little if she were, say, Arthur Stein—"the account of the unusual friendships of a literary genius in the center of European culture during the 1920s." However, when Elizabeth Cady Stanton becomes Alexander Stanton, *Eighty Years and More* becomes "the extraordinary career of one of America's leading social reformers." Mountain Wolf Man, instead of Mountain Wolf Woman (*The Autobiography of a Winnebago Indian*) becomes "the achievement of a Native American against all odds in the struggle for survival." As Jonathan McCarthy, Mary McCarthy's *Memories of a Catholic "Boyhood"* becomes "the childhood crises that formed this brilliant contemporary intellectual." When Lillian Hellman becomes Robert Hellman, *An Unfinished "Man"* becomes "the political and social forces that shaped one of America's leading playwrights." And when Kate Millett is transformed into Michael Millett, *Flying* becomes "the confessions of a contemporary Rousseau, a revolutionary thinker and artist." As men, these women's experiences would be described in heroic or exceptional terms: alienation, initiation, manhood, apotheosis, transformation, guilt, identity crises, and symbolic journeys. As women, their experiences are viewed in more conventional terms: heartbreak, anger, loneliness, motherhood, humility, confusion, and self-abnegation.

Even if we ignore the subjective biases of critics of autobiography, we find that most of their objective theories are not applicable to women's life studies. For example, James Cox argues that the history of America and the history of autobiography have developed together and that the periods of greatest productivity in autobiography correspond to important events in American history. By meticulously calculating the number of diaries and autobiographies listed in various bibliographies according to historical periods, one finds contrary evidence for women. The periods of increased diary writing by men, for example, during the Revolution and the Gold Rush, are periods of decreased productivity by women. During the Civil War period, there was an increase in autobiographies by military men, but women's autobiographies did not begin to be published in significant numbers until the end of the nineteenth century. Female diaries and autobiographies increased as literacy and educational opportunities for women improved. The peak periods of autobiographical productivity for women have been during the Progressive Era—1890 to the First World War, an era of unprecedented public service by women—and during the late 1960s and 1970s. The periods of greatest productivity for women's autobiographies have not been during revolutionary (male) times but during the high points of women's history. In *The Female Experience* (1977), historian Gerda Lerner notes:

> The periods in which basic changes occur in society and which historians commonly regard as turning points are not necessarily the same for men and women. This is not surprising when we consider that the traditional time frame in history has been derived from political history. For example, neither during or after the American Revolution nor in the age of Jackson did women share in the broadening out of opportunities and in the political democratization experienced by men. On the contrary, women in both periods experienced status loss and a restriction of their choices as to education or vocation, and had new restraints imposed upon their sexuality, at least by prescription. Thus, the traditional political and military chronology is largely irrelevant to the history of women. (pp. xxiv-xxv)

More significant are discrepancies between the critical canon and women's autobiographies on matters relating to their form and content. Despite the fact that women's life studies are excluded from the evidence from which the characteristics of the genre are drawn, it is assumed that they will either conform to them or else be disqualified as autobiographies. One may reasonably question whether including women's autobiographies in critical studies might force modifications in their definitions and theories. Or we might find that different criteria are needed to evaluate women's autobiographies, which may constitute, if not a subgenre, then an autobiographical tradition different from the male tradition.

Since "autobiography" is etymologically and in practice the story of a person's life, we shall first compare the content of women's and men's life studies before contrasting their stylistic differences. While not every autobiography may conform to the conclusions we have drawn here and readers will no doubt be able to cite examples to disprove every one of them, nonetheless, the patterns that emerge cannot be wholly ignored.

One such distinguishing pattern is related to the restrictive male view of history. The consensus among critics is that a good autobiography not only focuses on its author but also reveals his connectedness to the rest of society; it is representative of his times, a mirror of his era. This criterion is adequately supported by the many male autobiographies which concentrate on chronicling the progress of their authors' professional or intellectual lives, usually in the affairs of the world, and their life studies are for the most part success stories. Augustine's *Confessions* (400), an essential philosophical document of his time, traces the vicissitudes of his spiritual progress until his successful conversion. Rousseau's *Confessions* (1781), Gibbon's *Autobiography* (1793), and Goethe's *Poetry and Truth* (1812–31), though personal in some respects, are also success stories and can be read as histories of their eras. Mill shapes his *Autobiography* (1873) around the theme of his intellectual development, by means of which he traces the social and economic history of his century. In America the theme of progress or success in the affairs of the world is continued in Franklin's *Autobiography* (1791), a history of the stages of his rise to the career of international diplomat. Adams adheres so closely to this theme that he excludes twenty of his mature years as husband and professor in order to detail the conflict of his age between eighteenth- and nineteenth-century sensibilities. Others of such radically dissimilar origins as *Black Elk Speaks* (1932), *The Autobiography of Malcolm X* (1965), Willie Morris' *North Toward Home* (1967), and most obviously Norman Podhoretz' *Making It* (1967) stress their authors' successful professional life and concomitantly its relationship to their times, with little or a much smaller percentage allotted to their personal lives.

On the other hand, women's autobiographies rarely mirror the establishment history of their times. They emphasize to a much lesser extent the public aspects of their lives, the affairs of the world, or even their careers, and concentrate instead on their personal lives—domestic details, family difficulties, close friends, and especially people who influenced them. Agrippina's *Memoirs* from the first century A.D. depart radically from earlier autobiographical reminiscences by stressing her family members rather than the political affairs of state. In *The Book of Margery Kempe* (1436) the emphasis is on both the hostile and friendly people Kempe met on her pilgrimages rather than on her religious progress. Teresa's *Life* (1562–65) is addressed to other nuns, to convince them to persist in their faith in their visions as she had done for twenty years until she found a confessor who believed in their authenticity. In both English and American religious narratives and personal diaries of the seventeenth and eighteenth centuries, it is domestic details that comprise the larger proportion of their accounts. We recall the "lasting service" done autobiography by those eighteenth-century *vies scandaleuses* and their affective descriptions of people of the court and the men they loved. In Lucy Larcom's *A New England Girlhood* (1889) we learn little about her work in the Lawrence factory but much about her relationships with her friends and about their efforts to find personal diversions to their work. Later when she travels to the frontier to teach school, we get only glimpses of her classroom activities but detailed descriptions of the cultured people she met, to her surprise, in the supposedly barren Midwest. Even missionaries rarely write about the work in which they were engaged but emphasize the people they encountered and the hardships of frontier life. Most frontier autobiographies share this characteristic, as do the narratives of Indian captives, ex-slaves, and pioneers, which concentrate on efforts to be reconciled with their families, to acquire food, to build homes, to endure childbirth, and to survive emotionally and physically in the wilderness—all "domestic" details that Shumaker claimed were not the province of autobiography.

Even in the autobiographies by women whose professional work is their claim to fame, we find them omitting their work life, referring obliquely to their careers, or camouflaging them behind the personal aspects of their lives. Elizabeth Cady Stanton states in her preface to *Eighty Years and More*:

> The story of my private life as the wife of an earnest reformer, as an enthusiastic housekeeper, proud of my skill in every department of domestic economy, and as the mother of seven children, may amuse and benefit the reader.
>
> The incidents of my public career as a leader in the most momentous reform yet launched upon the world—the emancipation of woman—will be found in "The History of Woman Suffrage."

Though we do learn much about the history of the American woman's suffrage movement and Stanton's major role in it, she softens her political message to the predominantly female audience she is addressing with humorous and distracting anecdotes about her arduous travel adventures as a lyceum lecturer, with advice to young mothers about caring for their children, and with sketches of the many socially prominent and unsung pioneer women whom she met in America and abroad.

Stein goes to great lengths to place her concern for her work in the background by camouflaging it behind humorous anecdotes about others. Interspersed among her entertaining stories are some allusions to her actual writing, to Toklas' typing of her manuscripts, and to her failures and successes at publishing them, but the reader must struggle to piece together the progression of her literary output and to see it as a separate and important subject, which like an antiphonally recurring theme does persist until it emerges into fuller view in the last chapter.

Neither Edith Wharton's *A Backward Glance* (1934) nor Ellen Glasgow's *The Woman Within* (1954) tells us about the writing of their successful novels or of the recognition that resulted from them. *The Living of Charlotte Perkins Gilman* (1935) focuses on Gilman's struggles to overcome the severe emotional handicaps that plagued her work life in the reform movement. Hellman concentrates on portraits of friends in her three autobiographical works, and in the one chapter on the theater in *Pentimento* (1973), she tells us amusing stories about eccentric producers, directors, and actors but nothing about her writing. Carrighar is a frequently published naturalist, but she devotes her autobiography almost entirely to her depressing emotional life up to her mid-thirties, *before* her professional work began.

(She wrote *Home to the Wilderness* [1973] in her late sixties.) What Mead relates about her early field trips in *Blackberry Winter* (1972) is for the purpose of explaining the development of her interest in the maturation of children; she, like Adams, skips twenty years of her life, but they are her most active professional years—the time between the birth of her daughter and granddaughter—because her autobiographical intention is to outline the proper training of children. Even so historical an autobiography as Emma Goldman's *Living My Life* (1930) dilutes the political activities of the anarchists with portraits of their personal lives and details of her own relationship with Alexander Berkman and other close friends.

This emphasis by women on the personal, especially on other people, rather than on their work life, their professional success, or their connectedness to current political or intellectual history clearly contradicts the established criterion about the content of autobiography.

Another criterion of the autobiographical canon that is contrary to the evidence constitutes an autobiographical fallacy of the first order and applies equally to women's and men's autobiographies. This is the stipulation that the autobiographical mode is an introspective and intimate one and that autobiographers write about their inner or emotional life. The emphasis on an ideal of self-revelation that informs the mass of critical efforts to define autobiography derives from an urgency to legitimize autobiography as an aesthetic genre in order to distinguish it from mere historical document. However, despite the rarity of the introspective perspective or of personal intimacies, consciously shaped and artistic autobiographies do exist. Though we may not be surprised to find that life studies by public figures often lack both confidentiality and stylistic excellence, creative people, especially writers, though contributing proportionately little to the autobiographical mode, have produced some of the best autobiographies in the literature without conforming to the confessional ideal. Irrespective of their professions or of their differing emphases in subject matter, neither women nor men are likely to explore or to reveal painful and intimate memories in their autobiographies. The autobiographical fallacy of self-revelation is demonstrated not only by the similar subjects usually avoided in life studies by both sexes but also by the different means of detachment with which they treat the material they do include.

Let us first review some subjects that we would expect to generate the revelation of deep feelings but which autobiographers omit from their life studies. Shumaker made some efforts to isolate these subjects among the male autobiographers he treated, noting specifically the exclusion of siblings, children, mates, and romantic attachments. This happens to be true of women's autobiographies as well.

A possible explanation for the absence or near-absence of siblings in most life studies is the fact that most autobiographers are achievers with self-sustaining ego systems, and not surprisingly, therefore, most are only children or the oldest child. The self of the oldest child is rarely threatened or influenced by younger siblings, except perhaps to reinforce the oldest child's confidence, which explains this omission by practically all autobiographers with younger sisters and brothers. Younger siblings are most likely to treat their next older brother or sister, especially if they are of the same sex. James's and Adams' feelings of inferiority to their older brothers are familiar examples. But Gertrude Stein, who adored her older brother and followed him first to college and then to Europe, mentions him only briefly, and his name, "Leo," not at all. In one sentence, Podhoretz dismisses his older sister, who provided the "reality principle" to his indulged only-son status.

That few autobiographers write about their children may have to do with the fact that most do not have children or not during the time covered by their life studies. However, even when autobiographers do have children, and male autobiographers more frequently do than female, not unexpectedly women are more likely to include them to some extent. For example, Augustine, Rousseau, Franklin, and Podhoretz are fathers during the time covered by their life studies but mention their children only briefly. Stanton, Duncan, Gilman, and Mead were mothers and write about their children; for Stanton and Mead, the emotional and physical needs of children are essential aspects of their life studies. While Nabokov includes his child in an autobiographical essay in *Speak, Memory* (1960), it is much more a nostalgic rhapsody on his own childhood than it is a portrait of his son.

Shumaker's observation about the reticence of autobiographers to write about their mates applies for the most part to female autobiographers also. However, though fewer autobiographies have been written by married women than by married men, of those who cover the period of time of a relationship, more women than men discuss their mates to some degree. "Romantic love," Shumaker also noted, "Digby, Hazlitt, Moore, and female apologists to one side, . . . is usually treated as none of the world's business"—by women also. Though Augustine lived for many years with a woman who bore him a child, they are given one summary sentence. Franklin excludes his notorious courtships in the French capital from his memoirs, understandably, given his intention of depicting himself as a public figure of high honorable character. Even after marriage, autobiographers give us little or nothing about their courtships. Mill briefly eulogizes Harriet Taylor's influence on him, but only during their short life together. Adams excludes all mention of his wife before or after their marriage. Elizabeth Cady Stanton describes the joys of adolescent awakening and the fine impression Henry Stanton made on her as an orator and horseman, then is wed in the next paragraph. Gertrude Stein completely omits her relationship with Alice Toklas, and Lillian Hellman lives with Dashiell Hammett with no hint of their romantic beginnings.

The major exception to this reticence of autobiographers to discuss close family members is the subject of their parents. Stein is unique in appearing virtually motherless and fatherless, for most autobiographers at least touch on one or both parents; Hellman and, to a lesser extent, Podhoretz are examples of the latter. The pattern, however, is for autobiographers to emphasize one parent, often to the exclusion of the other one. Franklin, Mill, Adams, Gosse, and Elizabeth Stanton concentrate on their fathers, whom they view as authority figures who relate impersonally to their children, and ignore their mothers entirely. Women are less likely to focus on their mothers than men are; Augustine, Washington, and Dahlberg write adoringly of their mothers, an inclination among male autobiographers. Carrighar's portrait of her mother's physical and psychological brutality is a rare negative exposé, however apologetic. De Beauvoir's equal attention to both parents' bourgeois influence on her burgeoning intellectuality is atypical.

Also atypical is the frankness with which Gosse, Dahlberg, and Carrighar paint their filial relationships, for despite the inclusion of parents by most autobiographers, they are rarely described with emotionality. In summarizing the subjects usually excluded from autobiographies, Shumaker missed the implications of his findings, but William Matthews drew from his study of the affective matter of autobiography the following conclusion:

> . . . few autobiographers put into their books very much of that private, intimate knowledge of themselves that only they can have. Oftener than not, they shun their own inner peculiarities and fit themselves into patterns of behavior and character suggested by the ideas and ideals of their periods and by the fashions in autobiography with which they associate themselves. The laws of literature and the human reluctance to stand individually naked combine to cheat the expectations of readers who hope to find in autobiographies many revelations of men's true selves.[6]

The admission of intense feelings of hate, love, and fear, the disclosure of explicit sexual encounters, or the detailing of painful psychological experiences are matters on which autobiographers are generally silent.

Despite this reticence, autobiographers cannot entirely avoid recalling and writing about subjects that provoke uncomfortable memories. In order to deal with their feelings, they use various means of detachment to protect and distance themselves from the imagined or real judgments of their unknown audiences. It is this detached treatment of the subjects they include, even more than the omission of certain subjects, that most characterizes the genre for both sexes and explains the discrepancy between the critical ideal of autobiography as a genre of disclosure and the thousands of testimonies of a nonconfessional nature. However, men and women tend to distance themselves from their material in different ways, and this stylistic difference is an important distinguishing feature of their autobiographies.

Because most autobiographers of both sexes describe their child-

hoods, which are usually recalled as unhappy times, we can most easily see this difference in the way they handle their early years, but it
also pervades the accounts of their adult lives as well, whether they
stress careers or personal subjects. Men tend to idealize their lives or
to cast them into heroic molds to project their universal import. They
may exaggerate, mythologize, or monumentalize their boyhood and
their entire lives. Perhaps for fear of appearing sentimental, they often
desist from revealing crises in their childhood but are more likely to
relate adult crises, usually turning points in their professional lives.

Augustine's narrative dramatizes his sinful youth and culminating
conversion at the onset of middle age. Franklin idealizes his rise from
poor boy to international statesman and exalts himself as the first
American. He seems to see no necessity to dwell on the cutting short
of his education or of his inclination for the sea by his father's forcing
him to work at the age of ten; instead, the difficulties he encounters
are political ones as a career diplomat. Mill extols the superhuman
education he absorbed at the feet of his relentless father and also his
rise to intellectual giant of his age; his crises of identity occur first at
twenty-one when deciding upon his future career and later in his epi-
phanic marriage to Taylor in middle life. Booker T. Washington skips
over his deprived youth to document his role as the father of his race.
Foreseeing his destiny when his fortunes begin to change, he assumes
the surname of the father of his country. The turning point of his life
occurs at the kiln firing of the first bricks for his revolutionary Tuske-
gee Institute. Adams casts himself as a symbol for American history,
split between eighteenth- and nineteenth-century sensibilities and incapable of dealing with the twentieth—another crisis that comes in
middle age. Berkman barely sketches selective incidents from his
early teens in his native Russia to present the source of his unflinching
passion for the anarchist cause in America and instead concentrates on
documenting the traumatic fourteen-year prison ordeal he endured
from the age of twenty-three to thirty-seven. James responds equally
magnetically to all sensory impression in *A Small Boy and Others*
(1913); the interpretation of an obtuse paragraph in the sequel, *Notes
of a Son and Brother* (1914), as a "mutilation" experience at the age of
sixteen seems a futile effort by critics to account for his sexual ambiva-

lence. Kazin rhapsodizes about the Jewish ambience of his childhood neighborhood in Brownsville, within envying view of Manhattan, in a style that undulates and resonates with the sounds, smells, and sights of his adored city. Nabokov's yearning for the lost idyll of innocence as the indulged child of a pre-Revolution aristocratic family is monumentalized by his majestic prose. Dahlberg saturates his autobiography with classical and biblical allusions that cast him as a mythical hero and his life as a contemporary odyssey. Morris sprinkles his childhood adventures with tall tales. We cannot be certain how Malcolm X would have written the *Autobiography* himself, but under Alex Haley's shaping, we read a heroic narrative of Malcolm's rise to fame, from a childhood of extreme poverty and violence, and his catastrophic demise. Richard Wright converts a childhood of hunger and alcoholism, emotional suffocation, and racial trauma into a miracle of survival and salvation through literature.

This view of their childhoods as idylls of innocence and redemption and of their lives as heroic seems to be a male literary tradition. The proclivity of men toward embellishing their autobiographies results in the projection of a self-image of confidence, no matter what difficulties they may have encountered. This is contrary to the self-image projected in women's autobiographies. What their life stories reveal is a self-consciousness and a need to sift through their lives for explanation and understanding. The autobiographical intention is often powered by the motive to convince readers of their self-worth, to clarify, to affirm, and to authenticate their self-image.[7] Thus, the idealization or aggrandizement found in male autobiographies is not typical of the female mode.

Women's self-image is projected by the very means used to distance or detach themselves from intimacy in their life stories—a variety of forms of understatement. In place of glowing narratives, women tend to write in a straightforward and objective manner about both their girlhood and adult experiences. They also write obliquely, elliptically, or humorously in order to camouflage their feelings, the same techniques used to play down their professional lives. Even when they risk themselves by relating crises, usually in girlhood, it lacks that nostalgia men seem to experience (perhaps because, as Ellen Moers has noted of female fiction, it is more usually the "brutishness of child-hood" and the "savagery of girlhood" that are most remembered[8]). In-stead, the accounts of girlhood crises, while conveying their authors' awareness of their importance in shaping their later lives, are dis-tanced by this understated treatment.

Stanton wrote her autobiography to sway her readers to the cause of women's suffrage, and she dates her career as a fighter for women's rights from her traumatic experience at the age of eleven when she learned that her adored father valued only boys. Yet she recounts this incident objectively in the same reportorial style that informs all the trials of her fifty years of petitioning, lecturing, and herculean travel-ing on the lyceum circuit in her fifties and sixties, a narrative both relieved and distanced by her many humorous anecdotes.

Stanton's style could be attributed to her restrictive nineteenth-cen-tury upbringing were it not for the fact that this same kind of detach-ment continues among autobiographers in the twentieth century. All eight essays in Mary McCarthy's *Memories of a Catholic Girlhood* (1957) are directed toward examining the complex childhood influ-ences that shaped her adult personality, and though each one reveals a crucial turning point in every formative area of her girlhood—family, character development, intellectual growth, and sexuality—she skill-fully detaches herself from these events by utilizing an abstract and intellectual style, as well as by choosing to analyze each essay in a critical epilogue. In *I Know Why the Caged Bird Sings* (1969), Angelou consistently understates her girlhood experiences, like her first shock-ing encounters with racism and her rape at the age of eight, as well as her adolescent struggles to gain self-reliance and to attain womanhood. Carrighar, whose autobiography documents her successful resolution of the many traumas of her childhood persecution by her mother, also understates her experiences, as in the accounts of her mother's at-tempt on her life and of her command to "lose" a cherished dog. Hellman camouflages the trials of her childhood behind humorous anecdotes, especially in *An Unfinished Woman* (1969), like the nose-breaking incident, which diverts us from her school frustrations and loneliness, and her running away from home, which sidetracks us (for a time) from her budding sexuality. In *Pentimento* she relies heavily on an elliptical style and especially on oblique dialogue, both of which distance her and her readers from her uncomfortable childhood and adult memories. While Stanton and Hellman use humor on occasion to detract readers from their feelings, Stein relies almost entirely on this means of detachment in the many anecdotes about her expatriate life. In her case, it is an ironic and mocking humor, wholly untypical of the serious genre of self-portraiture.

A final autobiographical feature upon which critics agree is that autobiographers consciously shape the events of their life into a coherent whole. By means of a chronological, linear narrative, they unify their work by concentrating on one period of their life, one theme, or one characteristic of their personality. It is not surprising that with men socially conditioned to pursue the single goal of a successful career, we find such harmony and orderliness in their autobiographies. Such unity betokens a faith in the continuity of the world and their own self-images. The unidirectionality of men's lives *is* appropriately cast into such progressive narratives.

On the other hand, irregularity rather than orderliness informs the self-portraits by women. The narratives of their lives are often not chronological and progressive but disconnected, fragmentary, or organized into self-sustained units rather than connecting chapters. The multidimensionality of women's socially conditioned roles seems to have established a pattern of diffusion and diversity when they write their autobiographies as well, and so by established critical standards, their life studies are excluded from the genre and cast into the "non-artistic" categories of memoir, reminiscence, and other disjunctive forms.

Our earliest male autobiographer, Augustine, narrates his life story progressively up to the time of his conversion and then crowns it with three chapters of brilliant intellectual analysis. Rousseau's confessions, however excessively detailed, are persistently chronological and progressive. Franklin wrote his autobiography during several sittings over a period of eighteen years, yet he resumed the narrative each time where he had left off. Goethe's autobiography, also written over a number of years, is methodically chronological. Washington, Mill, Berkman, Wright, Koestler, Dahlberg, and Malcolm X all proceed linearly with no miscellaneous forms to disrupt the orderly time sequence or the style. Though Adams omits twenty years of his life, the hiatus causes no break in the continuity of his theme, whatever curiosity readers may have about those hidden years.

But as early as the fifteenth century, we find Kempe constantly interrupting her narrative with long apostrophes to God and with descriptions of her many weeping fits. Teresa's life story is broken with a long dissertation on prayer and with sporadic descriptions of her raptures. In Mary Rowlandson's account of her captivity by Indians (1682), frequent quotations from the Bible halt the narrative, and an exhortation on improved means for combating the Indians increases our suspense only sentences before her eventual release. Pioneer narratives and accounts by women disguised as soldiers and sailors in order to experience lives denied them as women describe their adventures and trials episodically and fragmentedly. Stanton's history is interrupted by anecdotes, portraits of people, and quoted letters and articles of her own and by others.

In the twentieth century, we find the situation unchanged. Stein's anecdotes of the famous artists and writers whose friendships legitimized her before she received public recognition are well known; so is her method of accreting details of her tales, and arranging many of her chapters, in nonchronological order. McCarthy's *Memories* are a collection of eight previously published essays. Hellman's *Unfinished Woman* starts off chronologically, but shortly becomes a pastiche of diary notes from her trips to Spain and Russia and concludes with studies of her closest adult friends. By the time she came to write *Pentimento*, subtitled *A Book of Portraits*, she had recognized that her forte in autobiography was the same dramatic character development that informed her playwrighting, and each chapter in her second work is a self-contained unit. Had she forced an orderly and linear narrative on the events and persons that affected the development of her personality and values, she would have destroyed the achievement of a cumulative, three-dimensional portrait of herself. Angelou's *Caged Bird* proceeds somewhat chronologically, but most chapters or groups of chapters are self-sustaining vignettes or short stories. Almost half of Tillich's *From Time to Time* (1973) consists of poems, playlets, dreams, dramatic allegories, diary extracts, and character sketches distributed throughout a narrative organized around the various towns and cities she inhabited as a child and adult. The controlled chaos of Millett's autobiography, with its mixed chronology, flashbacks within flashbacks, sometimes three times removed, and its stream-of-consciousness and associative narrative, clearly reflects the fragmentation she experiences in her multiple roles as writer, teacher, filmmaker, critic, sculptor, political activist, bisexual, and feminist.

Surveying quite a number of bibliographies from various countries and periods, one is struck by the number of women writing diaries, journals, and notebooks, in contrast to the many more men writing autobiographies proper. From earliest times, these discontinuous forms have been important to women because they are analogous to the fragmented, interrupted, and formless nature of their lives. But they also attest to a continuous female tradition of discontinuity in women's autobiographical writing to the present day. Fragmented narratives are not unknown among men's autobiographies, nor are progressive narratives absent in women's, especially in life studies which include more about their work life than the norm. But even when they are basically linear, as are Stanton's, Gilman's, and Goldman's, they exhibit the same anecdotal and disruptive characteristic we find in other women's autobiographies.

Thus, the final criterion of orderliness, wholeness, or a harmonious shaping with which critics characterize autobiography is often not applicable to women's autobiographies. No such restrictions adhere in defining or evaluating fiction, to which critics long ago adapted their standards to accommodate fragmented and stream-of-consciousness narratives, however chaotic, that are integral to their content. The various forms in which women write their life studies are often appropriate for rendering the authors' intentions and/or personalities, and autobiographical critics do a disservice to these many fine works and to the genre itself when they saddle the autobiographical mode with their confining criteria.

Perhaps this situation will change. In the late twentieth century, the autobiographical mode has been undergoing considerable experimentation, which may prod critics into modifying their standard definitions and theories, modifications long overdue for judging women's autobiographies. While linear and detached autobiographies by people who concentrate on their professional lives still dominate, more men are writing in less regular forms and are including more personal subjects; Merle Miller's *On Being Different* (1971), Mark Vonnegut's *The Eden Express* (1975), Jerry Rubin's *Growing (Up) at 37* (1975), and Mark Harris' *Best Father Ever Invented* (1976). In addition, autobiography is no longer the sole province of older people looking backward reflectively and consciously on their past, for young people are recording their lives as they live them.

Whatever their ages or circumstances, contemporary autobiographers are having more difficulty making sense of the past than did their historical predecessors. The complexity of the atomic era has made a wholistic view of life difficult, and it has affected the form and content of autobiography as well. But however much the gradual collapse of traditional values has made women's values more acceptable to the present male culture, what may appear new is, in fact, for women the culmination of a long tradition.

2.

The Emergence of Women's Autobiography in England

CYNTHIA S. POMERLEAU

Autobiography in the general form that we know it today is a relatively recent development. Even in antiquity, to be sure, it is possible to find isolated autobiographical passages in works of history or poetry. But as a distinct literary genre, representing an attempt to fulfill the author's conscious and primary intention of recounting and assessing his or her life to date, autobiography before the seventeenth century is practically nonexistent.

It is generally accepted that the rise of autobiography was associated with the increases in historical sense and self-consciousness which took place during the Renaissance. And because the winds of change which swept from Italy northward through Europe took awhile to blow across the channel, the appearance of autobiography in England, like other literary forms, came relatively late. In all, only a score or so autobiographies have come down to us which were penned in England before around the middle of the seventeenth century. After 1640 there was a sharp increase in the number of British autobiographies; some of this increase can be attributed to the incipient formation of a tradition of religious autobiography in the various Protestant sects.

It should come as no surprise that although women probably comprised more than half the population, their autobiographies make up roughly ten percent of the total produced in the seventeenth century. As might also be expected, seventeenth-century autobiographies by men exhibit more variety than those of their female counterparts; military memoirs, political memoirs, accounts of a religious calling, family histories, boasting self-exposés—all these can be found among the productions of men. Men of course had more educational opportunities than women and access to a wider range of experience; though self-revelation was in general thought of as inappropriate and requiring some justification, the men who undertook it were at least not subject to a prejudice against members of their sex writing at all.

What is noteworthy about the productions of women, whatever their numerical and other limitations, is that they are by no means anemic imitations of those of men. On the contrary, in many respects they seem more modern, more subjective, more given to self-scrutiny, more like what we have come to know as autobiography. Furthermore, writings by women are among the early examples of the form. Two of the most remarkable autobiographical works of the century were written by women before 1660 (Anna Trapnel and Margaret Cavendish). Indeed, autobiography must share with the novel the distinction of being one of the first literary genres shaped with the active participation of women (if the word "shaped" can be used to describe the creation of a form many of whose early examples went long unpublished). Heretofore even the most gifted female intellects had worked within forms already perfected and refined by male artists.

The women who produced secular autobiographies in the seventeenth century were largely upper class, and their mood was by and large one of acceptance. Because the old traditions of order and female subordination were still workable within this social context, these women could engage fairly comfortably in conventional relationships and submit to a subordinate role without being overwhelmed by a sense of oppression. For one autobiographer, Lucy Hutchinson, it was simply a matter of following the natural order of things:

> . . . never man had a greater passion for a woman, nor a more honorable esteem of a wife; yet he was not uxurious, nor remitted he that just rule which it was her honour to obey, but managed the reins of government with such prudence and affection that she who would not delight in such an honourable and advantageable subjection, must have wanted a reasonable soul.[1]

Especially after the political turmoil of the Civil Wars, a subject that looms large in the work of autobiographers of both sexes, clinging to the old patterns may actually have provided an element of serenity and stability in a world where the sanctity of these patterns could no longer be taken for granted. As the following passage from Margaret Cavendish's autobiography suggests, the differences between males and females and the importance of perpetuating those differences through education were part of a larger, divinely appointed pattern of order in society which was necessary for human happiness:

> As for my breeding, it was according to my birth, and the nature of my sex; for my birth was not lost in my breeding. For as my sisters was or had been bred, so was I in plenty. . . . Likewise we were bred virtuously, modestly, civilly, honourably, and on honest principles. . . . We did not riot, but we lived orderly; for riot, even in kings' courts and princes' palaces, brings ruin without content or pleasure. . . . For disorder obstructs; besides, it doth disgust life, distract the appetites, and yield no true relish to the senses; for pleasure, delight, peace, and felicity live in method and temperance.[2]

The superiority of males simply was not questioned. Alice Thornton remarked casually in her autobiography on her husband's hopes for a son; she explained to her four-year-old daughter her husband's grief over the death of one of their sons: "being a son he takes it more heavily."[3] Women not only accepted their subordination but actually found it a positive virtue, one which they could constructively work to achieve. Lucy Hutchinson proclaimed herself (writing in the third person):

> . . . a faithful mirror, reflecting truly, though but dimly, his own glories upon him, so long as he was present; but she, that was nothing before his inspection gave her a fair figure, when he was removed, was only filled with a dark mist. . . . The greatest excellency she had was the power of apprehending and the virtue of loving his; so as his shadow she waited on him everywhere. . . .[4]

They take pride in their husbands' accomplishments. In the following curious passage from Anne Fanshawe's *Memoirs*, the author's husband is even given credit for successfully delivered children, while she bears the onus for the abortions: "My dear husband had six sons and eight daughters, born and christened, and I miscarried of six more. . . ."[5] Mary Penington writes of her desire to be "serviceable" to her husband and finds a kind of exaltation in sacrificing for him: "I gave up much to be a companion to him in . . . his suffering."[6]

As one reads these works, one senses that the feeling of subordination sat relatively lightly on these women because the social system still allowed them a kind of dignity. They were not simply thrust under the thumb of any man who could successfully barter for them; they played an essential role and saw themselves as essential to the completion of the social unit. Anne Fanshawe called her husband her "better half" with no irony and asserted, "we never had but one mind throughout our lives. Our souls were wrapped up in each other's; our aims and designs one, our loves one, and our resentments one."[7] There was still a sense of connectedness with their husbands, a sense of linked and shared fates. She was not simply a part of him; rather, they were both a part of something larger.

It may also be that subordination was less onerous than it might have been because, as is evident from the autobiographies of the period, the social system permitted upper-class women to take some legitimate pleasure in their own achievements. Many of them evince self-satisfaction in their early precocity. And though a declaration of timidity is practically a badge of membership in the female sex, there is a certain amount of pride in Ann Halkett's description of herself fending off enemy soldiers; in Mary Rich's of her journey alone through the embattled countryside during the Civil Wars; in Anne Fanshawe's of facing Turkish pirates at her husband's side.[8] Such exploits offered a kind of escape valve to keep the sense of subordination from becoming oppressive. As long as women were willing and able to operate within the system of female subjugation, to see evidence of their own excellence as exceptional, individual marks of courage or intelligence did not threaten the social fabric and perhaps even reinforced it.

Moreover, the single life was still seen as an acceptable way of life, for the unmarried female relative could still be a productive member of a household. Almost every seventeenth-century female autobiographer eventually married, but before doing so many professed great aversion to the married state; "I did dread marriage," said Margaret Cavendish, "and shunned men's company as much as I could."[9] To be sure, such reluctance is not shocking in view of the realities of marriage: it represented not only a great burden of responsibility, but also the pain and extreme danger of repeated childbirth. But women also had genuine and positive feelings about the unmarried state for its own sake, not simply for the absence of the problems imposed by marriage. Mary Rich enjoyed "living so much at my ease that I was unwilling to change my condition, and never could bring myself to close with any offered match"; and Alice Thornton asserted, "I was exceeding sattisfied in that happie and free condittion, wherein I injoyed my time with delight abundantly in the service of my God, and the obedience I owed to such an excelent parent, in whoes injoyment I accounted my daies spent with great content and comfort. . . ."[10]

Since the single life at least appeared to be a genuine option, the decision to marry was felt to be a matter of choice rather than necessity. Even though marriage was, for the woman, a clear-cut matter of self-surrender—Mary Rich described her commitment as having "given myself away to him"[11]—the act of choice is of itself a kind of self-ratification. Certain financial pressures often exerted great influence in the selection of mates, but not as extensively and as explicitly as was to occur in the eighteenth century. Though women may not have been very free to choose their husbands, by and large they accepted the cultural myth which said that they were.

For seventeenth-century English women, much more than men, love acted as a defining force. Although it is not possible to say whether love was inherently more important to women than to men, we can assert with confidence that it was more crucial to the way women saw themselves, especially women whose orientation was primarily secular. The self, we may say, is largely defined by the choices one makes; but we must recognize that the choices realistically open to a woman were far more limited than those open to a man. The professions were virtually closed to women. For a woman to sustain any sort of a position of independence required a more radical social and intellectual posture than most human beings are willing to take. In other ways, too, women's lives were more restricted than men's. Because they lived in a world where men made the rules, and had for centuries, women were bound much more oppressively by tradition and prescriptions for behavior. Even biologically their lives were less under their own control. Sex within marriage meant pregnancy after pregnancy, a life of "female troubles," and very possibly early death from puerperal fever; sex outside marriage meant all these things and severe social stigmatization to boot; the alternative was celibacy. On every social level, however unfree the men were, the women were more unfree. But loving was something a woman could legitimately do.

Either because they weren't expected to or because they didn't have to, men simply did not define themselves in this way. Even those men whose marriages we know from other sources to have been happy and fulfilling make little or no mention of it. For example, Sir Richard Baxter, the great Puritan divine, has left in his *Reliquiae Baxterianae* a lengthy and thoughtful "Narrative of the Most Memorable Passages of his Life and Times"; he has also left a penetrating and sympathetic biography of his wife, Margaret—a work that stands as a touching memorial of his affection and respect for her. Yet it is significant that the two were conceived as separate works, and no hint of the latter appears in the former.

Love and sexual love, insofar as they are mentioned at all, are frequently synonymous in the works of men. Thomas Raymond tells us, "I was soe pestered by the foolish blynde boy with a young defte wench that waited on my aunte that I could not rest for it. And this being the proper age for love matters, I had a greate and vexatious share of them." Such "loves" are easily dispensed with: "still I had some pangs of the boy Cupids tricks about me for that pretty wench, but left hir now the more litly for my deere friend, honest J. Bouillon, whoe was almost madd for hir. We had some turnes about hir by letter. . . ."[12]

More often, a man will scarcely touch on his intimate or domestic relations. One can thumb through index after index in works by men and find only the most cursory references, if any, to wife and children.

Clarendon, if we are to believe his protestations, was most shaken by the death of his first wife; yet he disposes of courtship, marriage, and the death of his wife in a few lines. This marriage, it is true, lasted only a few months; yet Clarendon, barely a page later, gives us scarcely more of his second wife, "by whom he had many children of both sexes, with whom he lived very comfortably in the most uncomfortable times, and very joyfully in those times when matter of joy was administered, for the space of five or six and thirty years. . . ." He adds that from "the time of his marriage he laid aside all other thoughts but of his profession, to the which he betook himself very seriously. . . ."[13] However much he may have loved his wives, it is clear that he views the primary function of marriage as providing him with a stable sex life, so that his libido will not distract him from his career.

Clarendon, of course, is of lasting interest as a distinguished historical figure; but even men whose careers seem to provide less matter for autobiography do not dwell on their domestic relations. Sir John Bramston tells us matter-of-factly that, "On the 19th of Nouember followinge, I married, in the parish church, St. Diones Backchurch, London, vnto Alice, the eldest daughter of Anthony Abdy, alderman of London."[14] After the marriage we hear nothing of her beyond a list of the miscarriages and births of their children, until she dies. On this subject, he waxes more eloquent than most male writers do; still, the whole sequence of events from his marriage until his wife's death takes up some ten pages in a book over 400 pages long. These ten pages, nonetheless, are a volume compared with Sir John Reresby's only mention of his wife in an account almost as lengthy: "But to resume other things, I married, and was thereby prevented from being an eye witness of the Dutch war; and so I shall only say that his highness obtained a glorious victory over the republic."[15]

It hardly seems necessary to multiply examples of men *not* mentioning their home lives. The point is that for women, and not for men, the domestic choices were, partly by default, a medium for self-expression; and as men began gropingly to write about their public lives, so, amazingly, did a few women write about their private lives.

The idea that oneself, one's feelings, one's spouse and domestic relations were properly and innately worth writing about was essentially
a female idea, however tentatively conceived at the time. There is
little or no precedent for such a notion, at least in English, in male
thinking or practice—though a century later it was espoused and
elaborated upon by so eminent a man as Samuel Johnson.

Apart from interpersonal relationships, the other area in which
women could operate with relative freedom was religion. The role of
religion, even in the accounts we have been describing as primarily
secular, is clearly an extensive one. For one thing, it provides an explanation and consolation for the grief, pain, and loss that were inevitably associated with life in that period but most particularly with
childbearing. Nothing that can happen is so devastating that it cannot
be justified or redeemed by being the will of God. Moreover, seventeenth-century Christianity by its nature dispelled most stirrings of a
sense of injustice, for justice was to be sought in the next world rather
than in this one; and women were effectively encouraged to cultivate
a kind of undifferentiated piety.

It is also obvious, especially among a large number of Quaker autobiographies, that religion provided an emotional outlet and a legitimate alternative to humdrum existences:

> . . . I could not take comfort in Husband or Children, House, or
> Land, or any visibles, for want of the Marriage Union with the Lamb
> of God. . . . I was sensible that he is the Light of the World, that
> enlightens every one that comes into the World; and that it was striv-
> ing within me from my Youth, which was before ever I heard the
> name *Quaker*; and then I did believe that there was a People or
> Church over whom Christ Jesus was Head, though I could yet not
> find them, nor be a Member of them; yet long sought after it sorrow-
> fully, with many strong and fervent cries and desires: But the Lord
> in his own due time answered my weary soul. . . .[16]

In this passage Joan Vokins makes explicit what is implicit in many
religious autobiographies. The invidious comparison between her life
with her husband and her union with God suggests part of the function
of religion in her life: it allowed her to find by turning inward the
meaning, mystery, exaltation, and ceremony that were lacking out-

wardly. In effect, she could admit that she was not satisfied with her domestic lot without actually rebelling against it.

The burgeoning growth of Quakerism during this period, by the way, is an important event in the history of women and of women's autobiography, for it preached and practiced, as had no other widespread movement, the equality of women, albeit within a limited sphere. These intrepid Quaker women preached and traveled extensively. They also wrote numerous autobiographies, a practice encouraged for all Quakers on the premise that since all are children of God, the experiences of even an ordinary person whose life has been touched by God can be profitable to others.

In summary, it is significant that the women who wrote primarily secular autobiographies in this period came without exception from upper-class backgrounds, for their relatively comfortable circumstances undoubtedly mitigated some of the most overt causes of oppression. The preponderance of religious autobiographies strongly suggests that introspective women whose lot was less favored tended to retreat to religion rather than dwell upon the inequities of life in this world. Potential protest was muted, for women were propelled by the force of privilege and tradition to find the causes of any dissatisfaction within themselves and to interpret any restlessness as a failure of piety.

The eighteenth century saw many alterations in this picture. Economic developments and social dislocations related to the Industrial Revolution and the resulting population shifts from rural areas to urban centers began to disturb the equilibrium maintained by the force of centuries of tradition, and the "feminine sensibility" in autobiography underwent a corresponding change. In effect, the disparities between the traditional picture of women and the realities of their existence became too great to gloss over easily, and vague rumblings of dissatisfaction began to be heard.

To begin with, new elements of society found voices: women whose lot in life was less sheltered and whose married life was less idyllic than those of their aristocratic sisters; women for whom a religious commitment was not an adequate substitute for domestic satisfaction. Such women undoubtedly existed before the eighteenth century, but they were largely isolated and unheard; there was no joining of voices, no sense of a shared fate. The growth of literacy and of the publishing industry created a nonelitist audience and a tribe of authors eager to satisfy its tastes. Many female authors of the period were people who were forced to live either by their wits or their bodies to keep the two together and who found that they could make a shift to support themselves by writing. Autobiographies were written not only by respectably well-placed women such as Lady Mary Wortley Montague, the bluestocking Mrs. Delany, and Sarah Churchill, Duchess of Marlborough, but also by novelists such as Mrs. Manley, actresses such as Charlotte Charke and George Anne Bellamy, and literary hangers-on and demimondaines such as Laetitia Pilkington and Con Phillips.

Eighteenth-century England was not an easy time or place to be a woman. As single women became more and more of an economic burden to their families, the social stigma attached to the single state for women increased considerably. It was around this time that the term "old maid" came into vogue and the term "spinster" acquired its negative connotations. We no longer find women considering in a leisurely fashion whether or not to marry; the pressure on them to do so was tremendous and the life of an unmarried woman an unenviable one in which she was the butt of constant joking or denigration.

At the same time, it became more and more difficult to make a satisfactory marriage. The 1801 census showed a preponderance of women, a situation which had probably existed throughout the eighteenth century and which created what was perceived as a marriage crisis. Moreover, women were much more dependent upon men than men upon women. These factors made marriage more than ever a men's market. Marriages were more blatantly mercenary, as parvenus struggled to consolidate their newly acquired wealth and older families to maintain or strengthen their position. Mrs. Delany's description of her reaction to her first husband is strikingly reminiscent of Clarissa's physical aversion to Mr. Soames, but this did not deter her connections from pressing her into an uncongenial marriage. Repeatedly autobiographers assert that the forces which impel them to marry are often other than love; more often it is a need for financial security or for assurance that they are attractive and worthwhile. A typical comment is that of Con Phillips:

> . . . among the various Passions in Female Nature, Love is not always the principal one to which their Views are directed: How many more Instances of Fair Ones may we remember, who have fallen Victims to their Interest, their Pride, their Vanity, their Credulity, their Revenge &c. than to the rare and honest Simplicity of a mutual Inclination? And unless a Woman be endued with an uncommon Share of Understanding and Prudence, she inevitably becomes a Sacrifice to some of these.[17]

Love as choice became diminished, a less potent force for self-definition than it had been in the seventeenth century.

Women who couldn't snag a husband or who couldn't make a marriage that guaranteed economic security were frequently forced, especially in an urban setting, to take their wares to the marketplace to maintain a decent existence. Such a life was extremely precarious. Scarcely any profession in which women were allowed to engage had more than a very marginal respectability attached to it. The trajectory of a woman's life as it emerges from several of the autobiographies of the period is one of early peaking, when the woman is still fresh and pretty enough to attract men who will support or assist her temporarily; after that the path goes downhill, with monotonous episodes of frantic scrambling for money and frequently with periods spent in debtors' prison.

Love and marriage were still a woman's subjects, as they had been in the seventeenth century; this field was seldom extensively invaded by men. Gibbon, who "sighed as a lover, obeyed as a son,"[18] is almost a parody of male restraint and coolness. But the attitude of women had changed. Domestic love had in some ways fallen into disrepute and was not invested with much importance or dignity. As has frequently been observed, many of the major intellectual figures of the period— Swift, Pope, Gibbon, Burke, and so forth—never married at all; and the eighteenth century produced little lyric poetry of lasting value. Moreover, as the disenfranchised started making themselves heard, the stories they told of their less sheltered marriages were at odds with the domestic idyls of the seventeenth-century aristocrats. Women, as Con Phillips' lawyer gleefully told her, had no legal rights, and unless their husbands were men of good will, they could be subjected to monstrous indignities. The Countess of Strathmore, as she relates in her autobiography, was actually kidnapped and imprisoned by her husband. In some quarters the restraints of family tradition were breaking down; Con Phillips' husband was a Dutch merchant whose family lived in Holland, too far away to have any understanding of what was going on between their scion and his wife. Women like Laetitia Pilkington felt that they were formed for domesticity but had been thwarted in their true calling. Marriage had become so debased that in most cases the connectedness, the sense of a shared fate that characterized seventeenth-century secular autobiography, was lost.

So instead of love in domestic circles, we frequently find love taking its chances in the tougher world outside the home. Here the antagonistic nature of relations between the sexes becomes far clearer. The growth of the novel, with its structural demand for conflict, undoubtedly helped to throw the adversary relationship between men and women into sharper focus. There is no more succinct statement of the model for interaction between the sexes which the eighteenth century had inherited from the past and elaborated upon in its own way than Lovelace's: "Men are to ask; women are to deny."[19] Men were excused or even approved for being creatures of ungovernable passions. Any method of lying or playing on a woman's weakness was a fair tactic. Kidnapping and even rape do not appear in most cases to have been indictable offenses, though they may have raised a few eyebrows; the experiences of Con Phillips, George Anne Bellamy, and the Countess of Strathmore prove that Richardson's kidnapping episodes were not merely the fantasies of a repressed male. "Men in general are rascals," the actor James Quin told George Anne Bellamy.[20] The idea of male virtue and premarital chastity was so laughable that it formed the basis for Fielding's parody of *Pamela* in *Joseph Andrews*. Women, on the other hand, were to resist as though life depended upon it; for so, in effect, it did. A single slip, for whatever reason and under whatever pressure, meant a lifetime of dishonor; if she was drugged, intoxicated, or raped, she was still defiled. To succumb to passion was to be a whore, nothing less; it often meant resigning any possibility of achieving the security of marriage. Such a woman, said George Anne Bellamy, was truly "the martyr of an unguarded moment."[21]

A growing sense of the injustice of these disparities made resentment of the double standard and even outright hostility toward men a significant element in the autobiographies of eighteenth-century English women. "What is not a Crime in Men is scandalous and unpardonable in Woman,"[22] Mrs. Manley remarked early in the century, and this theme is picked up and elaborated upon by a number of women later in the century. Or contempt may be shown metaphorically; Catherine Jemmat, one of the bitterest of female autobiographers, compares her would-be rapist to a fox, an ass, a lap dog, a baboon, and a spaniel within the course of three short paragraphs.[23]

The other important women's topic, religion, still looms large in eighteenth-century autobiography. It accounts for a smaller proportion of the total output, however, and many of these works seem largely to be going over old terrain rather than breaking fresh ground. The general secularization of life, abetted perhaps by the increased availability of consumer goods, seems to have promoted a change of emphasis from the afterlife to the here and now. The new religions growing up, such as Methodism, were less committed to female participation than some of the earlier radical sects. Quakerism, however, still deserves a special note, for if its adherents were less likely to break new spiritual ground, they were more likely than ever to seize the opportunity to go far afield in the literal sense. As travel in America became somewhat less hazardous, missionary excursions became an increasingly common feature of the Quaker experience; many women traveled extensively, unaccompanied by men, and lived to tell of their adventures.

It would be a misleading anachronism to suggest that there was anything resembling a woman's movement in the eighteenth century; there was no organized effort, no clearly articulated goals. This is hardly surprising. Women had no role models for excellence outside their assigned sphere to emulate (even Mary Wollstonecraft in her most utopian visions cannot conceive of a society in which women op-

erate on an equal basis with men). There were severe social and economic consequences for deviation from the normal expectations. The
treatment of women as sex objects and the race for husbands tended
to divide women from one another, so that when they were discarded,
locked into an uncompanionable marriage, or otherwise deprived of
intellectual stimulation, they found themselves without class consciousness and with few friends among women. Several autobiographers of the period express their reservations about members of their
own sex in general. Men were quick enough to foster this separation;
the classic example is Swift's "Letter to a Very Young Lady on her
Marriage," in which he advises that young person to eschew the company of her own sex and sniffs that he "never yet knew a tolerable
woman to be fond of her own sex."[24] Except on the most superficial
level, women did not challenge the supposition that their subordinate
position in society was divinely and biologically ordained. Any evidence of superiority in a woman was declawed by being taken as exceptional; Dryden praised one autobiographer, Elizabeth Thomas, by
contrasting her to other women and setting her against her own sex.

There is, however, much evidence in the autobiographies of the
period of widespread feelings of dissatisfaction, isolated voices speaking out, and a burgeoning sense of (often unwished for) independence.
There is an increasing disparity between what women are told they
should be and life as they are actually experiencing it. The economy
did not require and therefore did not value productivity within the
home; the qualities needed to snare a husband were not skill and intelligence but rather such passive attributes as youth, beauty, submis-
siveness, and wealth. Yet the realities of existence often demanded
something quite different, as even genteel women were often forced
by a bad marriage, widowhood, or no marriage at all to enter the labor
force or in some way to live by their wits. By the same token, there
was an increasing awareness of the difference between what men are
and what they are supposed to be. Catherine Jemmat, looking at her
husband, comments:

> . . . as the unhappy victim I cannot refrain mentioning, that night
> after night, like a poor submissive slave, have I laid my lordly master

in his bed, intoxicated and indefensible: day after day have I received blows and bruises for my reward: in short, I thought I had married a man, I found I had married a monster.[25]

Though there is little direct challenge to the old system of subordination, many women cite educational differences as the primary basis for male superiority, and a few even flirt with more radical notions of social equality. George Anne Bellamy, only half-jokingly, tells of a conversation when she was in her teens with an old gentleman who found her reading Dryden's *Virgil*:

. . . he seemed to be surprised that a girl of my age should have either taste or erudition enough to understand works of that kind. Piqued at this supposition, I undertook to vindicate my sex from the want of knowledge in literature generally imputed to them. I told him there would not be the least room for such a reflection, did not the lords of creation take care that we should not eclipse them in this respect. The old gentleman then said, "As that is your opinion, I suppose you would have a *female* parliament." To which I replied, "I do not know that the present is much better. . . ."[26]

By the end of the eighteenth century women are beginning to realize that they will have to look elsewhere than in marriage for satisfaction and self-fulfillment. The bitter pill of subordination is no longer sugar-coated with protection, attentiveness, and the self-respect that goes with the knowledge that one is making a positive contribution to the functioning of the household.

The novel, as we have seen, contributed to this new awareness by helping to expose the assumptions underlying the traditional model for relations between the sexes. Perhaps equally important was its function as a medium for the spread of the cult of sensibility. To some extent the contribution may have been negative since it tended to substitute a strong emotional response to tragedy and injustice for positive action to rectify them. But self-justification and self-pity, for all their excesses, led women to an examination of the forces outside themselves which contributed to their problems and promoted self-forgiveness. By the end of the eighteenth century, autobiographers such as Mrs. Gooch, who was also a novelist, had become quite sophisticated in analyzing the apportionment of blame between self and society for their shortcomings and lapses. Moreover, the shift of attention from the object to the subject of love—to their own feelings—encouraged women to analyze the effect of the more cruel aspects of male behavior upon themselves; from here it is only a short step to a consideration of the psychology of subordination, as we find in Wollstonecraft's *Vindication of the Rights of Woman*. Finally, the exaltation of friendship could hardly fail to stir reflections about the limitations placed by society and by accepted male behavior upon the possibilities for friendship between a man and a woman; George Anne Bellamy comments wistfully that the distinction between friendship and love is "beyond the comprehension of the *million*" and that only a "truly delicate mind" will perceive it.[27]

With the increasing discontent came a shift in the social framework for expressing that discontent. The idea of natural rights superseded the soul as the basis for justice and equality. The American and French revolutions and the spread of democratic ideals affirming the rights of man inevitably raised the question of the rights of women. Though such radical notions are beyond anything expressed in women's autobiographies of the period, it is clear that women were becoming more interested in finding satisfaction in this world than in deferring until the next.

Within the context of this general ferment, Mary Wollstonecraft's outburst represents a distinct advance but not an entirely surprising one. The traditions which were still working after a fashion in the seventeenth century were breaking down in the eighteenth, shaken by major social and economic changes. It would be pleasant to report that once Mary Wollstonecraft had articulated the sources of female discontent and suggested a theoretical basis for social change, women were immediately spurred to free themselves from oppression. As we all know, no such thing happened. The history of women has always been retrogressive. The nineteenth century saw, if anything, a backlash; the fluffy, kittenish child-women in Dickens' novels sink below anything portrayed in the seventeenth and eighteenth centuries. Repudiation of Mary Wollstonecraft became, in early nineteenth-century autobiography, a way of establishing the respectability of the writer's views and forestalling or propitiating male criticism, much as a woman today might say, "I'm no women's libber, but. . . ." It is interesting to speculate whether the peculiar violence of British feminism, when it finally erupted in the twentieth century, might have been caused by a revulsion against the image of women promulgated in nineteenth-century England.

But that is a tangential issue. What, finally, can we say of autobiography in the eighteenth century? On the whole it is more varied, revealing more vigor and independence, than that of the seventeenth century. Yet in one sense the eighteenth-century showing is disappointing; unlike the century before, the truly outstanding names in autobiography are no longer those of women. Women with a serious, comprehensive world view seem to have channeled their energies largely into other forms. The novel and the autobiography grew up together; yet women produced novels that were the equal of any written by men, whereas there is nothing comparable to, say, Gibbon's autobiography among women's autobiographies of the eighteenth century.

The answer, I suspect, lies in the nature of the form itself. Dr. Johnson's "compliment" to Fanny Burney and Mrs. Thrale may give us a clue: "'Tis a terrible thing that we cannot wish young ladies well, without wishing them to become old women."[28] The traditional view of women is antithetical to the crucial motive of autobiography—a desire to synthesize, to see one's life as an organic whole, to look back for a pattern. Women's lives are fragmented; they start as young women and are successively transformed from without into either spinsters, demimondaines, wives, mothers, or matriarchs. The process is not one of growth, of evolution; rather, they enter each stage as a failure of the previous stage. Earlier and more decisively than for a man, the curve of a woman's life is seen by herself and society to be one of deterioration and degeneration. Men may mature, but women age. It is significant that the eighteenth-century novel often ended with the marriage of the heroine; the author's vision of life is not forced to accommodate the fate of the heroine as she ages.

Time after time, the eighteenth-century autobiographies of women make energetic and entertaining starts, but dwindle in the end to overly drawn-out sagas of dreariness and debt. The seventeenth-century author of secular autobiography escaped this dilemma by defining herself entirely as a wife and creating within the domestic theater a little stage for growth and maturation. The simplicity of such a limited solution was evidently less accessible to the eighteenth-century women who wrote autobiography. Nevertheless, the autobiographies of the period are well worth reading, from both a literary and sociological point of view. Their authors may not yet have found a way to integrate their lives into a society which discouraged women from doing so, but they were gamely groping.

3.

Quest for Community:
Spiritual Autobiographies of
Eighteenth-Century Quaker and
Puritan Women in America

CAROL EDKINS

The history of any literature is the history of a unique series of
quests, the story of the individual in search of external community
and internal harmony.[1]

Some of the earliest life stories by American women that we have
available to us now are the spiritual autobiographies written by Puritan
and Quaker women in the seventeenth and eighteenth centuries.
These spiritual autobiographies are narratives by Puritan women who
were seeking admission into the Church of Visible Saints (the Puritan
church) and by Quaker women who had been itinerant ministers for
the Society of Friends. The bulk of these narratives date from about
the middle of the 1700s,[2] although one Puritan autobiography, that of
Elizabeth White, was written around 1660 but published in 1741, during the Great Awakening. More Quaker than Puritan spiritual autobiographies are extant from this period[3] because (1) the Quakers were
avid believers in the power of the published word as a means of dis-
seminating the truth and of furthering the aims of the Society, and (2)
Puritan spiritual autobiographies, while required for church admission, were probably privately presented to a minister by the women

rather than publicly presented to the congregation. The reason for the private audiences was that "Reverend John Cotton arrived in Boston in 1633 and soon requested that women desiring church membership be examined in private since a public confession was 'against the apostle's rules and not fit for a woman's modesty.'"[4] Obviously, though, at least some women's confessions of faith and conversion were written down (sometimes for the benefit of their children) since today we have, at least in microprint, these documents of their testimony.[5]

These autobiographies are not timeless works of art, though they were published in part because of their ability to inspire. But if we go to them, looking at them comparatively in order to see more clearly the characteristics of each and to discern their meaning for the women who wrote them and their place in a history of women's autobiographies, we will find ourselves witness to the individual's symbolic confirmation of her bond with her respective group or community. For instead of individualistic statements of a life uniquely lived, which we might expect given not only our notions of the autobiographical act but also our contemporary worship of the individual, we hear echoed throughout these documents, whether Puritan or Quaker, the religious and spiritual experience of the community at large. At first, we might want to dismiss these documents because of their redundancy and because it is the Anne Hutchinsons, the women who stood apart from their community as protofeminists, who occupy our interest. But the women who wrote these autobiographies stood out in their communities as exemplars; otherwise they would not have been published. And it is important to think of women as having at least the symbolic power of verification, of deliberate yea-saying to the community to which they seek admittance.

It is also important from a critical standpoint to look at these women's spiritual autobiographies grouped together and considered as women's documents. In the literature written on spiritual autobiographies from this period in American history, the women's documents have been considered alongside the men's. From the broader perspectives of content and tone, this was justified. However, there were social differences, which should affect to some degree the way we consider these autobiographies. Puritan women, while esteemed and important members of the "little commonwealth" or the Puritan household, had in the church positions inferior to those of the men. Certain valued social functions, such as midwifing or aiding the sick, were given to widows;[6] otherwise, however, "the female role definition that the Massachusetts ministers and magistrates perpetuated severely limited the assertiveness, the accomplishment, the independence and the intellectual activity of Puritan women."[7] Quaker women had, relative to their Puritan counterparts, a much more equal position in the Society of Friends. They could be and were even encouraged at times to become ministers in and for the Society, which meant preaching during meetings and extensive, hazardous travels in outlying areas.

In the case of Puritan women, the initial bond with the community was created by going through the process of conversion, a process which a spiritual autobiography documents and a process which was the lifeblood of the early American Puritan settlement, since only the converted could be members of the Church of Visible Saints. Having testified to her community via an autobiographical act, either oral or written, she then became an acknowledged visible saint, a member of the Elect. Quaker women became members of the Society of Friends when they stood up for the first time to speak during a meeting of the Friends. The more public and deliberate confirmation of the autobiographer's initial bond with her community came with the autobiography, a confirmation effected by the formulaic nature of the document. Virtually every autobiographer of this period, Puritan or Quaker, follows, with some variations of course, a recognizable formula of religious experience; by adhering to this formula, she confirms the standard patterning of religious experience as established by each sect. This framing of the life stories around the group's tenets creates a symbolic bonding with the group and/or community that is significant because each autobiography tells us a story of spiritual and, in the case of the Quakers, social isolation and conflict. It is also significant because this bonding adds for the individual woman a new social role— that of church member. So there is both social and symbolic significance to following the community's given spiritual formula.

In story after story, we hear the autobiographer reciting her struggles to find the inner light, salvation, or grace. We find the individual attempting to establish some binding relationship with God, whether it is one of total submission as with the Quakers or one of passive activity as with the Puritans, who actively attempted to prepare themselves to receive God's grace. In their basic outlines, these narratives are formulaic and conventional.[8] The pattern of religious experience which centers around conversion is almost unerringly identical from one autobiography to another. However, since conversion is interpreted differently in each sect, it necessarily follows that the pattern of conversion and thus the formula will differ in the two sets of autobiographies.

Puritan autobiographies exhibit with varying degrees of complexity and depth the conventional states through which a person "passed as God brought him [or her] to grace."[9] These stages are conviction or illumination where the "individual perceived his [or her] helpless and hopeless condition [of sin] and despaired of salvation"; repentance or aversion where the heart turned away from sin; and finally conversion, the reception of grace from God, followed usually by doubt and despair of actual salvation (a positive sign to believers).[10] The detailing of this process functions as the backbone for Puritan autobiographies. In fact, these autobiographies contain little else of the woman's life; everything not directly relating to her spiritual development is omitted. Those topics relating to hearth and home which we might halfway expect to hear about are lacking. Even though Elizabeth White in *The Experiences of God's Gracious Dealings with Mrs. Elizabeth White* marks one period of her spiritual progress with the birth of a child, this is the exception. If any mention is made of the author's childhood or adolescence, it is made, of course, in a spiritual context. For instance, White, in the opening pages of her autobiography, briefly refers to her childhood by saying that her "father's chief care was to bring [her] up in the nature and domination of the Lord."[11] Later in the autobiography, White centers her adolescence around a crisis of conscience. Her father wanted her to receive the Lord's Supper, yet feeling unworthy, she feared she would be damned should she obey her father's wishes. In another autobiography, *An Account of Some Spiritual Experiences of Elizabeth Mixer* (printed in 1736), the author's only reference to her childhood is to say that between six and seven she became awakened to the duty of secret prayer, and to her adolescence that she was encouraged to come to God at thirteen—the stage of preparation of the heart. As these examples indicate, these autobiographies are restricted to those events which prominently figure in the conversion process, as though the Puritans have pared their existence, spiritual and otherwise, down to the essentials of this one crucial experience.

Variations, of course, exist in the experiences narrated and in the emphasis placed on the discrete stages. For example, turning again to Elizabeth Mixer, we find that her conversion, despite preparation at an early age, was sudden and unexpected. While sick, a number of years after her preparation, she had a vision of heaven where the gold of heaven, the light of the lamb, and angels in their white robes appeared before her. For Mixer this vision of eternity served as the second stage of conversion, repentance. A few nights later, the last stage revealed itself when Jesus Christ "visited her soul with light and love."[12] Mixer's conversion stands out from the rest as the only conversion experience to have a visionary and somewhat mystical theme.

In Elizabeth White's autobiography, we get a strong sense of the struggle and despair involved in the early stages of conversion. After the conflict with her father, White laments that her heart was "not right in the sight of God" (p. 15). She had asked the Lord to "turn her," but despite feeling unworthy, she had not yet had the thorough sense of sin which is part of the conviction/illumination stage of conversion. At this point of near utter despair, she is almost ready to surrender her soul to the unelected; she says: "If I were not elected, it was to no purpose to strive . . . yet I was unwilling to perish" (p. 17). Obviously, she does not give up; instead she sets about performing rote duties in the hope of receiving some comfort. At the climax of her struggles, White has a dream in which a ladder reaches up to heaven. She keeps struggling up the ladder only to be pulled down, until, at last, she is in heaven and filled with rejoicing. Nevertheless, after this experience she still vacillated between despair and joy—a common post-conversion state which for the Puritans connoted the vulnerability of man's perceptions of God's acts. Certain scriptures, however, which she includes for the reader's benefit, uplifted her "when [she] was in heaviness from want of the presence of God" (p. 17). White ends her autobiography by listing her principles of faith, another required part of the confession; and she says: "I trust the Lord will so fix me in them that I may never be tossed too and frow with contrary winds of doctrine as too many in these latter days are" (p. 20).

White's and Mixer's autobiographies are fair representatives of the standard Puritan spiritual autobiography. Their narrations, and thus the lives presented, are narrowly restricted to the three stages of conversion, including a Puritan brand of postpartum depression. The authors devote their narrative energies to detailing the doubts and successes of the soul in its search for peace and security as well as the fateful signs of election. The restricted area of attention is easily understood when we keep in mind what Alan Simpson says about the Puritans as a community: "The goals of regeneration and sanctification, common to Puritans everywhere, are to be sought within the tribal community. No diversity of opinion would be permitted . . . and the mission of the elect is to uphold an orthodoxy."[13] Seen in this light, it is completely understandable why Puritan women autobiographers fashion their life histories along relatively rigid lines. To be accepted into the Church of Visible Saints in which "no diversity of opinion would be permitted," one had to abide by the rules. To gain church admission, conformity to the traditional pattern was compulsory. However, this conformity to the standard formula not only indicates the willingness of the writer to be admitted by the community but also signals on a symbolic level the author's acceptance of the community.

Quaker autobiographies also centered around the conversion experience. Yet compared with the Puritans, the Quaker's definition or representation of conversion allows more flexibility in the scope of the spiritual autobiography. For the Quakers "the religious confession includes a record of successive steps by which Friends attained a spiritual sense of harmony."[14] Their narrations are fuller, more detailed, and give the reader a greater sense of pilgrimage, of time elapsed, of suffering and seeking steadfastly, usually in the face of great resistance from the external world. Compared with the Puritans, the Quaker women bring into their narratives more secular aspects of their lives, such as childhood reading of histories for Jane Hoskens or dancing for Elizabeth Ashbridge. Usually, however, a religious point is to be made by providing these details; this information functions not just as filler or social history but contributes to narrative verisimilitude.

The conventional stages of conversion, or steps in the quest of inner light and harmony with God, are a uniform series of experiences which appear in virtually all the Quaker autobiographies. These stages are (1) early intimations of religious questioning; (2) the attempt to ascertain from prevailing teachings an adequate basis for a religious life (usually at this stage the person is ignorant of the Quakers); (3) a record of the first knowledge of Quakers; (4) the struggle in the soul against surrender to God (and also the Quaker community); (5) submission; and (6) entry into the activity and defense of the Society of Friends.[15]

As with the Puritans, this schema provides the basic framework upon which Quaker autobiographers (male and female) lay their story. Depending on the autobiographer, of course, different phases of this process will be stressed more than others. Jane Hoskens, whose autobiography, *The Life and Spiritual Sufferings of That Faithful Servant of Christ*, was published in 1771, was born in 1693 in England into an Anglican household. At sixteen a brush with death "brought terror to her soul, as [she] remembered her failings,"[16] and as she says, she was ready to make a covenant with God. However, with regained health, she "went on her usual course," leading a normal adolescence which included music and dancing (two aspects of her life that she later rejects as frivolous). At about the same time as her illness, she had a visitation from God which was "like thunder to [her] soul" (p. 3). He urged her to go to America. So in 1712, against the wishes of her parents, Hoskens emigrated to Pennsylvania. During the first months and years in America, while living in a Quaker home, Hoskens "saw the rightness of the Quakers and was stripped of self-righteousness" (p. 5). She became "weaned from the gaieties of this fading world . . ." (p. 4). We see her in this period struggle in her attempt to submit body and soul to God's will: "O! the weight and exercise I was under during this time of refinement, days and nights of sorrow and penitential mourning are beyond my ability to set forth in words" (p. 8). Having passed through these stages of doubt and anguish, however, she begins attending Quaker meetings. It is here that Hoskens faces one of her worst battles, for when confronted with God's demand that she, a woman, speak forth in meeting, she is reluctant to obey, having "spoken much against women appearing in that manner" (p. 10). "I felt inexpressible anguish of mind, so that I could not shed a tear" (p. 10). Finally, after having renewed her covenant with God three times, after having fought off the Devil's constant suggestions that "the peace she enjoyed was a false one" (p. 11), and after having been heartily encouraged by the family with whom she was living, Hoskens begins to speak up at the meetings. The battle won, she ends this part of her narrative, the most detailed part, and goes on to list her travels as a minister for the Society of Friends.

For Hoskens the most demanding stages of her conversion to the Quakers were her final submission to God's will, the yielding of her will to the inner light, and her full and active entry into the work of the Society. She had difficulty believing that as a woman she could or should be a minister. This plight was unique to Quaker women who as ministers took on an active role in the church's well-being and future growth; for Puritan women there was an injunction against speaking in church.

Almost reversing Hoskens's pattern, Elizabeth Ashbridge in her spiritual autobiography, *Some Account of the Life of* . . . , stressed the early phases of the conversion process. Ashbridge was also born in England. At the age of fourteen she eloped with a young man and as a result was banned from her father's home. At fifteen she was widowed and went to Ireland to live with relatives. There she lived a short-lived free existence and decided to go to America instead of returning home. In America, living as an indentured maid, she began to doubt "whether there was any such thing" as religion.[17] "I became hardened and was ready to conclude that there was no God" (p. 13). However, when her "feet were on the brink of the bottomless pit, [God] pluchked [her] back" (p. 14). In the depths of despair and about to commit suicide, she heard God's voice tell her that there was indeed a hell beyond the grave. At this Elizabeth Ashbridge cried out for God's mercy, but she did not "give [herself] up to the heavenly vision" (p. 16). Rather, she married a man who fell in love with her because of her talents for dancing and singing.

At this stage, the "search to find the truth" began to absorb her. She went to services of various faiths and even consulted a priest; nevertheless, she found no relief and despaired for months. "My nights and days were continued scenes of sorrow; but I let no one know the state of my mind" (p. 23). One night, as she lay in bed bemoaning her condition, she beseeched God's mercy and promised to obey all that He should command of her. With this submission of her will to His guidance, "her heart was tendered and [she] was dissolved in a flood of tears" (p. 25). Ashbridge suffers through this "agony of mind" all alone. Her husband is unsympathetic, and she is not as yet affiliated with any church, so she has no succor from like-minded friends. She remembered that she had relations in Pennsylvania and went to see them. However, as she says, "I felt no small mortification on hearing that my relations were all Quakers, and what was worst of all, that my aunt was a preacher. I was exceedingly prejudiced against this people, and often wondered how they could call themselves Christians" (p. 27). While staying with her Quaker relations, she went to her first meeting of the Friends and felt like a stranger among them. Yet shortly her heart was changed and she "opened [her] heart to receive the truth" (p. 30). But rejoining her husband, who has discovered her change of faith, she was removed from her relatives, an event which began a series of battles between husband and wife. Despite her husband's many protestations and attempts to stop her, Ashbridge became a minister for the Society of Friends. Her husband, finally, came around and desisted from preventing her going freely to meetings. At the end of her autobiography her husband goes off to fight in Cuba where he is killed, leaving Ashbridge a widow and free to be an itinerant minister for the Society of Friends.

Ashbridge devotes the major part of her comparatively long narrative (fifty-four pages) to that time in her spiritual life when she searched for the right and true faith. At least two-thirds of her narration is spent detailing her pilgrimage, and the final third is devoted to her trials with her husband who had become the prime obstacle to her achievement of full communion with the Quakers. Vastly unlike the Puritan autobiographies, Ashbridge's spiritual autobiography presents her story within the context of the real world. The most vivid example of her narrative fidelity to her surroundings occurs in her description of an incident with her husband in a tavern. We learn that her husband announced to the people in the tavern that she was a new Quaker, but that before this time she had been a good dancer. Almost on cue someone picked up a fiddle and began playing, while her husband, against her wishes, pulled her up and "round the room, till the tears fell from her eyes, at the sight of which the musician stopped and said 'I'll play no more; let your wife alone'" (p. 36). Certainly in no Puritan autobiography do we see such a graphic portrayal of the individual's struggle not to disobey God's or the church's wishes. This incident does not demonstate the usual pull and tug between Satan and the doubtful soul within the inner chambers of the autobiographer's conscience, a scenario appearing countless times in both Quaker and Puritan autobiographies. Rather we witness a wife defying her husband within the very public sphere of a country tavern, an incident with a religious source and religious implications within the body of the autobiography, but rooted in a physical and social world. Ashbridge firmly grounds the narration of her vicissitudes. While staying faithful to the thematic thread of the inner light and the formula of the successive steps of Quaker conversion, she builds a full and sometimes graphic rendition of her troubles and glories. Once she had overcome the boundaries within her own spirit and submitted herself entirely to the inner light, everything else, while vexing, nevertheless was conquerable. This, of course, is the moral of her tale; this is what she wanted the formula to tell the community.

By adopting the formula, by fashioning their individual stories around the prescribed stages agreed upon by the community, both Ashbridge and Hoskens in part defer to the group's definition of spiritual experience. Yet by choosing to stress some stages over others and by grounding their journeys in the stuff of life, the individuality of the experience and the writer emerge despite the basically formulaic quality. It is almost as though the individual had not completely submitted herself to God's will. And this ambivalence can in part be attributed to the paradoxical nature of Quakerism: individuality is emphasized by reason of the doctrine of inner light and yet this individuality must submit itself to God's will. The autobiographies mirror this paradox by displaying individuality within the confines of conventionality. This tension between the individual woman's expression of her experience with its own peculiar stamp and the expression of the community's principles via its representative, the minister, produces a hybrid in this early manifestation of the autobiography. For, on the one hand, these spiritual autobiographies are very definitely products to some degree of a group experience—many ministers, male and female, shared similar types of obstacles from without and within. Yet these narratives are also very definitely products of women's lives lived in a somewhat unorthodox manner. Not many Quaker women, and certainly no Puritan women, went about ministering and traveling for their church, primarily because they were not allowed to, either by church elders or by resisting husbands.

The Puritan women adhere to a strict, orthodox conversion pattern in their autobiographies. Their narrations are almost purely restricted to the inner realm, where occasionally there may be beatific visions and dreams. "The more tangible stuff of Puritan autobiography was drawn from identifiable emotions appearing in discernible order and from events and experiences that bore the stamp of Providence."[18] We, as readers, feel the emotional stamp of experience but have little insight into the circumstantial aspects of these women's lives, as we do with the Quakers. "The Quaker autobiographer enjoyed a relative freedom; he [or she] was allowed to move about in the terrain of [his or her] past experience,"[19] and it is this freedom which permits the detailing of their lives. Since part of the conversion process involved searching for adequate religious beliefs, the Quaker autobiographer was forced to conduct her search both internally and externally, in the world, thus giving Quaker spiritual autobiographies a latitude not found in the Puritan documents.

Taken together, though, both sets of autobiographers, despite their differences, make their stories conform to a previously determined mold. Regardless of the marks of individuality, however significant they may be, time and time again we find the individual voice merging with the group voice. Wright claims that the motives of the Quaker autobiographer join with those of the group, which gives their autobiographies a distinctive quality.[20] This convergence of individual and group, though, equally applies to the Puritans; a conventional conversion pattern, representing the group voice, consistently and ultimately structures each individual woman's autobiography. Within the autobiographies each autobiographer establishes a positive, spiritual covenant with the community; she comes before the community either as a member of the Elect (one who has received grace and thus salvation) or as a minister—two roles quite distinct and separate from those of wife and mother. This bonding is crucial because the stories, while thematically dealing with the making of the spiritual covenant, center *in fact* around spiritual and, for the Quakers, social isolation and conflict.

Inherent in the early stages of the Puritan conversion process was that state where the soul is left abandoned by God's grace, where the soul is not only denied the promise of heaven but is also isolated from the Church of Visible Saints, the Puritan community. Usually we first encounter our autobiographer, at this stage, during that damp and drizzly November of the soul. This, for instance, is where we meet Elizabeth Mixer; before she has those rapturous visions of heaven, she is sick and in darkness. Oddly enough, her vision of election, instead of drawing her closer to the community, evokes statements from her which indicate her strength in solitude and, of course, the strength of her conviction. "And he gave me new assurance that I was in his favour then. I thought if all the world was against me, I should value it as nothing" (p. 23). In addition she says: "I thought that I had readily leave father and mother, brethren and sisters, to go to Christ" (p. 20). Given these statements at the end of her autobiography, the fact that she had read this document aloud seems doubly significant, if we grant that the autobiography represents an affirmation of community membership.

The Quakers also suffer from periods of doubt and isolation from God's presence. However, oftentimes their problems are compounded by a physical isolation from other Quakers. For example, Mrs. Chloe Willey in her autobiography, *A Short Account of the Life of . . .* , published in 1807, informs the reader that when she was young, her parents moved to New Hampshire, away from friends and "all of the comforts of life."[21] In this wilderness, there was not even a minister, and thus she spent much time alone and untutored. Catherine Phillips, an English Quaker minister who did missionary work in America in the mid-eighteenth century, continually comments on the isolation of the Quaker communities and the individuals in the wilderness. She says that the people she encountered "had few opportunities of religious instruction, no place of worship being near."[22]

The Quakers in both America and England faced a great deal of opposition and, in some cases, persecution; whereas the Puritans, in America at least, were an established and accepted community which had left opposition behind in England. Since the Quakers "demanded complete freedom for the religious conscience from civil and ecclesiastical authority"[23] and since they did not conform to formal ritualistic patterns of worship, they were outsiders. For the Quaker individual, and maybe even more for the woman who was venturing away from the traditionally sanctioned paths, the pilgrimage both to the Quaker community and to that state of submission to God's will was trying and difficult. Not only did they have to endure the inner hardships of religious doubt but they also had to withstand and overcome the resistance and prejudice of others, sometimes of those closest to them.

Trouble and conflict accompany the Quaker and Puritan autobiographer at every stage of the pilgrimage, and yet, ultimately, once the proper relations have been found with God and the community, the autobiographer offers her experiences to the public realm. But before the right relations have been discovered and before the autobiographer has made a public bond with the community, the individual retreats into herself. The Quaker autobiographer, however, before this stage, usually breaks with one community, usually her family, to pass into an intense period of isolation. Isolation for the Puritan autobiographer means exclusion from the Elect and from God's saving grace. The Quaker, on the other hand, oftentimes is not aware of an alternate community while she is alone and searching; all she knows is that she must find the path of truth. We are with these people most often during their trying times of solitude, and we see them, during the course of the autobiographies, re-emerging into a community of one sort or another, whether it be the Church of Visible Saints or the Society of Friends.

These autobiographies are not easily accessible or widely read today, and indeed they can be tedious reading. Yet when we look at the history of women's writings, it is important to keep them in mind, for as we examine these spiritual autobiographies, remembering the history of the documents within the community, a telling pattern emerges. The women mirror the community's standards and the community's struggles. In its broadest outlines, it is not the individual's voice that we hear but rather that of the community manifested through the peculiar stamp of the individual woman. Because of this, our expectations and maybe our hopes for highly individualistic and unique stories of spiritual questing are deflated. We are left with the sober reality that these spiritual autobiographies were not written by rebels or artists but by women who searched very hard and sometimes very long for a niche and who, once having found it, symbolically celebrated their sense of community via the written word.

4.

Harriet Martineau's Autobiography: The Making of a Female Philosopher

MITZI MYERS

Conceived as the final act of conscience by a woman who thought herself dying, *Harriet Martineau's Autobiography* is the emancipation proclamation of a female philosopher.[1] Characteristically, Martineau is concerned in her life story with demonstrating truths and elucidating principles through a comprehensive factual account. She is presenting the lessons of a life, a life which she rightly sees as having been lived in terms of an organic theme:

> I am more and more sensible, as I recede from the active scenes of life, of the surpassing value of a philosophy which is the natural growth of the experience and study,—perhaps I may be allowed to say,—the progression of a life. While conscious, as I have ever been, of being encompassed by ignorance on every side, I cannot but acknowledge that philosophy has opened my way before me, and given a staff into my hand, and thrown a light upon my path, so as to have long delivered me from doubt and fear. It has moreover been the joy of my life, harmonizing and animating all its details, and making existence itself a festival. (II, 112)

The imagery is significant, for Martineau's autobiography is organized around her stage-by-stage pilgrimage from darkness to enlightenment.

It is both a moving psychological study and a didactic success story, delineating in vivid detail the progress of a Victorian woman's mind from the paralysis of childhood fear to the serene freedom of full self-government. Its last sections are resonant with such passages as the one I have quoted. Finding herself at the close of life "under a new heaven and on a new earth," she tries urgently to realize for her readers what it means to have at last "got out of the prison of my own self" (II, 28).

Believing that she might die of heart failure at any moment, Martineau had hastened from her London doctors back home to the Lake District, where she wrote the *Autobiography* at breakneck speed in three months. So convinced was she of imminent death that she had it printed, illustrated, and bound, ready for publication in 1855, but the volumes waited for more than twenty years while Martineau lived on and on.[2] She never altered what she had originally written, for the *Autobiography*, despite its richness as a record of historical personages and events, is basically the story of an internal evolution—the active formation of a self as it responds to outer circumstances and painfully progresses toward an ever-developing inner ideal. The final stage of that self's freedom and self-knowledge once set down, Martineau left external addenda to the care of her close friend, Maria Weston Chapman, the American abolitionist and feminist who compiled the *Memorials* issued with the *Autobiography* in 1877. The *Memorials*—though often criticized for fulsome commentary (forgivable in a feminist determined to demonstrate a woman writer's importance as a statesman and philosopher)—complete Martineau's life history. More importantly, the letters, diaries, and miscellanea with which the volume is crammed supplement and clarify Martineau's own account of her intellectual and moral development. The *Autobiography* and the *Memorials* illuminate at what expense Martineau's always self-assured public image was erected and how late in her life public image and private self fully became one.

Martineau had long felt it a duty, a moral obligation, to tell the story of her life. As an unknown fledgling author from provincial Norwich, by late 1831 she had written her early mentor W. J. Fox, editor of the liberal Unitarian *Monthly Repository* (the chief recipient of most of her apprentice work) that she had made some progress.[3] She kept copious journals in preparation, and she recurred to the project again during her five years of invalidism at Tynemouth in the early forties. Each time she saw her autobiography as a duty, but the reasons behind the duty enlarged with the progress of her mind. The struggling writer in her twenties had the now familiar story of a miserable nineteenth-century childhood to tell. The Tynemouth invalid was the celebrated author of the *Illustrations of Political Economy* (1832–34) and many other political works, which had made her the conferee of government officials and significantly influenced reform legislation; a pioneer sociologist and early propagandist for abolition, who had produced six volumes on the theory and practice of American democracy; and a Unitarian reformer and rationalistic feminist with a host of causes to advocate and a most unusual achievement to relate. But the mature woman who finally completed the *Autobiography* was a freethinking philosopher less interested in self-justification and specific political controversies than in the progress of the mind and the future of society. Believing that humanity has no source of guidance from outside this world and that the all-important science of the human mind—the sole basis of our knowledge and action—is yet in its infancy, she presents herself as an experimental example, offering such testimony as she can to benefit that mental science for which she had already endured such a furor from the religious.

Like so many of Martineau's later concerns, her theory of life writing was clearly articulated during her long literary apprenticeship. Martineau's philosophical view of historical evolution and her lifelong interest in the comparative study of cultures led her to see biography and autobiography as of paramount significance. In 1830, she had already formulated an impressive rationale for life writing. Criticizing deception and panegyric, she called for emphasis on "internal machinery" rather than external deeds and insisted on richly detailed verisimilitude and absolute candor, a recipe linking aesthetic realization with educational value. If all the truth cannot be told, we should at least be given nothing but the truth. She recognized the pain that full life-records might give to those connected with the subject, as well as the difficulties inherent in the writer's bias. But the longing "to assist others" with the experience one has gained made the attempt worthwhile.[4]

The author of scores of outspoken biographical sketches (including her own remarkably unsparing obituary), Martineau was thus a champion of biographical candor in a period of reticence. She no doubt foresaw the clamor that would arise over her record of her childhood, her assessments of the public figures she had known, and her advocacy of "atheism" (what we would call agnosticism). But she was determined to tell as much of the truth about herself as she could, cost what it might, and in committing hoards of her private papers to Chapman with liberty to use them as she saw fit, Martineau knew that what she herself did not completely reveal—the extent of her ambivalence toward her mother, her quarrel with her brother James, for example— would be filled in by her friend. The result is a document of remarkable frankness, which is indeed a contribution to that "philosophical research, with a view to truth" (I, 322) which she so much revered. Like her longtime heroine Godiva, Martineau rather relished going naked for a cause; she was always audacious for what she saw as truth.

Indeed, for many, Martineau is the epitome of the woman writer as stern truth-seeker and scientific investigator. R. Glynn Grylls's summary in *Ideas and Beliefs of the Victorians* is typical: "Mary Wollstonecraft has to yield in feminism to Harriet Martineau. Much more prolific in the production of spiritual daughters, it was she who set the standard of the objective outlook and the scientific approach in place of personal rebellion and political passion—and set at the same time an unfortunate standard of personal plainness to which it was a heresy not to conform."[5] It is not hard to caricature Martineau as a cold-blooded, strong-minded spinster, critical of those who, like Wollstonecraft and Eliot, succumbed to illicit love, and to remember her chiefly for her deafness, her eccentricities (e.g., a taste for cigars and gossip), and her strenuous concern with improvement. But it is important to recognize that just as Wollstonecraft's personal rebellion generated a radical ideology based on the rights of humanity, so Martineau's objective outlook and scientific approach were fueled by private misery and revolt, were indeed very much a defensive response to personal pain. Far from being intrinsically objective and deficient in imagination and passion, the young Martineau was immersed in a nightmare world of subjective suffering; the mature woman's final achievement of a serene, distanced view is supremely valuable to her precisely because of its contrast with her starting point.

As a philosophic autobiographer who is also a woman, Martineau's attitude toward her experience is necessarily complex. She sees her life as at once representative and unique. Having learned to make sense of her own tormenting history, she wants not only to explain why and how she personally became a female philosopher—escaping into "the fresh air of Nature . . . after imprisonment in the ghost-peopled cavern of superstition" (II, 107)—but also to suggest that individual lives can both represent and recapitulate stages in the progress of civilization. She offers her life as an educational model, which she hopes will help her readers comprehend, accept, and transform their own existences: "The age in which I have lived is an infant one in the history of our globe and of Man; and the consequence is, a great waste in the . . . powers of the wisest of us; and, in the case of one so limited in powers, and circumscribed by early unfavorable influences as myself, the waste is something deplorable. But we have only to accept the conditions in which we find ourselves, and to make the best of them" (II, 106). The mature woman can assent to her life as a bit part in the pageant of human evolution and is content to rest her faith on natural facts and the principles that govern them, "the eternal laws of the universe" (II, 107).

Martineau is thus the narrator of a real-life female *Bildungsroman*, in which deplorable waste is converted into intellectual and emotional sustenance. She recognizes the typicality of her experience in an age of cultural transition, but she is also very much aware of its particularities: her infirmities, her gender, her family configuration. However philosophic, her approach to her story is quite different from, say, Mill's dispassionate intellectual analysis of his life. Where Mill is cool and concise, Martineau is garrulous, emotionally emphatic, and novelistically detailed. She understands that concrete domestic circumstances shape our lives as ineluctably as abstract ideas. Her autobiography is very much a portrait of the *woman* as intellectual.

Martineau's retrospective account of her childhood and youth is dual in perspective. Her narrative stance entails a delicate balancing act. She wants both to recreate what it was like to be that girl and to judge that younger self and the "early unfavorable influences" that impinged upon her from the vantage point of the disinterested philosopher. Because she is a reformer whose optimism assumes that people are wholly the products of secular facts and conditioning, she must realize fully the social mesh that marked her. She shows in this developmental record an unexpectedly acute psychological insight into the strengths and weaknesses of character that evolved under what she likes to call the "discipline of circumstance," always to her much more formidable in effect than express teaching.[6] Her description of her suffering is extraordinarily vivid, but her awareness of what a difficult and provoking child she must have been is no less keen. Although she was always very grateful to her parents for the excellence of her education, both academic and domestic, she wants also to show how parental mishandling of a proud, reserved child irremediably warped her personality—not so much to castigate as to suggest better methods for bringing out the full potentialities of every child. Before she completed the *Autobiography*, Martineau had already drawn largely from her own youth to enforce this self-realization motif in her *Household Education* of 1849, the personal aspects of which had led Charlotte Brontë to write Martineau that reading it "was like meeting her own fetch,—so precisely were the fears and miseries there described the same as her own" (II, 22).

The recognition was mutual. The closest analogue to Martineau's early girlhood, as she herself emphasizes, is *Jane Eyre*. In fact, she notes that she had been taxed with the authorship by some friends and charged by others with having supplied some of the material in the first volume from her childhood. Martineau "was convinced that it was by some friend of my own, who had portions of my childish experience" in mind (II, 21–22). (She was sure the unknown author was a woman—or an upholsterer—because of a passage about sewing on brass rings.) What Martineau and Brontë were creating and responding to in their respective works, what many women then and since have identified with, is an archetypal female success story, a passage from imprisonment to freedom. The novel and the autobiography have very different conclusions, but their youthful protagonists are remarkably similar: a plain, keenly intelligent girl, with delicate health, sensitive nerves, a strong will, and sharp, judging eyes. Each hides her fears and self-doubts under a hard, unchildlike exterior, and each can be goaded by injustice into passionate revolt, to the shock and dismay of her persecutors. As artistically as any novelist, Martineau has formed her youthful memories into powerful images of dependence and rebellion, images which both explain the shape of her own search for identity and independence and mirror the contours of every woman's existence in an oppressive society.

Always a rapid writer, Martineau could set down those early memories so deftly because of their long gestation; they had been used and reused in many earlier works and often told to friends, "almost in the very same words," George Eliot noted.[7] That first self-image had long since been replaced by a succession of others, but it was burnt into Martineau's brain as the key to what she became. Her estranged brother James and some biographers have disputed the literal accuracy or emotional coloration of her perceptions, but they are unquestionably valid indicators to the evolution of her character. Martineau's terrified responses to her mother's temper, for example, were psychological truths for her, no matter how much James may urge that his memories of Mrs. Martineau differ. Martineau remembered her childhood as "the most tremendous suffering perhaps of human life . . . the misery of concealed doubts and fears, and heavy solitary troubles,—the misery which makes the early years of a shy child a fearful purgatory."[8] Even while stranded on a sickbed for five years in what she thought was a hopeless illness, she could envision nothing worse than her girlhood, which she summarized as "a painful and incessant longing for the future . . . a longing for strength of body and of mind, for independence of action—for an escape, in short, from the conditions of childhood."[9]

Deprived of sympathy, encouragement, and justice, the young Harriet was miserable, jealous, and totally lacking in self-respect. Though apparently fearless and obstinate, a bold tomboy who would never own herself wrong, she was in reality sickly, morbidly self-conscious, and subject to irrational terrors of virtually everything. The starlight sky was perpetually coming down to stifle and crush her, magic lantern displays brought on "bowel-complaint" (I, 12), and the sound of feather-beds being beaten made her heart stand still. The milk diet her mother insisted on as proper for children gave her years of painful indigestion and recurrent nightmares. Harriet was the sixth of eight children—the unhandy, unobservant one, snubbed and ridiculed by her elder siblings and perpetually provoking her mother's sharp tongue. What Harriet calls the "taking-down" system (I, 15)—no overt affection and plenty of subjection to authority—flourished under her mother's hand. Mrs. Martineau had not the insight to recognize the emotional needs her daughter could not communicate. Though no orphan, Martineau, like Jane Eyre, perceived herself as an unmothered child. (She says little about her father in the *Autobiography*, but he seems to have been a gentle, supportive parent.) The girl took refuge in religion and books, fantasized about martyrdom (she came to believe that her deafness was partly occasioned by these vainglorious dreams), and mothered her younger brother and sister. She was so wretched that she wept every day for years, planned suicide with the carving knife, and frequently lied to her mother out of sheer terror. "The first person I was ever not afraid of," she writes, "was Aunt Kentish, who won my heart and confidence when I was sixteen" (I, 8).[10]

Martineau liked to say that her life began with winter, had no spring, and ended with a fruitful summer and autumn, and she carefully divided the *Autobiography* into "periods" (there are six) to mark her strong sense of stage-by-stage progression. She was very much aware of how her childhood had shaped her existence and directed her toward philosophy. In a letter of 1844, she calls herself "a sort of pioneer in the regions of pain, to make the way easier,—or at least more direct to those who come after. . . . what a continued series of disappointments & troubles my life has been, & how directly whatever I have been able to do has arisen out of this. . . . So do we stumble and grope onwards to the clear issues of our lives!"[11] These clear issues are implicit in the earliest periods of the *Autobiography*. Take, for example, her hatred of irresponsible power and her ardor for justice to all deprived classes and races—those "who dared not speak." It is easy to see the future feminist and radical reformer, the "national instructor" as Fox called her,[12] in what she says of herself as a child: "I had a devouring passion for justice;—justice, first to my own precious self, and then to other oppressed people. Justice was precisely what was least understood in our house in regard to servants and children." Always an intensely religious child, she found "my passion for justice baulked there, as much as any where. The duties preached were those of inferiors to superiors, . . . but not a word was ever preached about the justice due from the stronger to the weaker . . . a doctrine of passive obedience which only made me remorseful and miserable. I was abundantly obedient in act . . . but the interior rebellion kept my conscience in a state of perpetual torture" (I, 14, 16–17). These are of course verbalizations after the fact, orderings of experience already characteristically directed toward social action.

Even more impressive and significantly indicative of the future philosopher's lifelong obsession with facts, laws, principles—the way nature, society, and the human mind work—is the total gestalt of privation and suffering, rendered in painfully concrete symbols of physical and mental oppression. Selected events stand for a whole orientation toward the world, an existential situation in which this infant's experience recapitulates the infancy of the race. Martineau's memories go back to the age of two: she is standing at a threshold trying methodically to reach solid ground—finally she toddles uncertainly. She is perpetually bombarded by sensations of "monstrous" intensity, and perceived facts seem to have no connection with the sensations they inspire. At four, she is frozen with unaccountable horror by a dream of a stag and her mother offering her sugar; prismatic colors dancing on the wall made her heart race all her life, long after she understood how they came there. She was never afraid of ghosts, but "things as I actually saw them were dreadful to me . . . I had scarcely any respite from the terror" (I, 8). Martineau conveys with extraordinary clarity the frightful slipperiness and senselessness of experience to a child.

She is pursued, stifled, sealed in. Deficient in taste and smell, she also cannot see what the rest of the family can, even though her eyesight at least is perfectly good. Because she is perpetually miserable, she feels herself guilty; she must understand why, must try to make sense of things to remedy the pain. But with the constant physical lump in her throat and the familial injunction against the expression of feeling, she exists in a world of silent fear. Totally self-contained, she lives isolated with her anxiety in the midst of a large family, her "habits of life silent, and as independent as they could be under the old-fashioned family rule of strictness and the strong hand" (II, *Mem.*, 563). She has no way, no language, in the phrase of the time, to "utter herself." She has, however, those advantages which make the *Autobiography* a story of "how I found my way out" (I, 33)—a "desperately methodical" mind (I, 27) and a driving self-will, which she described shortly before her death as "such a helper to me in life. I did not dare to utter it, to express it in any way when I was a child, it so happening that our mother also was strong on that point . . . but in my silent way I did scores of things of which I should not have been capable, perhaps, under any other impulse or by any other strength" (II, *Mem.*, 552–53).

Autobiography, one critic argues, is essentially an "epistemological genre."[13] In no case is this truer than that of Martineau, whose life from early childhood was one long investigation of the origin, nature, methods, and limits of human knowledge. She describes with wry precision her early attempts to get a fix on experience—cutting the Bible up into little tabular rules for life, being overwhelmed with joy when her sister Ellen was born because she could now see the growth of a human mind from the very beginning, absorbing herself wholly in *Paradise Lost* for seven years. When very young, Martineau began what she calls "to take moral charge of myself." She was always in search of principles which would guide her out of the prison of herself, give her the "ease of conscience" and self-respect she pined for, and satisfy her longings for comprehension, sympathy, and justice. She ultimately found "moral relief through intellectual resource," but it was a long, difficult progression (I, 22, 31, 33). *Household Education* acts as a gloss on this early period of self-making. Embedding the episodes of her childhood in a discursive analysis, Martineau explains how the child proceeds from being the mere recipient of sensation to slowly learning to think for itself: how it becomes aware of itself, searches into the reasons of things, learns it can modify nature, and, more importantly, itself. With her usual deep reverence for human powers, she spells out the relationship between the child's ability to reason and its development of imaginative faculties—its capacity to conceive a moral ideal for itself and gradually advance toward it. It is no accident that six closely reasoned essays on the "Art of Thinking" were among Martineau's earliest publications or that she cites her working out for herself of the necessarian philosophy as the foreshadowing of her release from the constriction of childhood. Thinking, philosophizing, was her salvation, and necessarianism the bedrock of her thought as both Unitarian and agnostic.[14]

Theology was the meat on which the precocious eleven-year-old cut her mental teeth. Wanting desperately to be good, craving heroism (yet another nineteenth-century St. Theresa), she choked over the problem of how creatures could be blamed or rewarded for their conduct if God foreknew everything. It was a dilemma of pressing personal urgency, but she was put off by her eldest brother when she timidly broached it. Having sorted it out on her own a few years later, she felt as if she had been given a key to interpret life's mysteries. Necessarianism must not be confused with fatalism. Because it showed how every event, material or mental, has its causal antecedents, how humans are products but not prisoners of circumstances, the doctrine of necessity offered Martineau both an answer to her own psychological and moral quandaries and a rationale for her future career as didactic educator. People act as they do because of their previous training and environment; the way to amend them is not to pray for providential intervention, but to improve their education, surroundings, and associations. They can never escape their pasts, but they can turn their experience to advantage. By understanding the influences that act upon them, by controlling their own mental set, they can to some extent will themselves into what they want to be. Action is not "free"—divorced from motive and consequence—but proceeds in accordance with general laws, thus ensuring security of results. Instead of feeling that things were arbitrarily and capriciously governed, as under her mother's rule, Martineau started to believe that life does make sense. It was the beginning of her escape from passive subjectivity. Now she could see herself no longer helplessly faulty, but a self-governing individual capable of change: first, personal; later, social. This is the root of Martineau's radical optimism, her belief that "every human being," if all aspects of conditioning could ever be brought into healthy congruence, "might be made perfectly good."[15] Its implications for her feminism, reformism, and views of autobiography are obvious. Martineau speaks of herself as overwhelmed by the vastness of this new conception and the great alteration requisite in her management of herself. She is reborn, a "new creature," henceforth experiencing, she says, a steady growth in self-command, courage, and disinterestedness. Inspired by an encouraging minister to study David Hartley and Joseph Priestley, the necessarian philosophical heroes of her Unitarian heritage, she felt she had taken a giant step toward freedom, though it was a long time before the "last link of [her] chain snapped" and she became "a free rover on the broad, bright breezy common of the universe" (I, 83–89).

By the time she came to write her autobiography, Martineau saw her Unitarianism as a way station to something better, and she probably underestimated its importance, just as she consistently underrated her earlier works and personae. But while the peculiarities of her faith explain much about the course of her development, they do not, as some critics of her work imply, explain virtually everything. Not all Unitarians were necessarians, nor did all undergo the deconversion experience which is the leitmotif of the *Autobiography*. Martineau was indeed, as R. K. Webb, her most recent biographer, calls her, "Priestley's disciple," inheriting and revitalizing his Enlightenment attitudes, but she was also a young woman with a complex emotional history and a difficult family situation. Even though her sect was in general hospitable toward women's endeavors to use their minds and better their lot, Martineau did not find it easy to reconcile her ambition to develop her intellect and succeed in a public career with her need to live up to her mother's notions of what was proper for a dependent daughter. The Martineau girls were unusually well educated for their day, being expected to support themselves as teachers or governesses if necessary, but Harriet was also supposed to be a wizard at housewifery and to keep her studies strictly under wraps. She stitched mounds of sewing in public, but she also carried on a busy subterranean intellectual life with her then much beloved younger brother James. She was the leader in their eager discussions, but he was the one who went off to college, leaving her so bereft that he suggested she try writing something for publication. Significantly, her first essays discussed women writers and female education; she was working out a justification for her aspirations.[16] She was ecstatic when her eldest brother told her to leave shirts and stockings to other women and devote herself to writing, but she had to juggle both until she was past thirty and finally succeeded in establishing herself in London in an "independent position." For her, these long years from 1819 to November 1832 were a "marked period" (I, 75), the third stage of her progress and a key time of preparation for the following evolution. Because Martineau's life was essentially a working out of basic principles to their farthest conclusions, it is important to understand this period of Unitarian apostleship—what advantages and challenges her heritage offered her and how it contributed to the attitude toward the self which informs the *Autobiography*.

Lax on doctrine and heavy on social activism, Unitarianism was less a set of tenets than a model for the virtuous self's interaction with the world. A denomination of practical philosophers at once idealistic and scientific, Unitarians combined an optimistic belief in the gradual perfectability of man through rational reform with a rigorously intellectual approach to the examination of factual evidence. They were given to investigation of everything, from biblical miracles to the inequities in contemporary society. Dedicated to freedom, intellectual and political, they were vigorously individualistic, yet forever concerned with the good of the whole. They were temperamentally radical and devoted to education as the vehicle of social change. They often struck others as abrasive and egotistical in their contentious pursuit of truth; isolated and persecuted, they saw every day as an occasion for discipline, activity, and quiet heroism. However acidulous Martineau later became about this legacy, it clearly offered the anxious and ambitious young woman a great deal indeed. It furnished her with an order, a pattern for relating to the world into which she could meld her personal experience and needs, and an ethical ideal around which her own aspirations could crystallize: religion for her was always the pursuit of perfection, mutual and self. It provided tools for inquiry—she never tired of talking about the inductive method. It substituted an acceptable, outwardly directed channel for the self-consuming passion and imagination of her youth. Most importantly, it gave her a voice, a persona of energetic reason, serving as a protective shell within which she continued to grow and develop. Carlyle nicely catches the complex flavor of that early self-image: "One of the strangest phenomena," he exclaimed, "a genuine little Poetess, buckramed, swathed like a mummy into Socinian and Political-Economy formulas; and yet verily alive in the inside of that!"[17]

When the Martineaus lost their money and "gentility" in June 1829 and Harriet began to think about a wider and more remunerative audience than the Unitarian constituency of the *Monthly Repository*, she set down a most revealing set of rules for herself. They contain both a demanding program of self-improvement and a rational assessment of her capabilities and chances of succeeding in what she plans. She is determined to please her family, submit to her God, and control her very thoughts. Because circumstances had led her "to think more accurately and read more extensively than some women," she aims to become "a forcible and elegant writer on religious and moral subjects." Her goal is "to consider my own interests as little as possible, and to write with a view to the good of others." She warns herself against "heat and precipitation." It is a description of someone girding for a battle, in which possible enemies lurk within as well as without (II, *Mem.*, 166–68). But safely inside the combative conventions of her sect which she adopted and later secularized, Martineau could, paradoxically, find an identity—satisfying, if temporary—by losing herself. She escaped her self-consciousness and individual problems by total absorption in her chosen vocation. The *Autobiography* and the *Memorials* abound in accounts of her extreme pleasure in thought and composition, frankly recognizing the emotional compensations she derived from her intellectual mastery, while primarily conveying an urgent sense of vocation, a conviction that she had a mission to perform in the contemporary social crisis. Through writing, duty and self-realization became one, the fervent youthful desire for personal justice and self-government mutating into the effort to help the powerless "who dared not speak" free themselves from the oppressions of a patriarchal society through understanding the forces that acted upon them and gaining control over their own lives. Different from "normal" girls, shaped by the most persecuted and radical of dissenting sects, she would triumphantly turn to use the special knowledge of the outcast, making her own repressed rebellion and rage into a voice that would transform English society. As a Unitarian and political controversialist, Martineau had found something to say which utilized and enlarged her own hard-won experience, and she had found a mode of saying it.

Her strategies succeeded for quite a long time. The astonishing popularity of the political economy tales validated her bent for practical philosophy to her family and the world. She describes strikingly her difficulties in getting a hearing—endlessly trudging muddy streets in search of a publisher, weeping hysterically all night, and rising to write prose of complete self-assurance in the morning. Her characteristic mask—authority, verve, and cool common sense—and her mission sustained her. She might be inwardly nervous about the work she had taken on or riddled with domestic anxiety (her problems with her mother persisted long after she became famous), but the outward display of confident control seldom faltered. She went through an unprecedented lionizing and accomplished an almost incredible amount of work seemingly without turning a hair, but she worried constantly about succumbing to flattery or having her independence co-opted. She saw herself as purely the instrument of ideas whose time had come and her life as an extraordinary plot, which must not be sabotaged by any weakness of her own: "Here I am," she wrote her mother in the first flush of success, "placed in an unparalleled position, left to maintain it by myself, and (believe me) *able* to maintain it; and by God's grace I will come out as the free servant of his truth. . . the ground of my confidence is *principles* and not my own powers" (II, *Mem.*, 216). Her letters of the period display a tough-minded management of the anomalies of her situation as a woman and a radical. Recognizing that women could influence politics only through the pen, she strove for an image of such competence that her gender would be irrelevant. She could also use her sex to advantage on occasion, noticing that she could get access to people in power because the radicalism of a woman did not alarm them. Still, she fretted about chinks in her image. Offered the editorship of a magazine, she reflected in her journal that it would set women forward, always a prime object with her, but wondered if she could live up to her standards: "If I do this, I must brace myself up to do and suffer like a man. No more waywardness, precipitation, and reliance upon allowance from others. Undertaking a man's duty, I must brave a man's fate. I must be prudent, indefatigable, serene, good-natured" (II, *Mem.*, 322). All contemporary accounts agree that she had already fully demonstrated every "manly" virtue; considering the reputation for dauntless aplomb she had established, hers is a most surprising statement.

Finally, she fell ill from overwork and family problems. Five years were a long time to think. As ever with Martineau, adversity was a strong stimulant to self-discovery. She struggled to convert suffering into strength, to wrest disinterestedness out of the morbid self-concern of invalidism. Freed from her couch by a celebrated mesmeric cure, she was increasingly excited about the possibilities of a wholly secular mental science and dubious about her Unitarianism, which she saw more and more as simply a subjective stage of thought, a mere fact of human history. She felt the deficiencies of her earlier work and her former self; she was ready for a new philosophy, a final self-image. She had outgrown the buttress of religion; realizing that her conventional faith was quite eroded after a studious trip through the biblical lands, Martineau felt very lonely. In 1847, she wrote: "I know, as well as I ever knew any thing, that for support I really need nothing else than a steady desire to learn the truth and abide by it; and, for self-government, that it is enough to revere my own best nature and capabilities: but it will require a long process of proof before I can be sure that these convictions will avail me, under daily pressure, instead of those by which I have lived all my life" (I, 541). They did. By 1851, she identified her illness as the "turning point," the time "when I got not to care in the least what became of me,—otherwise than morally.

That is in our own power; & therefore a proper object of care."[18] Advancing from relying on God for support in her life and career to relying on herself, she had at last succeeded in coming to terms with who she was and could speak with her own voice—she was a completed woman.

Looking back, Martineau interpreted her life as a series of escapes from successive traps of subjectivity—the helpless egotism of infancy in which the whole world was contracted to a child's terrified vision, the metaphysical self-centeredness of early maturity which clung to a religion based on a human-oriented universe, a personal God, and a bait of individual immortality. Any "dogmatic faith," she concluded, "compels the best minds and hearts to narrowness and insolence" (II, 109). Martineau's *Autobiography* is firmly organized as a progress away from isolated I-ness, a pilgrimage toward a nurturing truth which would connect her with a larger whole. Its pervading image is that of gradual ascent, from inside a stultifying, paralyzing enclosure up and out to a wide, clear, farseeing view. From that elevation, the philosopher can take in the slow evolution of humanity's past and the endless vista of increasing knowledge and progress which the future would surely bring as diverse human capabilities and the material world were better understood and reverenced as they deserved. Leaving life, placed apart, Martineau described the condition of humanity as infantine, but hopeful because "the one essential requisite of human welfare in all ways is scientific knowledge of human nature," and attention is at last "fully fixed on the nature and mode of development of the human being" (II, 121). She looked forward to the extinction of crippling theologies and social structures, believing that the real "kingdom of Christ" would be manifested "in the new heavens and new earth of the regenerated human mind."[19] Her intellectual sense of growth and change leads, in its own way, to a textual conclusion as ardently romantic as that of *Jane Eyre*.

Martineau was obsessed all her life with the problem of what we can know and what we cannot, and it was an enormous relief to rid herself altogether of a theology which promised gloriously, yet delivered little of the self-respect and serenity she had so long and so urgently desired. To dismiss the soul, to check the nagging, importunate, never-satisfied self, meant for her the beginning of real fulfillment, of seeing herself in a true perspective and being responsible only for what she could actually understand and do. Bringing all she had learned from former stages of her life into a new coherence, she felt wholly free and in control at last. Understanding how she had become what she was, she could accept even her infirmities—her deafness, the early emotional warping that left her fitted only for a single life—as positive advantages. Selecting and creatively fusing the elements of her life into an integrated pattern, Martineau modulates the intensely individualized early periods of the *Autobiography* into a kind of philosophical confession, a history of the mind with larger implications.[20] Though her definitions of truth and philosophy might evolve, she correctly perceived the thematic continuity of her existence and its written record: "My business in life has been to think and learn, and to speak out with absolute freedom what I have thought and learned" (I, 101–02). Her own thinking mind and this one world were quite enough; she had absolutely no desire for the immortality which she had forfeited to win her freedom: "The real and justifiable and honourable subject of interest to human beings, living and dying, is the welfare of their fellows, surrounding them, or surviving them. About this, I do care, and supremely" (II, 108). It is a noble Nunc Dimittis.

5.

The Paradox and Success of Elizabeth Cady Stanton

ESTELLE C. JELINEK

In 1895, when Elizabeth Cady Stanton began her autobiography at the age of eighty, she was still a vigorous and active person, writing and publishing even during the last year of her life. *Eighty Years and More: Reminiscences, 1815–1897* (1898) followed close on the heels of two other of her major publications, *History of Woman Suffrage* (I–II, 1881–86) and *The Woman's Bible* (I, 1895; II, 1898), and she had been a prolific writer of articles and speeches during a period of fifty years of service to the cause that occupied most of her life—and shaped her autobiography—the women's suffrage movement.

Stanton was not a literary person, making her representative of most women who produced autobiographies in America and in England at the turn of the century—they were women who devoted their lives to careers in the reform movements of the nineteenth and early twentieth centuries. She was the major intellectual figure of her time, and her autobiography reflects both the excitement and the reserve of her era. It also bears the particular stamp of her personality and reflects her specific intent in writing her life story.

Stanton's intention as stated in her preface—to write about her "private life" as opposed to her "public career"—does not exactly give us the whole picture.

> The story of my private life as wife of an earnest reformer, as an enthusiastic housekeeper, proud of my skill in every department of

71

domestic economy, and as the mother of seven children, may amuse and benefit the reader.

The incidents of my public career as a leader in the most momentous reform yet launched upon the world—the emancipation of woman—will be found in "The History of Woman Suffrage."

The account of her private life as wife-housekeeper-mother is not given enough coverage in *Eighty Years* for us to believe Stanton's assertion. Though her marriage to Henry Stanton lasted for forty-seven years until his death in 1887, her role as his wife is hardly mentioned. Except for a brief sketch of their meeting and marriage journey, Henry himself is hardly present in the book; from 1848, when Stanton's political work started in earnest, until 1885—a period of thirty-seven years—he is never mentioned, and thereafter only three times, very briefly and insignificantly. Though Stanton offers many helpful suggestions on the subject of housekeeping, like the value of efficient stoves, of circulating heat throughout a house, of adequate ventilation, and of the joys of creative cooking, the anecdotes on these matters are scattered through the book and hardly constitute the major theme. Her own motherhood is barely covered and then only, after the birth of her first child, as a kind of handbook for other new mothers; she urges them to trust their own judgment rather than the dictates of rigid and ignorant doctors. Though Stanton bore seven children from 1842 to 1858 and did not undertake her out-of-state lecturing until 1869 when the youngest was eleven, we rarely hear anything about these children until the 1880s when they are all grown and married and pleasant people to visit in her less active years.

Stanton's actual intention is twofold. She wants to present herself as an *ordinary* human being, but *not* as a wife-housekeeper-mother. She is ordinary because she mixes easily with ordinary people, has a cheerful disposition, is self-reliant and healthy, and has varied domestic interests in addition to her political ones. This ordinary person plays an important role in the anecdotes she relates to relieve the narrative of its more weighty and actual though unstated goal: to educate her readers about the women's suffrage movement in order to convert them to her cause. Everything she includes or excludes in this autobiography, even the way she portrays her own self-image, is determined by this overriding educational aim. Her "public career" is indeed the major objective of the autobiography, but she tries to present it as painlessly as she can by means of her humorous, human interest anecdotes in order to persuade her readers to accept her and her reformist ideas.

When Stanton wrote *Eighty Years and More*, she was well known, actually a celebrity among reformists and a name that had figured prominently in the news for fifty years. By casting her views within the framework of an ordinary life, she was attempting to counter the unidimensional public image of herself as a brilliant, argumentative, sharp-witted, unrelenting reformer from a prestigious upper-class family. How was she to integrate this overdetermined image of herself as a superior human being—certainly one worthy of full citizenship as an equal with men—with a multidimensional image of an ordinary human being so that her readers would be receptive to the "most momentous reform yet launched upon the world"?

The dilemma that this paradoxical self-image presented for the writing of her autobiography derived from the two roles she played out in her life, one as wife-housekeeper-mother, the other as public, professional person. It was the struggle of her entire life as a feminist, and it still remains a dilemma for today's feminists. In every way, for Stanton, and for us, there is this dialectic between this ordinary woman, product of the conditions that produce women in this society, *and* at the same time, this *not* ordinary but exceptional woman who is not trapped in those conditions but can see her way out of them.

It is evident from reading her autobiography that Stanton was a success at both roles in her life. But in the autobiography itself, she needed to submerge the superior person in order to win over her readers. Yet in presenting herself as an ordinary person who could accomplish so much, she produces a narrative that is rife with paradox, contradiction, and, at the very least, ambivalence. While she writes an apparently linear and chronological narrative that emphasizes the stability of her personality and her faith in the order and progress of the world as well as in the successful outcome of her life's mission, the narrative is constantly interrupted by a variety of discontinuous forms—anecdotes, for the most part, but also letters and excerpts from speeches and published articles by herself and others. Though she is writing about weighty and controversial issues, she resorts to light and humorous anecdotes to make her points. While she wants to convince us that her childhood was a happy and normal one, she also must show the unusual emotional and intellectual sources of her dedication to the cause of women's rights. Though she treats her father with the greatest respect, it is apparent even at the age of eighty-two that she still thinks of him with fear and a great deal of unrecognized anger. While she regales us with her exploits aboard trains, bathing crying babies or airing stuffy parlor cars, she turns out speeches, lectures, petitions, and pamphlets undauntedly, traveling day and night under superhuman conditions. While in her travels on the lyceum lecture circuit, she feels comfortable and sisterly with ordinary women whose hospitality she accepts despite often unhealthful food and unsanitary sleeping accommodations, she has easy access to the homes of famous people in and out of the reform movement in her own country and abroad because of her family's social position. While she is completely reticent about her sex life, she is outspoken on such controversial issues as hypocrisy in the Bible, incompatibility as grounds for divorce, and the enfranchisement of former slaves only on condition of enfranchisement for women also—positions that brought the profoundest attacks upon her not only from the mass public but even from within her own movement.

The final paradox is that at the time Stanton wrote her autobiography, she had not achieved the goal to which she had dedicated her entire life—the enfranchisement of women. Yet campaigns, attacks on bills, struggles for propositions and amendments, petitions, speeches, etc., all the various efforts she describes here appear as victories. We complete this autobiography with the very positive impression that Stanton's public career was a success.

The primary means by which she conveys this image of her work, despite its immediate failure, are to omit anything that might cast a negative light on her achievements and always to emphasize the positive. She excludes anything about her personal or public life that is irrelevant to the movement or that might give detractors ammunition to undermine the cause. Stanton's unflinching self-confidence and her positive vision of her work—qualities that produce leaders and he-roes— made a success of her effort to educate her readers and to con-vince them of her cause and resulted in their acceptance of her two-pronged self-image. The resolution of her self-image—the dialectic between her being one with all women and at the same time above them—has contemporary overtones, especially in Kate Millett's ef-forts in her autobiography *Flying* to reconcile her individual needs with the collective goals of her cause.

Let us look at how Stanton develops her two unstated intentions—presenting herself as an ordinary human being and furthering the cause of women's suffrage. In the first third of the book, she deals with the influences that shaped her personality and character during her childhood, girlhood, marriage, and early motherhood, to the age of thirty-three in 1848. Here we see the most ambivalent or paradoxical treatment of her life study, for she is dealing with her personality more than the movement. In the second and longest section, the emphasis shifts to her efforts for the cause, from 1848 to 1881; here we see less ambivalence and more direct omitting of information to further her intention. In the final section, which continues the theme of her work for women's suffrage, she spends more time describing her travels and visits with her grown children; here, there is both omission and para-dox, but to a lesser degree than in either of the two earlier sections.

First, let us look at the ambivalence evident in Stanton's description of her early years. She pictures herself, on the one hand, as a healthy, romping girl full of enthusiasm and energy, enjoying her school work, her games with her two younger sisters, and all kinds of outdoor activ-ities at her central New York state home of Johnstown. Her upper-class family supported a number of servants, nurses, and tutors, and the three girls played joyfully in the attic or the cellar, where the many barrels of produce from her father's tenants served as playthings. She presents no terrifying experiences or a sense of deprivation either emotional or physical in these descriptions.

So intent is she on demonstrating that she had a happy childhood that whenever she does introduce a "sorrow" from her childhood, it is immediately followed by one of joy. Some complaints are common to children, like the starched collars that tore at her neck but about which she was rebuked for even complaining. Or the all-red outfits that she and her younger sisters wore throughout their childhood, leaving with Stanton a permanent hatred of that color.

Her more sorrowful memories are of the worms that dangled from the poplar trees of the town, the sight of which made her tremble, and the many bells that tolled on every conceivable occasion and seemed to her like "so many warnings of an eternal future."[1] Years later, in her sixties, she experienced the same frightened reaction that she had as a child to the mournful sound of church bells. Of the many festivities that early nineteenth-century Americans celebrated with such enthusiasm like the Fourth of July, it is the terrifying sounds of the cannon she most remembers.

Stanton evidences ambivalence not only toward the "joys and sorrows" of her childhood but also toward authority. On the one hand, she is incapable of defying her nurses until her younger sister convinces her that they will be punished anyhow, so they might as well have some fun. "Having less imagination than I, she took a common-sense view of life and suffered nothing from anticipation of troubles, while my sorrows were intensified fourfold by innumerable apprehensions of possible exigencies" (p. 11). On the other hand, she rails against the nurses who "were the only shadows on the gayety of these winter evenings. . . . I have no doubt we were in constant rebellion against their petty tyranny" (p. 6).

Her upbringing must have been strict and rigid though she gives us little clue to the rules which suffocated her enthusiasm and energy.

> I have a confused memory of being often under punishment for what, in those days, were called "tantrums." I suppose they were really justifiable acts of rebellion against the tyranny of those in authority. I have often listened since, with real satisfaction, to what some of our friends had to say of the high-handed manner in which sister Margaret and I defied all the transient orders and strict rules laid down for our guidance. If we had observed them we might as well have been embalmed as mummies, for all the pleasure and freedom we should have had in our childhood. As very little was then done for the amusement of children, happy were those who *conscientiously* took the liberty of amusing themselves. (p. 12)

But perhaps the source of her fear of authority came as much from a severe religious code of behavior as from the nurses in her home. At the time Stanton was writing this autobiography, she was also writing *The Woman's Bible*, an exegesis and attack on the Bible and the clergy who preached women's inferiority. Writing the *Bible* must have reawakened her anger against the tyranny of the church, one source of authority in her childhood about which she evidences no ambivalence. "I can truly say, after an experience of seventy years, that all the cares and anxieties, the trials and disappointment of my whole life, are light, when balanced with my suffering in childhood and youth from the theological dogmas which I sincerely believed . . . " (p. 24).

When in her teens she attended Emma Willard's Troy Seminary for girls, she was so overcome by the hellfire sermons of the Reverend Charles G. Finney, that "terrifier of human souls," that because of "my gloomy Calvinistic training in the old Scotch Presbyterian church, and my vivid imagination," she became one of the first of his "victims" (p. 41). She roused her father so often at night to pray for her soul that he, her sister, and her brother-in-law took her on a six-week summer trip where the subject of religion was tabooed and they talked about nothing but "rational ideas and scientific facts." She then concludes this unpleasant subject with a rather rapid recovery, lest her readers be too saddened by her account. After this trip, "my mind was restored to its normal condition" (p. 44).

Stanton's mention of waking her father at night to help her and of his taking her on a trip to cure her would seem to indicate a warm relationship. However, about her father she exhibits much ambivalence. He was, she writes, "a man of firm character and unimpeachable integrity," "sensitive and modest to a painful degree," and though "gentle and tender, he had such a dignified repose and reserve of manner that, as children, we regarded him with fear rather than affection" (p. 3). With her father, Stanton had probably the most traumatic experience of her childhood. When she was eleven, her only brother, who had recently graduated from Union College, died. "He was the pride of my father's heart. We early felt that this son filled a larger place in our father's affections and future plans than the five daughters together" (p. 20). Stanton yearns so much for her father's affection that

she accompanies him on his almost daily visits to the boy's gravesite.
When she tries to comfort him, he says:

> "Oh, my daughter, I wish you were a boy!" Throwing my arms about
> his neck, I replied: "I will try to be all my brother was."
> Then and there I resolved that I would not give so much time as
> heretofore to play, but would study and strive to be at the head of all
> my classes and thus delight my father's heart. All that day and far
> into the night I pondered the problem of boyhood. I thought that
> the chief thing to be done in order to equal boys was to be learned
> and courageous. So I decided to study Greek and learn to manage a
> horse. . . . They were resolutions never to be forgotten—destined
> to mold my character anew. (pp. 20–21)

Her efforts are futile, however, though she accomplishes her two
goals.

> I surprised even my teacher, who thought me capable of doing any-
> thing. I learned to drive, and to leap a fence and ditch on horseback.
> I taxed every power hoping some day to hear my father say: "Well,
> a girl is as good as a boy, after all." But he never said it. (p. 22)

In 1854 when Stanton was thirty-nine, her father asked to hear her
first speech on the issue of divorce that she was to deliver before the
New York legislature.

> On no occasion, before or since, was I ever more embarrassed—an
> audience of one, and that the one of all others whose approbation I
> most desired, whose disapproval I most feared. I knew he con-
> demned the whole movement, and was deeply grieved at the active
> part I had taken. (p. 188)

When she finished her rehearsal, Judge Cady offered no opinion for or
against her political work then or ever after but "gladly gave me any
help I needed, from time to time, in looking up the laws, and was very
desirous that whatever I gave to the public should be carefully prepared" (p. 189). But more important to this study is the fact that Stanton evidences no bitterness toward her father's disapproval of her as a
female. She treats him as one more influence on her life. At the above

meeting, Judge Cady's response on hearing her speech is primarily surprise at her emotional complaints.

> "Surely you have had a happy, comfortable life, with all your wants and needs supplied; and yet that speech fills me with self-reproach; for one might naturally ask, how can a young woman, tenderly brought up, who has had no bitter personal experience, feel so keenly the wrongs of her sex? Where did you learn this lesson?" (pp. 188–89)

And Stanton's response is, "'I learned it here, in your office, when a child, listening to the complaints women made to you'" (p. 189). Stanton does not want to remind her readers of her emotional crisis at eleven lest her readers attribute her devotion to her cause to merely a neurotic source.

Even her father's objection to her marriage to Henry Brewster Stanton did not seem to change her affection for him. Her cousin Gerrit Smith, the abolitionist, at whose Peterboro, New York, home she met Henry, also objected to the marriage and for similar reasons, that an abolitionist reformer and orator, as Henry was, would not be a good provider. After their wedding trip to Europe, however, Judge Cady took Henry into his law office to train him for the bar, and for three years the couple and their growing family lived in the Cady household. Apparently Daniel Cady was both a stern father and a reasonable man. Though Stanton does not include it in her autobiography, it is known that at one time he disinherited his suffragist daughter but changed his mind before his death in 1859.[2]

Of her mother, Mary Livingston, from the prestigious colonial family, Stanton writes hardly anything at all. We know that her mother "took the deepest interest in her father's political campaign for Congress, at which he succeeded during the year of her birth; this prenatal influence, Stanton suggests, may account for her own interest in politics. To her mother's side of the family, she attributes her self-reliance, derived no doubt from General Livingston, whose Revolutionary War fame came from using his own judgment and firing upon a British man-of-war. This action earned him not only General Washington's commendation because it saved many of his troops, but also a warning that under normal circumstances the action would have earned him a court-martial. Stanton describes her mother as a "tall, queenly looking woman, . . . courageous, self-reliant, and at her ease under all circumstances and in all places" (p. 3). One wonders how she evidenced her courage and what control was mustered to be at "ease under all circumstances and in all places." It is clear that Stanton, who was short and progressively stouter as she grew older, must have envied her mother's queenliness because she attributes this characteristic to women she most admires. Stanton never mentions her mother after the first early pages, a curious omission, for which she gives no clue.[3]

Stanton's relationship with her husband seems to have been a satisfactory one though she gives us very little to go on in this autobiography. When she met him, he was considered

> the most eloquent and impassioned orator on the anti-slavery platform. . . . Mr. Stanton was then in his prime, a fine-looking, affable young man, with remarkable conversational talent, and was ten years my senior, with the advantage that that number of years necessarily gives. (p. 58)

On their first outing together on horseback, they seem to have fallen immediately in love, though they had talked in groups on other occasions.

> When walking slowly through a beautiful grove, he laid his hand on the horn of the saddle and, to my surprise, made one of those charming revelations of human feeling which brave knights have always found eloquent words to utter, and to which fair ladies have always listened with mingled emotions of pleasure and astonishment.
>
> One outcome of those glorious days of October, 1839, was a marriage, in Johnstown . . . and a voyage to the Old World. (pp. 59–60)

That is the extent of Stanton's description of her courtship and marriage to Henry Stanton. We can only guess whether or not he objected to her taking out the word "obey" from their marriage ceremony, but she does tell us, quite objectively, that at the World's Anti-Slavery Convention in London in 1840, which they attended as part of their honeymoon trip, when the issue of women's participation in the proceedings came up for a vote, Henry cast his in the negative. She expresses no feelings on this early event of her marriage, but she does recount enthusiastically the position of abolitionist William Lloyd Garrison, who sat in the observation gallery with the women and refused to take part in the segregated proceedings.

She briefly mentions Henry when, because of his frequent travels to courts and abolitionist meetings, he delegates to her the complete management of their homes, first in Boston and Chelsea, later in Seneca Falls. After 1848, when Stanton's political work began, Henry is not mentioned until thirty-seven years later at his eightieth birthday celebration in 1885.

There must have been a policy of live-and-let-live during their forty-seven years together until Henry's death in 1887, which also is not mentioned. We know from sources other than this autobiography that he, like her father, though reformist in every other political cause, always objected to her work for women's rights. We know that he threatened to leave town if the first women's rights convention was held in their town of Seneca Falls, and he did.[4] We also know that Stanton's father frequently helped the couple financially and that she undertook the lyceum tours in part to earn money for their children's education. But Elizabeth Stanton does not include this information in her life study; it might discredit her husband, herself, and the movement. Writing in 1897, in *Eighty Years*, of their minister's superstitious objection to their marriage on a Friday, she sums up her view of her relationship with her husband:

> as we lived together, without more than the usual matrimonial friction, for nearly a half a century, had seven children, all but one of whom are still living, and have been well sheltered, clothed, and fed, enjoying sound minds in sound bodies, no one need be afraid of going through the marriage ceremony on Friday for fear of bad luck. (pp. 71–72)

Though Stanton also leaves out any personal references to sexuality, her awareness of it is evident. For one thing, she frequently notices the good looks or fine physiques of the men she meets in her travels, but even earlier, she writes of her experiences as a child when she studied with boys at the Johnstown Academy, then moved on to Emma Willard's Troy Seminary for girls only. She was flabbergasted by the intrigue stirred up by the girls there without boys present and argues strongly for coeducation, which most adults of her time opposed.

Stanton describes the period between her graduation from Willard's seminary to her marriage as "the most pleasant years of my girlhood" primarily because she "rejoiced in the dawn of a new day of freedom in thought and action" (p. 45). Her description of this time of her life is filled with echoes of sexual awakening:

> Then comes that dream of bliss that for weeks and months throws a halo of glory round the most ordinary characters in everyday life, holding the strongest and most common-sense young men and women in a thraldom from which few mortals escape. The period when love, in soft silver tones, whispers his first words of adoration, painting our graces and virtues day by day in living colors in poetry and prose, stealthily punctuated ever and anon with a kiss or fond embrace. What dignity it adds to a young girl's estimate of herself when some strong man makes her feel that in her hands rest his future peace and happiness! Though these seasons of intoxication may come once to all, yet they are seldom repeated. How often in after life we long for one more such rapturous dream of bliss, one more season of supreme human love and passion! (pp. 44–45)

Closely following this passage is Stanton's effusive description of her brother-in-law Edward Bayard, "ten years my senior . . . an inestimable blessing to me at this time" (p. 45). We know that Stanton was infatuated with Bayard, but she judiciously rejected his advances beyond a platonic attachment[5] and soon after fell in love with Henry Stanton, like Bayard ten years her senior. She excluded any hint of an attachment to a member of her own family, which might have been construed as an unrequited love affair "explaining" her "discontent" with the male way of running the world.

Of the intellectual influences on her life, we have already learned how, as a youngster, Stanton frequented her father's law office and heard the complaints of abandoned wives and mothers with no recourse to the law. Nonetheless, from these experiences and her frequent visits to the county jail, she writes, "I gleaned some idea of the danger of violating the law" (p. 14). Her respect for the law explains why Stanton was conservative when it came to tactics and deferred in that department to her complement Susan B. Anthony; it also explains why she was such a logical and thorough debator. But her respect never seems to have intimidated her or deterred her from fighting laws she felt were unjust or discriminated against women.

Stanton's political and reform spirit was nurtured in the home of Gerrit Smith, where as a late teenager she met her first runaway slave. But Stanton never felt the force of the tyranny of slavery as much as she did that tyranny of her own childhood and womanhood. When push came to shove, she opposed enfranchisement for male blacks when it was denied women after the Civil War, though she had given up her suffrage efforts for five years to help the cause of the North.

It is not surprising that the tyranny Stanton felt was exercised over her as a child was the foundation for her later rebellion against the tyranny over her and all her sex as female. And it is not surprising that she should use the very same phrase to describe those two areas of tyranny over her life: "the constant cribbing and crippling of a child's life" (p. 11) and "the most cribbed and crippled of Eve's unhappy daughters" (p. 204).

The crucial experience that ignited her already informed sympathies for the lot of women came at that antislavery convention in London on her honeymoon trip. It wasn't until eight years later, when longing for more intellectual challenges than those evoked by the management of a large house, servants, and many children, that she and Lucretia Mott placed a brief notice in the local newspaper. Four days later, fifty women met at the Methodist church in Seneca Falls, New York, and started the first feminist movement in North America.

At this point in her life story, female readers probably have no trouble in identifying with Stanton's frustrations after eight years of dedicating herself exclusively to domestic duties. She has convincingly proven herself an ordinary human being and justified her gradual involvement in a "public career." Perhaps now her audience will be receptive to her as a person and treat her ideas seriously.

We now turn to the bulk of *Eighty Years and More*, where Stanton concentrates on her public career, the stated nonintention of her book. While the first part was informed by ambivalence and paradox because of the need to convey the self-image of both an ordinary and superior person, with some omission to protect the women's movement, this second section is informed more by omission than paradox because her political work is the central focus. Her aim is to educate her audience about women's rights, and she does so by creating a positive image of the cause by leaving out anything that might devalue it in any way. There is still some paradoxical treatment or ambivalence in her presentation of herself, but it is less evident here than in the first section. Here everything is positively shaped for the cause.

All the chapters in this middle section have titles that refer to issues or events in the women's rights movement. Nonetheless, the subjects of these chapters are usually minimally treated. As in the first section, Stanton continues to use amusing and pleasant anecdotes, now to educate her audience painlessly about serious issues. The transition chapter "The First Woman's Rights Convention" deals less with that event than with Stanton's preconvention boredom as her duties become tedious, with her postconvention relief in talking to women about their rights, and with her door-to-door efforts for signatures to petition the state legislature for more liberal property and divorce laws. Her female readers, no doubt, could identify more with her concrete domestic experiences than with the convention itself, though she manages to convey its significance in bringing together for the first time an organized protest against women's inferior legal treatment. True to her determination to be positive, Stanton tells us nothing about her husband's negative reaction to the meeting.

The next two chapters, which constitute a portrait of Susan B. Anthony, break the chronology, for it extends from 1851 when the two women met, three years after the Seneca Falls convention, to the 1890s. By including this portrait of Anthony (a revision of one she wrote for *Eminent Women of the Age*, 1868), Stanton reveals how far from her stated intention this autobiography is. For Anthony was the lifelong friend of her public career, and her portrait emphasizes how closely the two worked together.

> In thought and sympathy we were one, and in the division of labor
> we exactly complemented each other. In writing we did better work
> than either could alone. While she is slow and analytical in compo-
> sition, I am rapid and synthetic. I am the better writer, she the bet-
> ter critic. She supplied the facts and statistics, I the philosophy and
> rhetoric, and, together, we have made arguments that have stood
> unshaken through the storms of long years; arguments that no one
> has answered. Our speeches may be considered the united product
> of our two brains. (p. 166)

Stanton omits any tension or problems with her friend. Their partner-
ship was, indeed, predominantly a harmonious one, but they did disagree at times. Though Stanton was more revolutionary in respect to
the movement's ideas, Anthony was more militant when it came to
tactics. Nonetheless, Stanton exposes none of the disagreements or
tensions in the upper echelons of the movement, nothing that might
give cause for dissention in the ranks or for gossip among their detractors.

In this chapter Stanton also reminds her readers that she is not neglecting her children while she and Anthony work. She describes the
mischievous games her children play around them that often require
quick rescues and adult participation. She also directly faces the issue
of Anthony's single life, which she knows her readers are curious
about. She uses the portrait as an occasion to praise all single women
who dedicate their lives to important causes: "All honor to the noble
women who have devoted earnest lives to the intellectual and moral
needs of mankind!" (p. 157). She quotes Anthony's stand on the question of marriage, thus educating her audience in the process:

> She could not consent that the man she loved, described in the Con-
> stitution as a white male, native born, American citizen, possessed of
> the right of self-government, eligible to the office of President of the
> Great Republic, should unite his destinies in marriage with a politi-
> cal slave and pariah. "No, no; when I am crowned with all the rights,
> privileges, and immunities of a citizen, I may give some considera-
> tion to this social institution; but until then I must concentrate all my
> energies on the enfranchisement of my own sex." (p. 172)

It is unstated, but one may infer that Stanton is aware that *she* had accomplished what few women before, during, or since her lifetime had accomplished, and that is the total dedication to a political cause *and* the achievement of a career as wife and mother.

It is in the next chapter, "My First Speech Before a Legislature" (in 1854 on behalf of the civil rights of married women), that Stanton gives her father her intellectual explanation for her sense of "keenly felt wrongs" against women—hearing the complaints of women in his law office—not the "negative" explanation of her traumatic emotional experience at eleven. Certainly, it was a common experience in her day for female children to be treated as inferiors to boys, but Stanton's explanation reflects her preferred emphasis on the law as the basis for her struggle.

In chapter after chapter, Stanton treats her material with this positive emphasis. In "Views on Marriage and Divorce" she manages to convey the impression of success in 1860 as she traveled around New York state trying to get a liberal divorce bill passed. We hear amusing anecdotes about generous people and her pleasant experiences while traveling from one city to another, but nothing of the results of the bill. In "Westward Ho!" she describes her trip in the early 1870s to lecture throughout the state of Nebraska for a proposition to strike the word "male" from the state constitution. She gives a favorable description of the results of her efforts, but we really do not know if the proposition passed or not.

For the 1876 centennial celebration, she attempted to get enough tickets so that every state was represented by a woman, but received only six tickets in response to her polite but firm letters, which she quotes in their entirety. She concentrates, however, on Anthony's daring rush to the platform to shove the Woman's Declaration of Rights into the presiding officer's hand, thus succeeding in making it a part of the day's proceedings. Of the Woman's Pavilion at the centennial, though she praises the woman engineer who ran its turbine to the surprise of the male organizers, she was obviously not satisfied with its contents. Rather than criticize what was in it, however, she lists all the things that *should* have hung on its walls: "the yearly protest of Harriet K. Hunt against taxation without representation," "all the laws bearing unjustly upon women," "the legal papers in the case of Susan B. Anthony, who was tried and fined for claiming her right to vote under the Fourteenth Amendment," and "decisions in favor of State rights which imperil the liberties not only of all women, but of every white man in the nation" (pp. 316–17).

It is only in the case of the proposition to extend suffrage to women in Kansas in 1867 that Stanton evidences any anger at the failure of their efforts. She blames the failure on those in the East who "feared the discussion of the woman question would jeopardize the enfranchisement of the black man" (p. 247). But women also learned another

> important lesson—namely, that it is impossible for the best of men to understand women's feelings or the humiliation of their position. When they asked us to be silent on our question during the War, and labor for the emancipation of the slave, we did so, and gave five years to his emancipation and enfranchisement. . . . I am now . . . sure that it was a blunder. . . . (p. 254)

The issue of black enfranchisement without women's suffrage spilt the women's movement into two factions, those who were willing to wait and take a back seat to black (male) suffrage and those who were not willing to support one without the other. Stanton led the latter camp, but nothing is mentioned in *Eighty Years and More* of this split in the movement nor of the establishment of two rival women's organizations in 1869. The union of the two groups eleven years later, in 1890, is easily missed in a quoted letter in which she mentions her election to the presidency of the new national organization.

Though Stanton expresses some anger about the Kansas failure early in the chapter "Pioneer Life in Kansas," the dispute over black and women's suffrage is pretty much buried thereafter as she concentrates on her harrowing experiences among settlers in the backwoods, sleeping in soiled and flea-ridden beds and eating starchy and sometimes inedible foods, but always admiring the frontier women whose sacrifices in settling the west go unrecognized. Many of the anecdotes in these chapters where Stanton is touting her seemingly successful efforts focus on her encounters with people, usually women, whom she praises with obvious pride in their accomplishments.

Many of the anecdotes, however, have to do with her own experiences traveling around states as a lyceum lecturer from 1869 to 1881, from the age of fifty-four to sixty-six, from October through June, enduring an extremely physically demanding regime with crowded schedules, often twelve-to-eighteen-hour train rides with no time to rest or eat before appearances, even frequent blizzards that snowbound the hardiest. But not Stanton: "As I learned that all the roads in Northern Iowa were blocked, I made the entire circuit, from point to point in a sleigh, traveling forty and fifty miles a day" (pp. 261–62).

Stanton never complains about the many difficulties she encounters in her travels but describes her experiences with enthusiasm and cheerful good humor. For example, in Dubuque, she arrives by train at a desolate station in the early hours of the morning but manages to attract attention by shouting, "John! James! Patrick!" When her feminist friends rib her for not hollering for "Jane, Ann, and Bridget," she retorts, "as my sex had not yet been exalted to the dignity of presiding in dépots and baggage rooms, there would have been no propriety in calling Jane and Ann" (p. 281). In Kansas, where her experiences seem to have been the most trying physically, she writes, "In spite of the discomforts we suffered in the Kansas campaign, I was glad of the experience. It gave me added self-respect to know that I could endure such hardships and fatigue with a great degree of cheerfulness" (p. 252).

The amazon image that Stanton conveys throughout this second section of her autobiography sits side by side with her image as an ordinary person. She sleeps on a lounge in the woman's salon of a ship during a two-week voyage because she can open a window there and avoid the stuffy staterooms. While all others are suffering with seasickness below, she enjoys the ocean breezes while strolling or reading on deck. She precariously descends a mountain in Yosemite National Park, grabbing for roots and branches to steady herself, an undignified but impressive picture for a heavy woman in her sixties. Stanton never mentions a single illness in her life study; she rarely, and then discreetly, refers to her weight which grew considerably each year; and only parenthetically does she refer to her lameness from a "severe fall" in her seventies.

Not only do we get this paradoxical self-image of Stanton as both an ordinary person and one of almost superhuman physical stamina, but in her descriptions of the people she meets and stays with, we also get a double message. On one hand, she stays with poor pioneer women in cabins in the midwest and west; on the other, she is hosted by famous people in the United States and abroad. Her egalitarian attitude came from her genuine political commitment, whereas her pleasure in meeting the famous came from her upper-class family background, which opened doors to her not open to the usual suffragist. It is also clear from the many names listed, most of which are unknown to readers today, that she is using this autobiography to thank these people for their generous support of the women's movement in hosting her and financing her efforts. There is no question, finally, that her name-dropping is meant to indicate her superior status not just in intelligence but also in social position, which should certainly entitle her in any just society to full citizenship with the right to vote and hold office.

In her travels Stanton emphasizes the women she meets rather than their usually more famous husbands. And on only one occasion does she deviate from her usual tolerance for women who are unable to support the movement:

> The history of the world shows that the vast majority, in every generation, passively accept the conditions into which they are born, while those who demanded larger liberties are ever a small, ostracized minority, whose claims are ridiculed and ignored. . . . That only a few, under any circumstances, protest against the injustice of long-established laws and customs, does not disprove the fact of the oppression, while the satisfaction of the many, if real, only proves their apathy and deeper degradation. That a majority of the women of the United States accept, without protest, the disabilities which grow out of their disfranchisement is simply an evidence of their ignorance and cowardice, while the minority who demand a higher political status clearly prove their superior intelligence and wisdom. (pp. 317–18)

Such an outburst, which might antagonize those she most wants to win to her cause, is the exception rather than the rule in *Eighty Years*. Generally, the presentation and tone of the autobiography are mild and low-keyed. Stanton explains how she and the other women, often writing as a group, would argue, discuss, and plan their strategy in order to prepare speeches with acceptable arguments and ones that would not reap the abuse so often leveled at them:

> so long as woman labors to second man's endeavors and exalt his sex above her own, her virtues pass unquestioned; but when she dares to demand rights and privileges for herself, her motives, manners, dress, personal appearance, and character are subjects for ridicule and detraction. (p. 241)

Anyone reading Stanton's *History of Woman Suffrage* or *The Woman's Bible* will be startled by the comparison with *Eighty Years*. The effort not to antagonize readers of her autobiography made her soften the presentation of her ideas here with anecdote. Her other writings are complex and brilliantly argued expositions; this life study appears simple and straightforward, almost childlike, by comparison. Where her public writings express the full force of her anger and rage at the injustice of the laws against women, here there is no anger, no rage, and no bitterness.

While some men have felt uncomfortable reading the autobiography, it is not because she ever affronts them personally but because of the force of her very logical attacks on the laws which discriminate against women. She is no man-hater and often expresses her appreciation for men who supported the movement and her understanding for those who could not. Though she wore the bloomer outfit for two years, she desisted when it was apparent that it caused her male companions too much embarrassment. When she reflects on how much abuse and ridicule men have suffered in supporting the women's movement, she understands, even in her eighties, why so few have been its supporters.

The third section of Stanton's autobiography, after 1881 when she was sixty-six and had retired from her lyceum lecturing chores, relies on the diary she began keeping at the suggestion of friends. The result is a more precisely documented narrative with notations of day, month, and year scrupulously recorded. The narrative thus becomes choppy and less integrated, with fewer extended anecdotes and much less humor. Though she continues to write, deliver speeches, and attend the annual meetings of the National American Woman Suffrage Association, the emphasis in this last section is once again on her private life. In the ten years between 1881 and 1891, she made six trips to Europe, primarily to visit her two children most active in women's work, Harriot Stanton Blatch and Theodore Stanton, who together edited her letters and other writings in 1922.

The emphasis here returns to the two-faceted image of ordinary woman and exceptional person. Though in 1881 her youngest child was twenty-two, she describes the joys of spending time with her "seven boys and girls dancing round the fireside, buoyant with all life's joys opening before them . . . " (p. 322). Invited to give an address at the sixtieth anniversary of her graduation from the Troy Seminary, she regales her audience with the memory of the time when she and a friend woke the entire school by ringing bells in the middle of the night without being caught. Her observations on differences in domestic accommodations between England and France continue her image of a woman concerned with ordinary matters. But she clearly wants to keep alive her exceptional image as well. Even in her seventies, she boasts of hiding her fatigue after a long trip when she arrives at a friend's house. And wherever she goes all over the world, she is treated as a celebrity with receptions in her honor and invitations to give keynote addresses at women's convocations.

Stanton ends her autobiography with a chapter on her eightieth birthday celebration in 1895, when she was honored for her fifty years of service to womankind with a gala reception at the Metropolitan Opera House. She leaves her readers here with the final paradox of the autobiography, the impression that her efforts were a huge success. She achieves this effect here by quoting several pages of an effusive article that reviewed the occasion, and then by quoting her own address where she summed up her life's work. Now it no longer required courage "to demand the right of suffrage, temperance legislation, liberal divorce laws, or for women to fill church offices—these battles have been fought and won and the principle governing these demands conceded" (p. 467).

As to the most important effort of her life, women's suffrage, rather than conclude with what still needed to be accomplished, she summarizes the victories: "municipal suffrage has been granted to women in England and some of her colonies; school suffrage has been granted to women in half of our States, municipal suffrage in Kansas, and full suffrage in four States of the Union" (p. 465). Though it wasn't until 1920, seventy years after her first call for suffrage in 1848 and eighteen years after her death in 1902, that the Nineteenth Amendment was finally passed, yet the reader closes this autobiography with the distinct impression that Stanton's life was a success.

For after all, it was, and *Eighty Years and More*, indeed, *is* a success story. Without Elizabeth Cady Stanton, ordinary *and* exceptional woman that she was, the present women's liberation movement would now be in the dark ages. She provided the foundation and the tradition for contemporary feminists, who are closer—because of her—to an amalgam of the sexual with the political, the private with the public.

6.

The Autobiographer
and Her Readers:
From Apology to Affirmation

ELIZABETH WINSTON

From the seventeenth century into the twentieth, women writers have shown an acute self-consciousness of the criticism they often aroused simply because they were female. One finds an interesting pattern of response to this criticism in the autobiographies of professional women writers, British and American, who were born in the last century. Those whose autobiographies were published before 1920 tended to establish a conciliatory relationship to their readers, by this means attempting to justify their untraditional ways of living and writing so as to gain the audience's sympathy and acceptance. Women who published autobiographies after 1920, however, no longer apologized for their careers and successes, though a few still showed signs of uneasiness at having violated cultural expectations for women. These more recently published writers openly asserted their intellectual and aesthetic gifts and their serious commitment to the literary life.

This change in the autobiographer's relation to her readers reflects an important change in the writer's self-image and in the kinds of autobiographical intentions she exhibited. That is, the more confident these women became of the legitimacy of their way of life, the more freely they used autobiography for explicitly personal and, thus, more self-validating reasons—to express strongly held beliefs, explore and understand the self, or experiment with the conventions of the genre.

A sample of fourteen autobiographies of professional women writers, published between 1852 and 1965, demonstrates this progression in self-image and intentions. Women writing between 1850 and 1920—Lady Sydney Morgan, Mary Mitford, Margaret Oliphant, and to a lesser extent, Mrs. Humphry Ward, youngest of the four—show ambivalence about being professional writers at a time when the usual pattern for a female was immersion in domesticity. Their need to assure readers of their womanliness results in apologies, disclaimers, and words of self-deprecation. These autobiographers express their desire to interest and entertain their readers, defend past actions, or leave a record for their children—intentions directed mainly toward satisfying others.

Harriet Martineau, who rightfully belongs in this early group (the autobiography came out in 1877), is a transitional figure, somewhat ahead of her time. She is the only woman among the autobiographers in this early period who sometimes assumes a didactic role in telling her story, an act which reflects her sense of authority vis-à-vis her readers. Yet she does resemble other women writing at this time in that though she never apologizes for the record of her life, she minimizes her "selfish" needs to write the autobiography by stressing the moral obligations which prompted her. At the beginning of the narrative she says she felt it a "duty" to record her personal history—it was a way of repaying other autobiographers for the pleasure and benefit they had given her. By invoking duty as her reason for writing, she transforms the fundamentally self-assertive autobiographical act into what she viewed as a commendable gesture of gratitude appropriate to a lady.

The women who published autobiographies after 1920 show a stronger professional commitment and belief in the value of their work than the earlier women writers, though a few still offer somewhat defensive explanations for their divergence from traditional female roles. Among their reasons for writing autobiography are the desire to present and recommend the ideas for which they have lived (Charlotte Perkins Gilman and Harriet Monroe), to show the improvement in women's lives since Victorian days (Elizabeth Haldane), to pay tribute to a way of life that has vanished (Edith Wharton and Edna Ferber), and to achieve self-understanding (Ellen Glasgow). The most confident writers in this later group—Edith Sitwell, Mary Austin, and Gertrude Stein—openly affirm their achievements, in tones ranging from the playful self-advertisement of Stein in *The Autobiography of Alice B. Toklas* (1933) to the defiant emphasis of Sitwell in *Taken Care Of* (1965). Not only do they use their autobiographies to inform and exhort their readers or to clarify the past for themselves, but also to assert their personal superiority (Stein and Sitwell) and to experiment with the autobiographical form (Austin and Stein). Yet even in these vigorously self-affirming narratives, especially in Sitwell's angry autobiography, one detects the signs of struggle, the force spent in challenging criticism and fighting restrictions. One gets a glimpse, in other words, of the price of success for a woman writing.

All of the women in this sample had succeeded in their careers. Even the early writers (Morgan, Mitford, and Oliphant), though little known today, enjoyed an enthusiastic reception during their lifetimes and were thus able to support themselves and their families through writing. That these successful women should have felt the need to justify their actions is a measure of the strong pressures on women to fulfill cultural expectations for their sex. The feminine stereotypes were pervasive: women were not autonomous individuals but dependents of their fathers and husbands, whether these men really "provided" for them or not; women were intellectually inferior to men and born to express their limited creativity through reproduction rather than through art; a "true woman" was modest and self-effacing and would never invite unseemly publicity by writing for publication. Given these limiting expectations, even highly gifted women would have had difficulty sustaining their self-confidence as artists. They needed continual confirmation of their work from people whose opinions they respected, to quiet the doubts within and to challenge the negative voices without. It is not surprising, then, that in autobiography—that most self-assertive and self-revealing of genres—these professional women writers should feel particularly vulnerable to criticism.

Women have traditionally experienced a conflict of values in deciding whether or not to write autobiographies. In *The Female Imagina-*

tion, Patricia Meyer Spacks refers to Margaret Cavendish, Duchess of Newcastle, whose autobiography of 1656 reveals its author's intense struggle with opposing inner demands: the desire to uphold traditional "feminine" values of self-effacement and suppression and the compelling need to assert herself in writing. In seventeenth-century Britain, says Spacks, "the propriety of feminine autobiography is dubious."[1]

Two centuries later, in Lady Sydney Morgan's *Memoirs* of 1862, one can still discern that writing an autobiography is for a woman a distinctly political act requiring careful justification. Though as a novelist and popular historian Lady Morgan has chosen a life that in some ways deviates sharply from the traditional feminine pattern, she projects the image of a woman who accepts the stereotypes and socially sanctioned roles for women. She justifies the writing of her memoirs by offering herself to her "dear, kind, fair-judging public" as an example of a female who has managed to realize her literary ambitions while at the same time fulfilling her desire "to be *every inch a woman*."[2] For Lady Morgan this meant being a devoted daughter, an attentive wife and hostess, but—surprisingly for her time—not necessarily a mother.[3]

In *Passages from My Autobiography* (1859), Lady Morgan reinforces the conventional belief in women's intellectual inferiority to men when she compares her husband's "clear Anglo-Saxon intellect and profound reflection" with her own "flimsy, fussy, flirty Celtic temperament, by courtesy called Mind."[4] In her 1862 *Memoirs*, she assures her audience that

> ambition and vanity, and social tastes have led me much into that chaos of folly and insincerity called the world, but domestic life is my vocation—unfortunately, my high organisation, and my husband's character of mind, our love of art, and all that is best worth knowing, renders *la vie domestique* impossible. (II, 417)

Here Lady Morgan reveals her dilemma regarding her identity as a woman. She seems to pay lip service to traditional feminine stereotypes and social expectations for women, but at the same time she recognizes and rejects the severe limitations inherent in the orthodox female's existence.

At least Lady Morgan was able to earn money by publishing her works. The Duchess of Newcastle's remuneration came in the form of psychological release, distraction from cares, and the admiration of some of her readers. Lady Morgan, writing at a time when literary women were no longer limited to the status of amateurs, commanded good prices for her novels and histories.

Yet in the two hundred six years between the publication of the duchess's and Lady Morgan's autobiographies, although many women in Britain and America began to support themselves through writing, they seem to have made slow progress in accepting the legitimacy of their new public and professional roles.[5] As Ann Douglas Wood points out, most of the American "scribbling women" (so named by Hawthorne) followed the advice of ministers, male reviewers, and certain influential writers of their own sex and used their talents to uphold the current limited notions about woman's nature and proper sphere. They published mainly in ladies' magazines and annuals, satisfying the demand for sentimental fiction and pious, imitative verse. They took pains to show their subordination of literary activities to domestic tasks and their unconcern for literary style or for recognition. In other words, says Wood, these women writers assuaged their guilt at succeeding in the "masculine" roles of bread-winner and public person and enjoying this success, "by hiding behind a conventional 'feminine' facade." In this way they avoided viewing themselves as serious professionals. Writing was simply a means to express themselves or to earn money in one of the few occupations open to educated women at the time.[6]

Lady Morgan took herself more seriously as a writer than these women apparently did. The editor of her *Memoirs*, Geraldine Jewsbury, notes that Morgan was a hard bargainer with her publishers and never sold herself short. In contrast to the "scribbling women" Wood describes, who tried to fulfill the feminine ideal of domesticity and self-effacement, Morgan took an active interest in liberal politics and championed the cause of oppressed people—the Irish and the Greeks—in some of her novels. She certainly believed herself superior to the nonliterary wives whose less finely nerved "organisations" allowed them to tolerate *la vie domestique*. But she was still ambivalent enough about what constituted the appropriate female vocation to use what could be called a "rhetoric of justification" to charm and placate those people of both sexes who might find her behavior audacious.

Like Lady Morgan, other women autobiographers writing before 1920 address their readers in conciliatory tones. In *Autobiography and Letters* (1899), Margaret Oliphant explains that she was prompted to make "a little try at the autobiography" after reading a biography of George Eliot. Ruefully comparing her achievements with Eliot's, she admits that her practice of always subordinating her career to maternal duties and family interests has negatively affected the quality of her work, and she reasons that since probably no one will want to write her biography, she will write it herself. Thus, the initial motive for the autobiography is what Oliphant calls "self-compassion" and "self-defence": showing the hardships she has endured and the financial burdens under which she has constantly labored in order to educate her own and her brother's children. Nine years later, Oliphant cites another motive for the autobiography: she had meant to leave it for her sons, and now, in 1894, both are dead. She apologizes for her frequent expressions of grief and eventually breaks off without completing the narrative.

Many readers of Oliphant's *Autobiography* would surely have approved her sacrifice of literary excellence to the claims of family and friends and her wish to leave an account of her life for her sons. These same readers also would have deemed appropriate the modest way in which Mary Mitford and Mrs. Humphry Ward referred to their professional achievements in their autobiographical volumes. Mitford says almost nothing about her career in *Recollections of a Literary Life* (1852), and when she does occasionally speak on this subject, her tone is self-deprecating. For example, she gratefully records receiving encouragement from a Mr. and Mrs. Kenyon, whose patronage of her "poor writings" has enabled her to support her improvident father and herself. Generally we learn about her writing indirectly, through the literary extracts she includes and the criticism she gives of these works.

In her two-volumed memoir, *A Writer's Recollections* (1918), Ward declares her intention of treating events "broadly" and "with as much detachment as possible," so as to maintain interest in her narrative. Accordingly, she devotes most of the first volume to descriptions of famous relatives and their friends (her grandfather, Dr. Arnold of Rugby; her uncle Matthew Arnold; William Wordsworth) and prominent people she knew at Oxford (the Mark Pattisons, Walter Pater, Benjamin Jowett). Yet when she comes to the point in her story where she should describe the writing of the novel with which *she* first achieved national prominence, Ward apologizes beforehand:

> If these are to be the recollections of a writer, in which perhaps other writers by profession, as well as the more general public, may take some interest, I shall perhaps be forgiven if I give some account of the processes of thought and work which led to the writing of my first successful novel, *Robert Elsmere*.[7]

It is difficult to imagine such a statement coming from a man! For years, male novelists have described the genesis of their writing in great detail (Henry James, a contemporary of Ward, comes to mind), automatically assuming that this material was both interesting and important. Ward does focus more attention on her novels in the second volume of the *Recollections*, but always with the proper feminine modesty.

Harriet Martineau is modest, too, about her successes as a political economist and writer. In *Autobiography* (1877) she rejects any claim to genius, saying that what "facility" she possesses was developed through discipline and years of translating. Nor does she emphasize her special status as a professional woman. At one point she admits to having been "provided with what is the bane of single life in ordinary cases to want—substantial, laborious and serious occupation."[8] But the passive construction of this statement conveys her characteristic reserve in referring to her literary vocation.

To explain her divergence from the feminine ideal of marriage, Martineau says she was "unfit" to marry because of a personal "disability"— her lack of the self-respect needed to fulfill familial duties without encroaching on her husband's and children's freedom (I, 132). Thus, she justifies her choice by pleading her own unsuitability to marriage and family life rather than by criticizing the institutions themselves.

When she turns to the issue of justice for oppressed people, however, Martineau exhibits a more positive sense of self. At these times she speaks authoritatively, revealing a didactic purpose. She voices particular concern for children, describing her childhood sufferings (her gradual loss of hearing) in order to alert parents to conditions about which they might otherwise remain ignorant. And she champions the cause of Catholics, American slaves, and women. Like her sister novelists, Harriet Beecher Stowe and Elizabeth Gaskell, who spoke out against the oppression of slaves and factory workers, Martineau had "access, via a sense of personal injustice," to collective problems of economic and religious discrimination.[9]

Martineau also seeks justice specifically for herself in the autobiography, giving her version of some controversial acts. She defends her participation in antislavery activities in America, justifies her refusal of a governmental pension, and defends her authorship with H. G. Atkinson of the *Letters on Man's Nature and Development*. This collaboration caused her to be called, rightly, an atheist and, wrongly, a victim of her male coauthor. (People did not seem able to accept the idea that a man and woman with similar philosophical views would freely enter into a cooperative publishing venture.) On the whole, her work of self-vindication is convincing.

Charlotte Perkins Gilman also had unconventional views and actions to defend. In *The Living of Charlotte Perkins Gilman* (1935), she records the growth of her ideas and principles, especially her views on the need for women's economic independence and the professionalization of domestic work and child care. Like Martineau, Gilman's concern for the plight of children originated in her own suppressed childhood. As children, both women had experienced an acute lack of parental tenderness. As adults much in the public eye, both had also provoked vehement opposition—Martineau for her antitheological convictions and her advocacy of mesmerism (she had recovered from a supposedly fatal illness following mesmeric treatment); Gilman for preaching "heresies" about women's domestic and sexual roles and for sending her daughter to live with her former husband and his second wife, Grace Channing, with whom she continued to enjoy a warm friendship.

An outspoken feminist, Gilman portrays her young self as a persistent questioner of the established order, who built her own humanistic religion, challenged the stereotype of woman's inherent weakness and dependence, and flouted the conventions of feminine coquetry in her relations with the opposite sex. Gilman the grown woman comes across primarily as a teacher. In fact, the author explicitly defines herself in this way[10] and also admits that she enjoys "preaching better even than lecturing, which is mostly preaching too" (p. 138). The autobiography, like the speaking engagement, is an occasion for expressing her controversial ideas.

Yet mixed in with her authoritative statements of principle are frequent references to the mental debility which plagued her from her mid-twenties, an incapacity resulting from the nervous breakdown she had after the birth of her only child: "So much of my many failures, of misplay and misunderstanding and 'queerness' is due to this lasting weakness, and kind friends so unfailingly refuse to allow for it, to believe it, that I am now going to some length in stating the case" (p. 97). She mourns the years lost, the work never done because she had lacked the mental strength to do it. In view of her extensive publications, these references to diminished productivity are revealing. They suggest her great need for achievement and recognition to reinforce her sense of worth.

Spacks calls *The Living of Charlotte Perkins Gilman* "a paradigm of feminine anger"—anger at the limitations of women's lives—and observes that Gilman's breakdown provided a way for her to escape the socially expected roles of wife, mother, and domestic servant, to do what she most desired: to labor, through lecturing and writing, not for one man and one child, but for the whole human race. Spacks's comment on the significance of Gilman's repeated references to her psychic pain is especially illuminating:

> It is as though, paying in mental suffering, she gains the right to personal fulfillment. Her desperate insistence that the suffering has been unrelenting, that she has never regained youthful power or

happiness, propitiates the fates. She permits herself to do what she
wants because her enjoyment of it is never complete, always angry
about that fact even while using it for self-justification. . . .[11]

The self-image Gilman projects in the autobiography is an ambigu-
ous one. At times she impresses this reader as a confident teacher and
committed exponent of feminist ideas. At others, she comes across as
an emotionally damaged, guilt-ridden woman, who seeks pardon for
her many failures. These conflicting images reflect Gilman's own
changing views of herself. Corresponding to these shifts in self-esti-
mation are changes in her relation to the audience. She moves back
and forth from an authoritative to a defensive position. For this reason,
despite her vigorous feminism, she seems closer to the transitional
figure Harriet Martineau than to contemporaries like the feminist
Mary Austin or the aesthetic innovator, Gertrude Stein.

In contrast to Gilman, Elizabeth Haldane shows few signs of personal defensiveness in her highly informative memoir, *From One Century to Another* (1937), though she consistently notes the restrictions
young women of her class encountered and celebrates the victories
contributing to their emancipation. In her preface, however, she allows herself one sardonic reply to those people who viewed her unmarried state as unfortunate. Perhaps, she says, her memoir will show
how a woman "may have a perfectly happy and full life, though devoid
of some of the ameliorations that novelists and psychologists tell us
make life worth living."[12]

Haldane's autobiography amply fulfills this purpose. The only
daughter in an upper-class Scottish family with a strong tradition of
public service, she responded to her country's discriminatory laws regarding women by pursuing the opportunities for service that were
available to her. Denied the right to vote or hold office,[13] she served
as treasurer of the Scottish Women's Liberal Association and worked
to get her brother Richard elected to Parliament. She became a member of the Edinburgh Royal Infirmary's board of management and also
worked for the improved administration of British poor houses. Haldane realized the wish she had expressed as a child: to become a doer
herself, instead of merely helping others who acted.

Though she characterizes herself as a person with special interests and talents, Haldane focuses more attention in her memoirs on the typicality of her life—on the experiences she shared with other British women—than on her singularity. For example, she does not mention being "the first woman to be made a J. P. in Scotland (1920), the first to receive the honorary degree of L. L. D. from St. Andrews University (1911), and the first to become a member of the Scottish Savings Committee."[14] Haldane neither underlines her modesty as do Mitford and Ward nor claims personal superiority as do Stein and Sitwell. She simply tells her story of "how a woman passed from the restrictions of one century to the interests of another" (p. vi).

In *A Backward Glance* (1934), Edith Wharton, like Haldane, places her life in historical perspective, but with a more personal focus than does the British writer. Wharton writes to preserve a record of a vanished order: the "old New York" of her childhood, with its traditions of gracious living and principled conduct—a society destroyed by World War I. Yet she writes for her own sake as well as for posterity. She hopes to "atone" for the many years she failed to recognize the value of this lost way of life.

A Backward Glance is also Wharton's record of her professional development and of the friends (notably Walter Berry and Henry James) who influenced and encouraged her growth. She found what she called her "awakeners" outside the immediate family, for the New York social group into which she was born had limited intellectual and aesthetic interests. Wharton clearly distinguishes herself from these Philistines and also from "authoresses" like Sarah Orne Jewett and Mary Wilkins, beloved of her mother's generation, who in her view wrote "rose-and-lavender" fiction.[15] She aimed to depict life realistically; her quiet pride in succeeding at this task is evident in the autobiography.

Wharton appears in *A Backward Glance* as a woman convinced of her literary vocation. She declares that with the publication in 1899 of her first book—a collection of short stories—her future was irrevocably determined: "The Land of Letters was henceforth to be my country, and I gloried in my new citizenship" (p. 119). At several points later in the narrative, she reaffirms the centrality of writing in her life. One of these passages is in the chapter describing her literary methods. Like the earlier autobiographer Mrs. Humphry Ward, Wharton is somewhat diffident about speaking of her "processes of thought and work":

> I have hesitated for some time before beginning this chapter, since any attempt to analyze work of one's own doing seems to imply that one regards it as likely to be of lasting interest, and I wish at once to repudiate such an assumption. (p. 197)

Yet she is quick to point out the necessity of including this chapter: without it, her self-portrait would be no more than "a profile." In another passage she states her desire not to "burden" the autobiography "with an account of every book" she has written (p. 140). Her solicitude for the audience, however, never causes her to belittle the literary efforts she does describe.

Wharton's relation to her readers is straightforward, her intentions directly stated. She writes to commemorate a life now extinct and to satisfy her own needs. Ellen Glasgow's attitude toward readers of *The Woman Within* (1954) is less clearcut. At times she turns away from the audience and directs her gaze inward. In the preface to the autobiography, she says she wrote for her "own release of heart and mind."[16] This statement seems to imply that she wrote without thought of an audience, in a spontaneous attempt to understand her past. Though the claim to spontaneity is clearly a pose (a year after beginning the book, she contracted to have it published posthumously), her assertion that she was writing primarily for her own sake is evidence for her positive sense of self. She considered the satisfaction of her needs an acceptable aim in writing an autobiography for publication. This stated purpose distinguishes her from women autobiographers writing before 1920.

During the nine years she spent in writing *The Woman Within* (1934–43), Glasgow wavered in her resolve to have the book published. Ultimately, however, she justified her decision for posthumous publication on the grounds that her story, told "without vanity or evasion" might "shed some light, however faint, into the troubled darkness of human psychology" (pp. 130, 161). This is surely a more self-assertive claim for the work than ones expressed by Ward or even by

Haldane. These women claimed a historical interest for their memoirs. Ward commemorated her famous relatives and friends and placed her narrative in the context of important religious and social developments in Victorian England. Haldane described her experiences as representative of the lives of other young British women. Whereas they offer readers information, Glasgow offers insight—into the complex world of her psyche.

It is a world of secret suffering and fierce pride. Glasgow presents herself as having been victimized by life—through deafness, her mother's chronic depression, the deaths of all the people she most loved, the belated recognition of her work. But she also portrays herself as having survived these "indignities" courageously and, until now, in silence. Her message to readers is that she is an exceptional person—more sensitive than others to injustice and pain, more truthful in her writing, whether autobiography or fiction. Her best novels— *Barren Ground, Vein of Iron,* and three others—are "some of the best work that has been done in American fiction" (p. 270). At the end of the autobiography Glasgow reaffirms her work and life. She has come through the painful experiences undefeated, with a still "unreconciled heart."

In contrast to Glasgow, Edna Ferber clearly acknowledges her desire for an audience for the autobiography *A Peculiar Treasure* (1938). Though she denies writing the book because she is "fatuous enough to think that anyone is interested," this disclaimer is neutralized by its position at the end of a section in which she firmly establishes her authority with her audience. Regarding the scope of her recollections, for instance, Ferber asserts that while she promises to tell the truth, she makes "no promise to Tell All."[17] She will offer, on her own terms, "the story of an American Jewish family in the past half-century"—her family, because it is the one she knows best. And she affirms the value of this story, even though her life may strike others as unpromising material for autobiography. True, she has met no royalty, known few powerful people, experienced no extremes of wealth or poverty. She is unmarried, childless, middle class, and "conventional." Nevertheless, Ferber declares optimistically, "if I were to die tomorrow (which, being middle-aged and neurotic, I feel fairly certain I shall), I should say today that I have had an enchanting time of it; a rich, gay exciting and dramatic life" (p. 19).

Ferber's yea-saying is seasoned with a piquant self-irony. In both *A Peculiar Treasure* and her second autobiography, *A Kind of Magic* (1963), she deftly uses irony to establish a casual, colloquial tone and easy relation with her readers. More important, irony is her device for safely expressing strong feelings, for controlling her emotions even as she admits them. What Ferber seems continually to be fighting in these pages is the label "sentimental woman writer," or to use another term she disliked, "romantic regional novelist." Very early in the first autobiography, she announces her distaste for literature of the Elsie Dinsmore variety; thereafter, she undercuts potentially sentimental remarks by mocking the "lachrymose" and pious Elsie.[18]

Ferber takes pride in her realistic portrayal of life in her short stories and novels. She recalls being "grimly pleased" when reviewers of *Buttered Side Down*, a volume of her short stories published in 1912, declared "that obviously these stories had been written by a man who had taken a feminine nom de plume as a hoax." The reviewers' comments pleased her because they supported her claim that many of her stories and some of her novels "could never be designated as feminine writing in theme, characterization, style or attack. They were written by a cerebral human being who had a knowledge of the technique of writing and of the human race. That is as it should be" (*APT*, p. 176). To Ferber "feminine writing" means sentimental writing; hence she does not want the term applied to her work. In her two autobiographies she consistently opposes literature of this type.

Like Ferber, Harriet Monroe had to contend with the widespread notion that women were weak, sentimental creatures. *A Poet's Life* (1938) shows that she was neither. The autobiography describes her persistent efforts to have poetry included in the dedication of the World's Columbian Exposition at Chicago in 1892 and records her success at being commissioned to write "The Columbian Ode." In five chapters at the center of the autobiography, she tells the story of *Poetry* magazine, which she established in 1912 and edited for twenty-four years as an organ for innovative, experimental verse. Monroe is justly proud of having disproved the pessimistic predictions that *Po-*

etry would be "a worthless assemblage of petty rhymesters under soft feminine editorship."[19] The magazine's record of publication firsts and her own intelligent, challenging editorials (from which she quotes freely) show that she managed to uphold high critical standards without forfeiting her kindness to struggling poets. Monroe sees her life and the cause of poetry closely intertwined and affirms them both in her autobiography.

Mary Austin explicitly acknowledges writing her autobiography, *Earth Horizon* (1932), as a means to self-clarification. The book also has a didactic strain, for which she neither apologizes nor offers justification. Says Austin, "I don't see why it should be so much the literary mode just now to pretend that ideas are not intrinsically exciting and that one's own life isn't interesting to oneself."[20] She declares that the "major business" of her story is to show how she "shed all the moralities that interfered with her soul" and found the "true Middle" of experience in herself, rather than in orthodox Christianity or the sanctities of hearth and home (pp. 119, 283, 280). The title of her autobiography is also the title of an American Indian song which describes this search for the "Sacred Middle" where the human spirit, "no longer deflected by the influences of false horizons," exists in free and natural relation to the Cosmos (p. 274).

Austin experiments with point of view in telling her story. In the first four of the five books composing *Earth Horizon*, she refers to her earlier self mainly in the third person. Occasionally, she shifts into second person to stress Mary as receiver of information or Mary as object of directives from people in authority, especially her mother.

Referring to her earlier self in Books I–IV as "Mary," "she," or "you" enables Austin to recount experiences of frustration and loneliness without sounding full of self-pity. She thus avoids the insistent tone of *The Living of Charlotte Perkins Gilman*, while still communicating the pain of those lonely years. As an example, with the second and third person Austin can describe a scene of parental favoritism and rejection that is poignant without being pathetic:

> When she [mother] sat down at twilight to rock the baby, and Jim leaned against her shoulder while she told stories about the war and

old times, and you forgot and leaned against her knee until you felt it subtly withdrawing . . . "hadn't you better get your stool, Mary?" . . . So Mary sat on her little stool, Jim leaned against Mother's shoulder, and Jennie sat in her lap. (p. 47)

When Austin does use simple first person in Books I–IV, it is to designate a more recent self, the self as writer. She says "I" when citing her authority for statements and when defining the extent of her knowledge about an event. She also refers to herself as "I" when describing memories so vivid that they cause time to collapse, bringing together the Mary of childhood and young womanhood and the Mary of 1932. In the last book of *Earth Horizon*, which takes her story into the present, Austin consistently refers to herself as "I."

By shifting from a predominantly third-person perspective in Books I–IV to first person in Book V, Austin calls attention to her development as a woman and writer. She distinguishes between the Mary still in the process of moving beyond false horizons and the author/narrator who has found the "true Middle" in herself. Usually her technique works, though occasionally, when the changes in viewpoint occur in a single paragraph and for no clear reason, they disconcert the reader. But generally the shifts in grammatical person effectively express Austin's journey from the restrictions of girlhood and young womanhood to the freedom of a literary career.

Gertrude Stein uses a third-person point of view in referring to herself in *The Autobiography of Alice B. Toklas* (1933). But unlike Austin, Stein maintains this perspective throughout the book and speaks through a narrative persona. With the first word of *The Autobiography*, Stein asserts her independence from the traditional autobiographical form. The opening sentence seems perfectly commonplace: "I was born in San Francisco, California," but the reader knows from the title page that the relation between the book's persona and the author of the work is not the usual one of identity. The "I" of the narrative and the autobiographer are two separate people—"Alice Toklas" and Gertrude Stein. In the Toklas narrative, Stein upsets conventional literary categories by simultaneously producing third-person autobiography and a first-person biography of her friend.

By flouting the conventions of autobiography, Stein accomplishes several aims. As "Alice Toklas" she promotes an audience for her work more effectively than through blatant self-advertisement. The third-person perspective also gives her a legitimate reason for omitting a full account of her painful girlhood since Toklas would not be expected to know the details of Stein's past. (By the time the two women met in 1907, Stein was already well along in her career as a writer and presiding genius of the rue de Fleurus salon.) Furthermore, using a persona allows her to avoid revealing her inner life. Through "Toklas" Stein can distance herself from the audience and protect her privacy. At the same time, by impersonating Toklas, she can pay tribute to her devoted friend and attest to the fundamental importance of their relationship without revealing the true nature of their intimacy.

Finally, and most significant for the present study, the third-person viewpoint enables Stein to declare herself a genius—a claim that none of the women autobiographers writing before 1920 dare to make. As I suggested earlier, the cultural stereotypes regarding women discouraged female writers from asserting themselves as serious artists. How much more difficult it must have been to consider oneself a genius!

Stein was lucky in having been born into a family with money and some artistic taste. She was doubly fortunate in having a brother, Leo, who supported her rejection of the traditional female domestic vocation[21] and, at least during her formative years, shared her intellectual and aesthetic interests. But perhaps most important in securing her confidence in her literary gifts was the thirty-three-year-old Stein's meeting with Alice Toklas, who immediately hailed her as a genius and through the remaining thirty-nine years of Stein's life believed in Stein probably more firmly than Stein herself. Readers of the 1933 autobiography see Stein through Alice Toklas's believing eyes. The Stein they see is a writer supremely self-assured and convinced of her genius. When she speaks in her own voice in *Everybody's Autobiography* (1937), Stein admits her need to be reassured of her place among "the masters of English prose."[22] Yet she is still convinced of her primacy in twentieth-century literature: "I know that I am the most important writer writing today" (p. 28).

Of the autobiographers sampled here, Stein makes the boldest assertions of personal superiority. But other post-1920 writers also openly express their belief in their singularity. In *Taken Care Of* (1965), Edith Sitwell reports that when she was less than five years old, one of her mother's friends asked her what she planned to be when she grew up, and she replied, "a genius."[23] Sitwell portrays herself as a born artist, isolated in the hostile world of her parents' mediocrity and tastelessness. About her divergence from the feminine norm she is not apologetic but proudly defiant. Sitwell speaks with scorn of those who have tried unsuccessfully to force her into the conventional mold. She impales her enemies on a satirical pen and vents her rage at the stupid, vulgar people who have dared to call themselves art critics.

In a chapter of the autobiography entitled "Eccentricity," Sitwell aligns herself with the eccentric "only insomuch," she declares, "as I do not suffer fools gladly and I am adamant in refusing to allow ignoramuses to teach me the spiritual and technical side of the art which I have practiced for nearly half a century" (p. 154). One cannot imagine her brother Osbert speaking with this defiant emphasis, even though he, too, was attacked by critics and relished a good fight with them. In his multivolumed autobiography, *Left Hand, Right Hand!*, he manifests an urbane good humor toward old opponents and troublesome parents alike. That he could record his past with such equanimity must be owing at least in part to his happier experiences as a child and his greater self-acceptance as a man of letters. Osbert's memoir shows that he enjoyed the money and deferential treatment accorded a male heir and the favoritism of both parents. Edith, on the other hand, was a disappointing daughter, and, according to Osbert, the elder Sitwells "mismanaged" her terribly. The combative tone of *Taken Care Of* conveys the message that it has been harder for Edith Sitwell than for her brother to succeed in a literary career. She is continually embattled, but defiant to the end.

Women autobiographers writing before 1920 consciously worked to establish a special relation to their audience. They sought primarily to justify their ways of living and the fact of their writing. The particular acts they felt compelled to defend reflect the cultural stereotypes which inhibit women from fully realizing their potentialities. Reacting to the prevailing belief that women found their true vocation as wives and mothers, these women defended their choice of a career or their deviation from the traditional marital and maternal roles. In response to the notion that "good" women were modest and self-effacing, they understated their achievements, disclaimed interest in personal recognition, or stressed the broad historical value of their life stories. Generally, it was only later in this century, as stereotypes became less rigid and women writers began to experience fewer negative reactions to their untraditional assertive behavior, that female autobiographers acknowledged more personal reasons for writing and affirmed their achievements without apology.

Contemporary writers like Mary McCarthy, Lillian Hellman, and Maya Angelou have exhibited even greater self-confidence in their autobiographical works. Their self-assertive, gender-affirming narratives are encouraging models for female readers and give promise of a future in which a woman's right to write will be assured.

7.

Selves in Hiding

PATRICIA MEYER SPACKS

Autobiographies, almost by definition, make the private public. Even men and women who live much of their lives before the public eye undertake, when they set down stories of those lives, to account for what the world sees at least partly by revealing what the world has not previously known. The writer who displays himself or herself in print claims the authority of individual personal experience, asserting unique knowledge of that unique subject, the self. The act of autobiography, the dynamic process of recorded choice, necessarily although sometimes inadvertently uncovers at least some aspects of personality and experience which normally remain hidden.

Commitment to formal autobiography, a story of the self written with the intent of dissemination, implies also a claim of significance— a fact that troubled early practitioners, who felt obliged to defend themselves against the charge of vanity by asserting the exemplary shape of their experience or the didactic intent of their prose. Women, for obvious social reasons, have traditionally had more difficulty than men about making public claims of their own importance. They have excelled in the writing of diaries and journals, which require no such claims, more than in the production of total works offering a coherent interpretation of their experience. Most female autobiographers, until recently, have been artistic performers by profession—dancers, actresses, writers—their demand for public attention in modes relatively acceptable for women predating their written self-description. The housewife seldom offers her life to public view.

During the last century, women have begun to fill significant political roles, and a few have written about the experience of assuming such places in public life. The stories they tell of the tensions between private and public demands often have something in common beyond the obvious facts on which they are based: a special kind of shaping, a distinctive tone. I want to speculate about what they share and what that sharing means, to try at least partially to think about the form of the stories rather than the lives.

The texts that concern me emanate from women born in the nineteenth century, so historical as well as gender determinants presumably account for the common elements in these accounts of work, love, and friendship. Their authors all won not only fame but notoriety, each the object of bitter attack for her public achievements. Emmeline Pankhurst, the English suffragist; Dorothy Day, a founder of the radical *Catholic Worker*; Emma Goldman, the fiery anarchist; Eleanor Roosevelt; Golda Meir; all have written accounts of their lives in which they describe themselves, implicitly or explicitly, as gaining identity from their chosen work. They reveal in addition, through the structure, language, and detail of their narratives, a painful fact: the identity of public performance may cause its female possessor to experience intensely, or at any rate to reveal emphatically, pre-existent uncertainties of personal identity. Such uncertainties, I suspect, take special form and receive special emphasis in women's accounts of their lives.

Thinking about these autobiographies in conjunction with one another, one may notice first the qualities they do *not* display. None of these women relies on any distinct sense of individual destiny, although some seek in memories of early experience the sources of later commitment. Although each author has significant, sometimes dazzling, accomplishment to her credit, the theme of accomplishment rarely dominates the narrative. Pankhurst, in fact, ends her account in a dying fall, stressing the failure, at the time of writing, of her battle to achieve women's suffrage; Golda Meir pleads the case of Israel rather than stressing her achievements on behalf of her country. Several of the autobiographers pride themselves on their unflagging energy, but they do not emphasize the importance of what that energy has enabled them to do. Indeed, to a striking degree they fail directly to emphasize their *own* importance, though writing in a genre which implies self-assertion and self-display. Although several find indirect means of declaring personal power and effectiveness, they do so, as it were, in disguise.

Yet each of these women seems to wish to make rather special claims for herself. Hannah Arendt, writing in *The Human Condition* about distinctions among political, social, and personal action, suggests that "goodness, . . . as a consistent way of life, is not only impossible within the confines of the public realm, it is even destructive of it," since good works, if known, lose their character of goodness, which depends on their being done for their own sake.[1] The five women we are considering all function as public beings, inhabitants of the public world. None openly prides herself on "goodness," yet all hint a dominating wish to define themselves as "good," mainly in the sense of "altruistic." The impossibility of laying public claim to essential virtue generates a curious tension in these records: their authors, for the reason Arendt suggests, can never openly value the image of a selfless self, yet they convey this ideal of selflessness and their frustration at the impossibility of achieving it; and they hint, paradoxically, that they themselves have come pretty close.

Goodness *is* selflessness, these autobiographies suggest; and vice versa—a notion by its nature unlikely to make for effective autobiography, since autobiographies are about selves. Women required to offer reactions to standardized accounts of moral dilemmas, I am told, sometimes have trouble with a problem which bothers virtually no male respondents. Asked whether a man has the right to steal a drug desperately needed for his dying wife, they usually say he does, and explain why: human life has more value than property. Would he have the same right if he needed the drug for himself? Women often find themselves uncertain, accustomed as they are to believe in subordinating the demands of the self to those of others. Whether such habits derive from socialization, from nature, or from the one intensified by the other, they prevail among many twentieth-century women, and their power over our female predecessors seems yet more obvious. Eleanor Roosevelt, who claims a desire to help others as a principal motive of her autobiography, offers a lucid account of the force of "duty" as a guiding idea. "A certain kind of orthodox goodness was my ideal and ambition," she explains, speaking of the early years of her marriage.[2] She adds that she expected the same ideal to dominate her husband. He, however, considered politics a career, not a mode of service, interested in government as a science and in "the play of his own personality" on other people (p. 66). His wife, seeing everything from the point of view of what she ought to do, ignored the question of what she wanted, concerning herself with politics solely because the subject preoccupied her husband and she felt it her duty to share his interests. She learned to transcend such restrictions on her sense of possibility—but the last section of her autobiography, dealing with the years long after her husband's death, opens with an explanation of why she finds it difficult to "slow down" as others urge her: "Even when a new project makes demands on my already crowded schedule, I find it difficult to reject it, so long as it serves a useful purpose" (p. 359). Conversely, she feels untempted by any course of action unlikely to prove useful. The shift from the notion of duty to that of useful purpose suggests a more flexible definition of obligation, but the same motivating sense of responsibility to others.

Dorothy Day and her sister, in their girlhood, would "practice being saints."[3] Golda Meir, faced with her first conflict between private and social responsibility, chose to fulfill her duty to husband, home and child rather than to pursue the kind of life she "really wanted." "Not for the first time," she explains—"and certainly not for the last—I realized that in a conflict between my duty and my innermost desires, it was my duty that had the prior claim."[4] Emma Goldman rose to political consciousness at the hanging of the Chicago anarchists, feeling their death as a personal loss, understanding "that something new and wonderful had been born in my soul. A great ideal, a burning faith, a determination to dedicate myself to the memory of my martyred comrades. . . . "[5] Such identification of her own awakening with commitment to the memory of martyred comrades represents one more version of goodness. Eleanor Roosevelt's interest in politics, Dorothy Day's imitation of the saints, Golda Meir's devotion to husband and child, Emma Goldman's conversion of the anarchists' suffering to political inspiration, Emmeline Pankhurst's total identification with a cause which destined her and her daughter to risk and to physical misery—all embody modes of self-transcendence or perhaps self-denial.

Of course commitment to a cause necessarily implies subordination of self. The value of such commitment, however, may be predominantly different for women—or so the evidence of these autobiographies hints. Instead of using the cause ultimately to enlarge the sense of self, these women seem to *diminish* self in their reports of their causes. The omissions and the inclusions of the texts alike offer clues. One notices, for example, a distinct lack of affect in much of Roosevelt's account of accomplishment. "I spoke to vast audiences and visited many hospitals, rest homes for our nurses, and recreation centers for our men" (p. 256). How did this routine of speaking and visiting feel? We do not know; the narrative fails to tell us. Sometimes the author confesses to having tired; sometimes she acknowledges that at least some of her anxiety derived from inner impulse, from her varied interests. But she implicitly denies, for purposes of the autobiography, all emotional response to her own public importance and accomplishment.

Summarizing the White House years, Roosevelt writes, "On the whole, I think I lived those years very impersonally. It was almost as though I had erected someone outside myself who was the President's wife. I was lost somewhere deep down inside myself" (p. 280). Summarizing more inclusively, from the perspective of her late seventies, she explains that she "was not a gifted person," just someone interested in life, with three and only three assets: her keen interest in various matters, her willingness to accept challenge, her energy and self-discipline (p. 410). Her objective in life, she says, evolved only gradually, less by choice than by experience: to help achieve a peaceful world. Earlier, her objective was to help Franklin. Earlier still, she suffered intense shame because she could not master the role of belle. She didn't care about slanderous attacks as long as they didn't hurt Franklin. She didn't believe in her own competence, even when she became U.N. representative; her colleagues were right, she feels, in assigning her to a committee where she could do the least possible harm. Although she refers the description of herself in hiding specifically to the White House period, the entire narrative supports the same characterization. Her declared subordination to her husband and to the interests of others, her refusal to dwell on, perhaps even to recognize, her own feelings, her systematic self-deprecation: all emphasize her unwillingness to make verbal claims for herself, to declare a powerful sense of self. Although she considers herself to have evolved far beyond the timid and dutiful young woman who, she says, wanted everyone to love her, she never conveys a distinct mature identity. However loudly she proclaims the range of her interests, she fails to communicate their reality or what they mean to her. The reader has trouble finding the *self* the autobiography purports to depict.

Golda Meir's total identification with the state of Israel becomes ever more striking as her book proceeds. The dynamics of this identification receive unconscious attention in her autobiography—one would love to hear about it—but one can sense in the story a struggle about selfhood rather different from Roosevelt's. Meir reports the advice she offered in 1971 to the children of the Milwaukee school she had attended fifty years before:

> It isn't really important to decide when you are very young just exactly what you want to become when you grow up. . . . It is much more important to decide on the way you want to live. If you are going to be honest with yourself and honest with your friends, if you are going to get involved with causes which are good for others, not only for yourselves, then it seems to me that that is sufficient, and maybe what you will be is only a matter of chance. (pp.34–35)

This clear statement that what one does in the world matters little, how one commits oneself to a cause matters a lot, amounts to an explanation of Meir's career. Always she stresses the accidental nature of her assumption of ever higher office; she can discount her own importance by emphasizing her identification with a larger institution. Receiving an honorary degree from the Catholic University of Manila, she comments, "I have never forgotten that I came from a poor family or ever fooled myself into thinking that I was honored anywhere— Manila included—for my beauty, wisdom, or erudition" (p. 343). Denying that her personal qualities merit reward, implying that the degrees honor Israel through its representative, she avoids the discomfort of taking full responsibility for ambition or even for accomplishment. As Eleanor Roosevelt's sense of self merged in her sense of mission, so does Golda Meir's, despite the fact that she sounds more confident, more clearly focused from the start, less subordinate to any specific individual than Roosevelt was to her husband. What one does in the world, her career demonstrates and her advice insists, gains personal validity only inasmuch as it involves commitment to a cause "good for others."

Dorothy Day—a more powerful and personal writer than the other two—exemplifies the same point, explicitly glorying, as she recounts an early episode of imprisonment, in the fact that she "lost all feeling of [her] own identity" as she felt herself merging with other prisoners "all over the world": "women and men, young girls and boys, suffering constraint, punishment, isolation and hardship for crimes of which all of us were guilty" (p. 78). Such achieved selflessness, a triumph of total empathy, provides emotional fuel for her ardent efforts on behalf of the unfortunate. Emmeline Pankhurst, far less self-aware (or perhaps only less willing to share her self-awareness), also claims to operate on the basis of sympathetic identification which she believes characteristic of her sex. Only new laws, she believes, will ameliorate the lot of the powerless, and only when women have the vote will such laws come into existence. "Women guardians [i.e., administrators of the Poor Law] have striven in vain to have the law reformed in order to ameliorate conditions which break the hearts of women to see, but which apparently affect men very little."[6] Pankhurst's experience of relative futility in pursuing her selfless aims differentiates her from the others, but her denial of identity apart from the common lot of her group reiterates a theme of the other autobiographies.

In this context Emma Goldman presents something of an anomaly. Her enormous two-volume autobiography demonstrates no difficulty in self-assertion; on the contrary, self-glorification, often explicit, dominates it. Although Goldman, too, proclaims her absolute involvement with the cause of other people—her "ideal," she repeatedly calls it—she appears often to use that involvement for self-display. Like the others, she suffered long and arduously for her beliefs; unlike them, she acknowledges fairly openly the narcissistic gratification even of the suffering, certainly of the performances before enormous audiences which made her a larger-than-life heroine or villainess for press and public. If she resolved her struggle differently from the others, though, she demonstrates at least as clearly as they the degree to which involvement in public life implies, for some women, peculiarly intense conflicts about identity.

Goldman provides more detailed data about her experience than any of the other autobiographers we are considering. She reveals, for example, not only her intense conflict with her father but the fact that this conflict originated in his powerful desire, before her birth, that she be a boy. Her commitment to anarchism, as it developed, afforded her opportunities to project diverse versions of herself, highly colored images of female sexuality, but also on occasion equally romantic traditional male roles.

The link between the sexual and the political apparently felt so close for Emma Goldman that she hardly knew the difference between them. Typically, she goes to bed for the first time with her long-term lover, Alexander Berkman, because she has been stirred by a political meeting offering "a fierce call to battle against the enemy, a call to individual acts, to vengeance" (I, 43). Earlier, she and Berkman have disagreed over the action of a woman revolutionary who refused to escape when she could, preferring to die with her lover, Berkman insisting that the woman's love for the cause should have motivated her to live for the sake of further anarchistic activity, Goldman believing "that it could not be wrong to die with one's beloved in a common act—it was beautiful, it was sublime" (I, 37). Sharing a platform with a sixteen-year-old Italian girl anarchist, she responds primarily to the girl's physical attractiveness. Goldman speaks after Maria, also to great applause, but she comments, "I sensed that the people were spontaneously responsive to my prison story, but I was not deceived; I knew intuitively that it was Maria Rodda's youth and charm that fascinated them and not my speech. Yet I, too, was still young—only twenty-five. I still had attraction, but compared with that lovely flower, I felt old" (I, 150). The same sexual competitiveness emerges when she complains that she had no female friends in the movement because other women envied her appeal to men. When she needs money for Berkman, she enacts a fantasy of noble prostitution, possessed by the image of Sonia in *Crime and Punishment*. Her political success and her sexual attractiveness merge in her mind, confirming one another; she makes little distinction between her private life of extensive sexual activity and her public career of speechmaking.

But the public arena also represents escape from the restrictiveness of the female role. She expresses this notion most dramatically when she uses a horsewhip to chastise a political opponent for his failure to acknowledge Berkman's heroism, finally breaking the whip in pieces and flinging the fragments in her victim's face. The typically "male" gesture of thus punishing an enemy—and punishing him, as it proved, with relative impunity—embodies for Emma Goldman a fantasy of the freedom to act created by her political involvement. From the beginning she glimpsed the possibility of transmuting personal feeling into public action and thus escaping painful consequences of emotion. As a young girl, she heard a woman speak about the fate of the Chicago anarchists. The speaker, Johanna Greie, observed to Goldman, "I never saw a face that reflected such a tumult of emotions as yours. You must be feeling the impending tragedy intensely. Do you know the men?" When the girl admitted that she did not, although she participated emotionally in their plight, Greie told her, "I have a feeling that you will know them better as you learn their ideal, and that you will make their cause your own" (I, 9). To "know" people by identifying with their cause became Emma Goldman's life course. When someone demanded too much of her personally—particularly when a man demanded some version of traditional female compliance—she could retreat into her larger involvement, always justified in her refusals by her great acceptance. Conversely, she could readily tolerate the intensities of her nature when they expressed themselves in political passion. The public sphere supplied both an extension of and an escape from the personal.

The overt sexuality of much of Goldman's self-presentation differentiates her sharply from such women as Eleanor Roosevelt and Golda Meir. Of them too, however, it might be said that they found in public

life not only expansion but refuge from private feeling. Unlike Goldman, they do not claim passionate involvement in every relationship,
but like her they try to identify themselves acceptably by submerging
their own interests in larger concerns. Eleanor Roosevelt did not have
to be a belle; Golda Meir could explain and transform her hostility to
her parents, because both could dramatize their primary concern with
others. In these life stories one can see how public commitment may
help to solve personal problems; more specifically, how it enables the
teller to find an acceptable definition of self almost without declaring
individuality. And it appears to resolve issues which one may consider
particularly crucial for women: how to channel strong feeling appropriately, how at once to use and to disguise aggressive impulse, how
simultaneously to deny and achieve personal striving.

Yet such a solution itself generates difficulties; these too assume
analogous shapes in several narratives. The conflicts which these
women present as central to their experience characteristically involve
clashing responsibilities toward other people. Although Golda Meir at
one point pits duty against desire—what she wants as opposed to what
she should do—even for her the tension comes to center on obligations to her husband and children versus obligations to the nation.
Dorothy Day provides the clearest statement of felt oppositions,
which of course belong traditionally to the seeker after spiritual life.
Her commitment to her husband, antireligious by nature and by politics, opposes her love for her daughter, for whom she wants the security of baptism. Her acceptance of the Catholic Church, a spiritual
community, clashes at first with her desire to do immediate good
within the secular community. Her need for "a cause, a motive, a way
to walk in" (p. 141) leads her to communism, then to Catholicism; but
that need merges with the yearning for community which accounts for
her autobiography's title, *The Long Loneliness*.

Loneliness, Day suggests, threatens women particularly. She
speaks of her daughter's recognition of "how alone a mother of young
children always is," and of an elderly woman who complains of suffering loneliness after having "lived a long and full life." The only solution
to the problem, Day believes, involves "living together, working together, sharing together, loving God and loving our brother, and liv-

ing close to him in community" (p. 241). But such a life choice deprives her of other kinds of fulfillment, other fruitful commitments. "I was thirty-eight, wishing I were married and living the ordinary naturally happy life and had not come under the dynamic influence of Peter Maurin" (p. 236). Although she values and glorifies the way she has chosen, she recognizes its costs: depriving her of life in a nuclear family, it deprives her of a woman's traditional mode of responsibility and of happiness.

Happiness, as these women implicitly or explicitly evoke it, derives from relationship, a point of view often considered particularly "feminine." Emmeline Pankhurst, severely impersonal in much of her account, goes out of her way to claim nineteen years of ideally happy marriage and to justify herself by her *husband's* belief that women should fill social as well as domestic functions; she found fulfillment from both and avoided most clashes between them by delaying her militance until after her husband's death. Eleanor Roosevelt followed in some respects a similar course, accounting for her every public activity in terms of Franklin's interests until he died. She articulates lucidly how social commitment for her represents an extension of personal feeling, its gratifications accordingly related to those of other kinds of interpersonal relationship, its responsibilities correspondingly inescapable. "I have always seen life personally," she writes;

> that is, my interest or sympathy or indignation is not aroused by an abstract cause but by the plight of a single person whom I have seen with my own eyes. . . . Out of my response to an individual develops an awareness of a problem to the community, then to the country, and finally to the world. In each case my feeling of obligation to do something has stemmed from one individual and then widened and become applied to a broader area. (p. 413)

Such a progression of feeling and idea does not, of course, belong uniquely to Eleanor Roosevelt, or uniquely to women. But it certainly differentiates her from her husband, as she evokes him; and the movement she describes characterizes this entire group of female autobiographers, all proclaiming themselves moved by the sight or the idea of suffering individuals, enlarging the perception to include its social implications, responding in action to perceived social dysfunction, understanding such response as another version of a pervasive inclination to react to the needs of others. Happiness derives from relationship; unhappiness follows when obligations conflict or cannot be fulfilled.

Meir and Goldman speak of frequent conflicting obligations. Even before her marriage, Meir tells us, "The idea that I might have to choose between Morris and Palestine made me miserable" (p. 64). (Significantly, she coped with this misery by throwing herself into Zionist activities, always able to find "something that took precedence over my private worries and therefore served to distract me from them" [p. 65].) Her desire to fulfill herself through the community of the kibbutz clashed with her need to work for a larger community; her worries over whether she was neglecting her children generated constant guilt although she also answered to other worries about the welfare of the state. Asked to be prime minister, she shrinks from "the responsibility, the awful stress and strain," accepting the job only because her family urged her to, disclaiming all volition (p. 378). "I became prime minister because that was how it was" (p. 379).

Confusion about motivation often emerges in these texts. Emma Goldman expresses it most vividly. Her conflict over opposed responsibilities and desires emerges in her accounts of successive relationships with men. Captivated by the eminent revolutionary Johann Most, a man much older than she, the youthful Goldman, by her account, responded ardently to his plea of loneliness. "Something gripped my heart. I wanted to take his hand, to tell him that I would be his friend. But I dared not speak out. What could I give this man— I, a factory girl, uneducated; and he, the famous Johann Most, the leader of the masses, the man of magic tongue and powerful pen?" (I, 35). The formulation, "what could I give?", has a familiar ring; in different versions it dominates all these narratives. As Most himself becomes aware of the necessities of Goldman's political involvement, he realizes that her need to give extends beyond a single man; he promises, therefore, to make her into a great speaker who will ultimately take his place. Goldman, however, finds this Svengali-fantasy unappealing, although she accepts the authority of Most's personality and position, characteristically confusing the personal and the political in her description of him. "His own rich personality meant far more to me—the alternating heights and depths of his spirit, his hatred of the capitalist system, his vision of a new society of beauty and joy for all" (p. 40). Gradually the satisfactions of contemplating someone else's rich personality pall. She feels hurt that he does not inquire about or allow her to report her own successes as public speaker; he wants her to be "his little girl-woman." At this, she observes, "I flared up, declaring I would not be treated as a mere female" (I, 53). The relationship founders over her desire to give, and to be given to, both as woman and as political force. She refuses to acknowledge the conflict between the two roles, although her narrative dramatizes precisely this clash.

Gradually the text begins to raise questions about the forces driving the narrator and about the possibility of reconciling them. The autobiography offers no explanations beyond the insights which the protagonist possessed at the time of reported action. Her early sexual connections raised for her the possibility of motherhood, a possibility she rejects not simply because of her own memory of a "tragic childhood" but because she wishes to give herself to all mankind, not only to a single child or a few children. Her absorption in her "ideal" constitutes a mission; to achieve it, she must reject personal fulfillment. "I would endure the suffering," she concludes, "I would find an outlet for my mother-need in the love of *all* children" (I, 61). All very well in theory; but when a man comes into her life who wishes her to bear his child, her conflict becomes intense. Her lover, Ed, shares her ideals but believes them impossible to realize in the predictable future. He suggests the desirability of arranging one's private life for satisfaction, since social amelioration represents an unattainable hope; and he suggests that "the strongest motive in [Goldman's] devotion to the movement was unsatisfied motherhood seeking an outlet" (I, 153).

The question of motivation has not previously concerned Goldman, beyond her rather naive insistence that sympathetic identification with the Chicago martyrs accounted for her political course. Now, however, she recognizes the plausibility of Ed's argument. She understands her devotion to humanity as "the all-absorbing passion of my life" but acknowledges the existence also of other forms of passion; she

cannot deal intellectually or emotionally with the dilemma of "unsatisfied motherhood," so she retreats into a fantasy that "it must be possible for a man and a woman to have a beautiful love-life and yet be
devoted to a great cause" (I, 154). She and Ed endeavor to live out this
fantasy; for a time they succeed. But experience repeatedly offers
Goldman a lesson which she never fully incorporates: devotion to the
masses mixes badly with devotion to a man, conflicting responsibilities
and conflicting desires for gratification proving impossible to reconcile. And she never succeeds in answering to her own satisfaction the
argument that desire for motherhood underlies all her commitment.
Partly she finds it flattering; certainly she finds it persuasive.

Public commitment and activity manifestly feel necessary to Emma
Goldman, but not altogether "natural": she never refutes Ed. Hence,
perhaps, the strain in her prose as well as her life, her account of
herself a sequence of poses, her writing an imitation of romantic and
sentimental models, second-hand in its phraseology. The uncomfortable artificiality of her style reiterates the impression of indistinct
identity. Her continuing report of her relationship with Ed describes
a painful erosion of her sense of personal substance, a paradigm of how
the central conflict can play itself out and how it damages the personality. Her career as public speaker suffers. Sometimes she refuses
speaking engagements; often she finds herself working for weeks to
prepare a presentation, hampered by her fantasies of whether Ed
would or would not approve. Never does she actually try her ideas out
on him, for she knows that he has "no faith in [her] work"—a fact
which, she says, eroded her faith in herself until she succumbed to a
series of "strange nervous attacks" which would fell her to the ground,
conscious but unable to speak, deprived of the power that had defined
her public role (I, 187). When Ed denounces Nietzsche in an anarchist
gathering, Goldman takes the attack personally. "It was not his differing from me that had stabbed me to the quick; it was his scorn and
ridicule of what had come to mean so much to me. . . . My own lover
made me appear silly, childish, incapable of judgment" (I, 194).

Even before the problem with Ed developed, Goldman appeared
aware of the internal conflict which the clash with a lover only objec-
tified. Like Eleanor Roosevelt, she claimed the dominance of the per-

sonal in her thought; unlike Roosevelt, she feels the fact to reflect weakness. She compares herself unfavorably to such male revolutionaries as Berkman, "heroic figures," "hewn of one piece." She, on the other hand, feels herself "woven of many skeins, conflicting in shade and texture." "To the end of my days," she concludes, "I should be torn between the yearning for a personal life and the need of giving all to my ideal" (I, 153). As she demonstrates the point over and over, and demonstrates also her confusion between the personal and the political, her inability to keep them in distinct realms, she evokes her uncertainty about where to locate her sense of self—a problem characteristic of this group of women, despite their authority of action and sometimes of phrasing.

Golda Meir, born latest of the five, appears to face the least difficulty in defining herself in print, perhaps because she accepts with greater equanimity than the others the idea of definition by public action. Emma Goldman, faced with personal crisis, lost the capacity to speak; Golda Meir, on the other hand, discovered that her gift for public speaking could avert personal crisis. In an emblematic episode when she was twenty, Meir clashed violently with her father over her soapbox speeches supporting the Labor Zionist platform. "Moshe Mabovitch's daughter, he stormed, was not going to stand on a box in the street and make a spectacle of herself" (p. 61). After a furious argument, the girl defiantly left the house, beginning her speech "not without some panic." Her father had sworn to come after her and pull her home by her braid; she believed him. But in fact he came, heard, and was conquered, "so carried away listening to me perched on my soapbox that he had completely forgotten his threat." Meir already believed in herself as an orator; she comments, "I suppose I had more than my fair share of self-confidence in this respect, if not in others" (p. 61). The telling final phrase underlines an important point: able to feel confidence in her public performance, able even to triumph through such performance against her father, Meir early learned the advantage of avoiding private problems by escape into the public.

Yet a residue of uncertainty about the nature and value of her private selfhood emerges in an occasional episode and affects her narrative structure and style. One paragraph begins, "But work was not everything for me during that period. There were also the private joys and sorrows of every life" (p. 271). The writer substantiates the flat vagueness of these assertions by reporting two of her sorrows, one of them her husband's death. "I flew back to Israel to attend his funeral," she explains, "my head filled with thoughts about the life we might have lived together if I had only been different." But she doesn't really want to talk about it; she will say only that, "standing at his graveside, I realized once again what a heavy price I had paid—and made Morris pay—for whatever I had experienced and achieved in the years of our separation" (p. 271).

Two hundred and seventy pages into Meir's autobiography, the reader has attained little insight into the author's experience; her curious use of *whatever* in the sentence above, in a context where one expects *what*—"whatever I had experienced"—suggests her own uncertainty about the nature of her experience and achievement. What feels certain is her self-blame. She thinks about how much better life might have proved had she been different, not about the possibility of her husband's being different; she accepts full responsibility for her marriage's failure. Proclaiming her confidence in her public self, she betrays her conviction of an absolute dichotomy between public and private and reveals serious doubt about the self responsible for intimate relationship. It is, of course, the private self that experiences; the failure of Golda Meir's account of herself to communicate convincingly how life has felt to her, what her experience has meant, evokes a writer out of touch with her own feelings. Like Goldman, she relies heavily on clichés. The autobiography's interest derives most obviously from its personalized account of recent Middle East history. Its frequent apparent identification of Golda Meir with the state of Israel generates once more the disturbing and confusing impression of an autobiography with no self at its center.

The same impression emerges yet more overwhelmingly from Emmeline Pankhurst's account, in which Victorian decorum partly accounts for the inadequacies of self-revelation, but the emphasis on "we" rather than "I" finally convinces the reader that Pankhurst hardly knows or cares about her distinguishable separate self. She declares that early experience accounts for her later militance, but tells almost nothing about her childhood. Like Emma Goldman, she considers her political awareness to have originated in sympathetic identification with the victim of an unjust hanging. But she also remarks "while still a very young child, I began instinctively to feel that there was something lacking, even in my own home, some false conception of family relations, some incomplete ideal" (p. 5). One can only guess what she found lacking, and what caused her to feel the lack. Her own formulation moves, even within the single sentence, toward increasing abstraction and enlargement: not a statement that her mother treated her badly or her father ignored her but an assertion of "false conceptions," "incomplete ideal." Her interest continued to center on conceptions and ideals.

On page twelve of a 364-page book, the autobiographer remarks—making the single sentence into a paragraph—"My marriage with Dr. Pankhurst took place in 1879." The next, much longer, paragraph generalizes from Dr. Pankhurst to the group of which he was part, a group working ardently for female suffrage. All we ever learn about the writer's husband is contained in these few statements about the group. Pankhurst then proclaims the happiness of her marriage, making of the proclamation a political point, and summarizes her married life: "My home life and relations have been as nearly ideal as possible in this imperfect world. About a year after my marriage my daughter Christabel was born, and in another eighteen months my second daughter Sylvia came. Two other children followed, and for some years I was rather deeply immersed in my domestic affairs" (p. 12). She never alludes again to the two later children or identifies them by sex or name; Christabel and Sylvia receive further mention only insofar as they involve themselves with the suffrage movement. In a book entitled *My Own Story*, this paragraph marks virtually the last personal reference. The writer mentions her husband's death, but not her reaction to it; she describes herself entirely in relation to her passionate political conviction. She writes more vividly about the sufferings of others in the cause than about her own; she expresses no doubts, fears, or personal resentments, although her political anger energizes much of her statement. The denial of private reality, more intense and more total than Golda Meir's, raises doubts again about the connection between autobiography and self.

Eleanor Roosevelt, reporting her relationship with Queen Elizabeth, recalls a conversation with a palace secretary in which she commented sympathetically on the difficulties of the queen's lot, having to function in relation to so many official responsibilities and also as wife and mother. The secretary, looking surprised, denied the difficulty, explaining that "The Queen is very well departmentalized." "How does one departmentalize one's heart?" Roosevelt wonders (p. 297).

This uncharacteristic episode—uncharacteristic because it directly reveals the writer's emotional response to an apparently trivial happening—emphasizes Roosevelt's awareness of the public-private dilemma and suggests her own difficulty in transcending the personal. But that difficulty rarely supplies material for her autobiography. Toward the book's end, the writer observes, "I find that, as I have grown older, my personal objectives have long since blended into my public objectives" (p. 416). Recent biographical revelations about the Roosevelts have disclosed much pain in her life which the autobiography entirely conceals. The reader can surmise its presence only by the ardency of the author's escape into the public, yielding up personal desire—"personal objectives," as she puts it—for her notion of larger good.

Transcendence of the personal, of course, may represent a triumphant, a truly heroic, achievement. In emphasizing the deprivation and loss that emerge in these books, I do not mean to deny the heroism, also vivid in all five accounts. These women have sacrificed and suffered in the service of their ideals; they make those ideals more compelling than they make themselves. Dorothy Day, unlike the others in this group, appears to have thought seriously and impersonally about what must be yielded for the sake of spiritual gain. (Emma Goldman, as we have seen, is sharply aware of conflicting desire and purpose, but she sees the issue entirely in relation to her emotional life.)

Day's autobiography opens with memories disguised in the second person: "When you go to confession on a Saturday night. . . . " That *you* isn't quite identical with *I*; it includes the reader in significant shared experience and in a continuing present. As the account relates events of Day's early life, it renders compellingly the emotional determinants of religious impulse. Making no grandiose claims, Day reports her childish reactions. "I didn't see anyone having a banquet and calling in the lame, the halt, and the blind. And those who were doing it, like the Salvation Army, did not appeal to me. . . . I wanted life and I wanted the abundant life. I wanted it for others too" (p. 39). The directness of statement convincingly evokes personal feeling. As Day's responses become more complicated, her capacity to render them straightforwardly continues to indicate the presence of a writer in touch with her self. But the sense of self creates problems. Day objects to Emma Goldman on the ground of her promiscuity, basing her stated objection to sexual looseness on its "emphasis on the personal." Then she generalizes about the special danger of the personal for women. "I am quite ready to concede now that men are the single-minded, the pure of heart, in these movements. Women by their very nature are more materialistic, thinking of the home, the children, and of all things needful to them, especially love. And in their constant searching after it, they go against their own best interests" (p. 60). The observation exists in a context of self-castigation: for "my own self-love, my own gropings for the love of others, my own desire for freedom and for pleasure," for "ambition" and "self-seeking." When Day reaches the narrative climax of her conversion, she reports it as motivated by love of a remarkably personal sort. She gives up her love for a man and for the radical movement in order to fulfill an almost erotic commitment to God. Her intense religious involvement, to the very end of her story, replaces intense personal relations and throbs with the energy of personal passion; the need for personal life continues to seem to her a weakness. Unlike the other autobiographers we have considered, she has a clear sense of self—but struggles constantly to lose it.

Partaking of an ancient, highly elaborated tradition, Day finds in her religion answers to the questions that plague her and appears to rest content in the identity she has forged. The clarity of her prose indicates less ambivalence of feeling than one senses in the other women, but like them she blames herself for lapses into kinds of private emotion she has taught herself to reject. Although the story she tells in its large outlines belongs to a pattern as characteristic of men as of women, fitting the well-established genre of conversion narrative or spiritual autobiography, although self-castigation for excessive self-love characterizes her male as well as female predecessors in the form, her identification of her sex as particularly prone to the weakness of personal feeling and her readiness to declare the superiority of men suggest the possibility that this genre has some special affinities for women.

I would argue, in fact, that all five of the books we have been considering represent a female variant on the high tradition of spiritual autobiography, although only Day's possesses the clarity of conscious commitment to an established formal tradition. The political involvement of the other women, like Day's religious passion, has spiritual meaning for them; the striking lack of acknowledged personal ambition in all these accounts makes clearest sense in a spiritual context. Barbara Hardy has written, "In order really to live, we make up stories about ourselves and others, about the personal as well as the social past and future."[7] The events of the autobiographers' lives, of course, are given, pre-existing the setting down of the narratives. But to organize events into stories, not merely sequences of happening but sequences of meaning, requires "making up," of patterns if not of events. To understand one's life as a story demands that one perceive that life as making sense; autobiographies record the sense their authors hope their lives make.

Spiritual autobiographies specifically declare meaning to inhere in the process of discovering and sustaining commitment to God. Their form and rhetoric characteristically speak of certainty, drawing energy and conviction from the affirmation of transcendent meaning. But the autobiographies of the women we are considering exploit instead a rhetoric of *uncertainty*: about the self, about the value of womanhood, about the proper balance of commitments. Only Dorothy Day writes convincingly about feelings, and she blames herself for her emotions. The others sound out of touch with their own personal reality, ignoring their feelings (Pankhurst), flattening them out by vague rendition (Meir, Roosevelt), or exaggerating and overdramatizing them (Goldman). Their stories profoundly contradict themselves, opposing to the manifest narrative of salvation through faith and hope (in anarchism, world peace, women's suffrage, the state of Israel) a hidden tale of doubt about the integrity and value of the self. Stories of unusual female achievement, these narratives convey singular absence of personal satisfaction in achievement. Even Emma Goldman, forever boasting, expresses also a constant level of self-doubt and dissatisfaction. These autobiographies remind me of a recently published collection of photographic self-portraits by women.[8] Of 120 self-renditions in that volume, only two depict women directly confronting the camera without obvious irony, self-deprecation, or disguise. The photographs gain power by their ingenuities of indirection, although they also suggest some female problems of self-presentation. They do not necessarily express in any simple sense how the photographers *feel* about themselves, only how they choose to convey themselves. I am trying to make the same point about these autobiographies, again not as lives but as stories about lives. In writing of themselves, these women of public accomplishment implicitly stress uncertainties of the personal, denying rather than glorifying ambition, evading rather than enlarging private selves. They use autobiography, paradoxically, partly as a mode of self-denial. Although they have functioned successfully in spheres rarely open to women, their accounts of this activity emphasize its hidden costs more than its rewards and draw back—as women have traditionally done—from making large claims of importance. Even as they tell of unusual accomplishment, in other words, they finally hide from self-assertion. Their strategies of narrative reflect both a female dilemma and a female solution to it.

8.

In Search of the Black Female Self: African-American Women's Autobiographies and Ethnicity

REGINA BLACKBURN

Both before and after the Civil War, the status of African-American women as a class of human beings has been determined by their blackness and their womanhood rather than by their creative, intellectual, and psychological composition. However, the common experience of racism and sexism notwithstanding, black women led greatly diverse lives—being black and female in America is a complex matter—and it is a mistake to study African-American women only as a group. Yet, while these women do not lend themselves to easy generalizations, their identities and conceptions of self are greatly shaped by their blackness and their womanhood.

One effective approach to viewing and analyzing African-American women is to study their autobiographies. When these women use the autobiographical mode, they reveal themselves in a unique way, one not typical of white autobiography. In *Black Autobiography in America*, Stephen Butterfield asserts,

> The "self" of black autobiography, on the whole, taking into account the effect of Western culture on the Afro-American, is not an individual with a private career, but a soldier in a long, historic march toward Canaan. The self is conceived as a member of an oppressed social group, with ties and responsibilities to the other members. It is a conscious political identity, drawing sustenance from the past

> experience of the group, giving back the iron of its endurance fash-
> ioned into armor and weapons for the use of the next generation of
> fighters. The autobiographical form is one of the ways that black
> Americans have asserted their right to live and grow. It is a bid for
> freedom, a beak of hope cracking the shell of slavery and exploita-
> tion. It is also an attempt to communicate to the white world what
> whites have done to them.[1]

Of black female autobiographies, specifically, it should be observed
that they also communicate to the world what the black world has
done to them.

Each author's work, while individual and unique, is, therefore, part
of this special category of the autobiographical genre. The very events
in their lives have been affected by racist and sexist forces that permeate American society. Their perspectives of themselves, first as individuals, then as individuals within the black community, and finally
within the general society, determine what they do with their lives,
how they look at life, what they demand of life, and, perhaps, most
important, what they demand of themselves.

There are those who aspire toward black nationalism; those seeking
total integration; those who attack the economic, political, and social
system; and those who succeed within the system and have no desire
to change it. Hence, they possess different perceptions of reality—
which helps explain why some African-American women rebel and
others seek to excel; why some emphasize ethnicity while others find
it the source of their disadvantaged lives; why some make a virtue out
of antiblack sentiment and realities, distilling from it racial pride,
strength, and solidarity, while others feel a pervasive sense of inferiority.

None of the autobiographers denies her blackness, although each
places a different emphasis on its importance. Concern with blackness
is not a recent fashion. Blackness has always been an issue, as the
earliest writings indicate. Most African-American female autobiographers confess to one incident in their early years that awakened them
to their color; this recognition scene evoked an awareness of their
blackness and of its significance, and it had a lasting influence on their
lives.

The black women whose autobiographies I will consider in this paper represent a variety of professions and lifestyles. Ossie Guffy (*Ossie: The Autobiography of a Black Woman*, 1971), "the mother," had many children, most of them out of wedlock, and developed into a political fighter as the result of fighting for her children. Delle Brehan (*Kicks Is Kicks*, 1969), a black prostitute who succeeded economically, decided that her personal power was more significant than the fact that she was black. Zora Neale Hurston (*Dust Tracks on a Road*, 1942), a professional writer, did research on black folklore and history. Entertainer Pearl Bailey (*The Raw Pearl*, 1968) sought to have everyone love and understand everyone else and saw her ethnicity in humanness. Nikki Giovanni (*Gemini: An Extended Autobiographical Statement of My First Twenty-Five Years of Being a Black Poet*, 1971) described herself as a revolutionary poet in a prerevolutionary age and analyzed the conditions of black life in America. Gwendolyn Brooks (*Report from Part One*, 1972), critic, poet, novelist, wrote about incidents that shaped her development. Lorraine Hansberry (*To Be Young, Gifted, and Black*, 1969), a poet and dramatist, wrote of the deep heartaches and sources of pride for African-American people. Helen Jackson Lee (*Nigger in the Window*, 1978), a white-collar worker, described the conditions she was forced to endure as a black female in her immediate environment and in the labor force. Author and entertainer Maya Angelou (*I Know Why the Caged Bird Sings*, 1969) fought against the negative self-image that gives rise to self-doubt and weakness. Anne Moody (*Coming of Age in Mississippi*, 1968), after experiencing a troublesome childhood, entered adulthood as a social activist dedicated to changing the American social system. Angela Davis (*Angela Davis: An Autobiography—With My Mind on Freedom*, 1974), a Communist, a rebel, and an educator, was also active in the black struggle for survival, but she sought change through Marxist analysis. Congresswoman Shirley Chisholm (*Unbought and Unbossed*, 1970) recalled her Barbadian roots and sought to change the fate of black America through political means.[2]

African-American female autobiographies are essentially formally written self-reports that offer analysis of self virtually neglected by critics. They consist of objective fact and subjective awareness.[3] Several interrelated and recurrent themes appear in these works. First is the issue of identity, of defining and understanding this black self. Second is the assigning of some value to the black self; it could be a source of pride and contentment, but more often the sense of blackness brought shame, self-hatred, and self-depreciation. This low or negative self-evaluation caused some women to exist in an ambivalent state, torn between pride and self-hatred, the latter often prompting a desire to be segregated from other blacks and a corollary desire to be white and reap the benefits of whiteness. Third is the bind of double jeopardy, being both black and female, with sexism displayed by black males toward black females. These three themes usually overlap and quite often evolve from one another.

These writers as blacks and as females offer insight into their immediate environment. The world described in these autobiographies reveals a great deal about the writer's perceived place in it. For some women, their problems and joys are derived from their personal experiences rather than from the larger society. Some acknowledge the social and political forces which shape their lives. Some feel they are weak and powerless, no more than pawns, incapable of controlling their lives or of changing their environment. Others come on as determined individuals who will make a difference or die trying. Their social perceptions of and comments on the greater environment add an essential dimension to the autobiographical genre.

Butterfield states that a black autobiographer must "rend the veil of white definitions that misrepresent him to himself and the world, create a new identity . . . ."[4] These women must define themselves in order to repair the damage inflicted on them by other women, white and black, and by men. Since the self is influenced and shaped by both external and internal forces,[5] these writers take on the task of unifying their public and private images in order to express their understanding of self.

Our concern here is with the source of the self-image of African-American women. It is uncertain whether self-images develop or whether they are adopted.[6] Most likely, for African-American women, it is a combination of both. We should consider that "'men and women are not only themselves; they are also the region in which they were born, the city apartment or the farm in which they learned to walk, the games they played as children, the old wives' tale they overheard, the food they ate, the schools they attended, the sports they followed, the poems they read, and the God they believed in.'"[7] These influences admittedly operated on the aforementioned black women as they grew and developed.

Black Self-Statement

Response to the initial realization of blackness was often uncertainty. Ossie Guffy admits that she does not know how to respond:

> I guess you can't say what it's like to be *born* black, because when you're born—and for a long time after—you don't know you are black. When you look in a mirror, you see a little girl with dark skin, but it doesn't mean anything special to you because when you're little you haven't learned yet that the color of your skin is going to be the most important fact of your life, the prison that locks you out instead of in, the package around your soul that sets up an immediate reaction in the white world and makes you forever an inferior, unless proven otherwise. No, when you're very young, you're just Ossie, a little girl with one brother and three sisters, a mother who doesn't live with you but visits you every Thursday and every other Sunday, and no father. (p. 13)

The conscious level of a child, she points out, is underdeveloped or at best primitive. A child is aware only of its immediate environment. Guffy saw only her reflection in the mirror, not what it signified to the outside world. She eventually learned that her skin was the most crucial fact in her life; and she learned through experience that there was a certain defined life-style for those who were black but that such a style was partially controlled by the self; she had to determine how her life would be different. As a writer, Guffy realized that the process of growth and development and change was ever present in her life.

In *Kicks Is Kicks*, Delle Brehan asserts her power to define herself and selects the labels she accepts for herself. Brehan writes:

> I am colored. No question about that because my mother was dark as you could wish and my father, although very light, was a colored

> man. Today, some people want me to say I am black. Not Negro or
> colored, but black. Well, screw them. When I want to be colored,
> that is what I will be, because it is my life and I can be the most
> independent creature you ever saw. And if you have not learned that
> nothing is all black or all white, that is because you have not gradu-
> ated yet from my kind of college. (p. 8)

Independent, possessed of a strong personality, Brehan rejects labels
others assign her and does not emphasize her blackness:

> The color of my skin has been about as interesting to me as the fact
> that I have two ears. I mean it is nice, and I am glad about it but I
> am not all choked up one way or the other. Because I am female and
> attractive, I had to get used to the sidewalk and subway creeps who
> vomit their sickness by muttering obscene words at passing girls.
> Some of these jerks try to patch up their mustered manhood by call-
> ing me "nigger." (p. 18)

Being a woman led to disrespect, she learned, and when men did not
succeed with sexual advances, they showed disrespect for her color.
Thus, as female and black—the totality of self—Brehan suffered. But
she went beyond the natural environment, where blackness was sub-
ordinated, to determine her goals by her own power; and she saw
herself as an independent person.

For Zora Neale Hurston, the environment itself contributed to the
shaping of a positive black self. Hurston's life was rather unique in that
she grew up in an all-black town, Eatonville, Florida. She learned
naturally to take pride in and be confident of blackness within herself.
Around her were self-ruling blacks. Perhaps living among them produced a sense of pride that could not be fostered elsewhere. Possibly
this accounts for an observation she made about herself: "Sometimes,
I feel discriminated against, but it does not make me angry. It merely
astonishes me. How can anyone deny themselves the pleasure of my
company!" (p. vii). Unlike so many who wrote about the South, she
always considered the region home. She never desired to escape from
it, and she was spiritually revived upon returning to it.

Hurston makes the following statement regarding her heritage:

I maintain that I have been a Negro three times—a Negro baby, a Negro girl and a Negro woman. Still, if you have received no clear cut impression of what the Negro in America is like, then you are in the same place with me. There is no *The Negro* here. Our lives are so diversified, internal attitudes so varied, appearances and capabilities so different, that there is no possible classification so catholic that it will cover us all, except My people! My people! (p. 237)

Despising labels, Hurston sees no logic in grouping people on the basis of skin color.

Being an observer of life in both worlds allows Hurston to compare accurately the makeup of both races. She declares:

My interest lies in what makes a man or a woman do such-and-so, regardless of his color. It seemed to me that the human beings I met reacted pretty much the same to the same stimuli. Different idioms, yes. Circumstances and conditions having power to influence, yes. Inherent difference, no. (p. 206)

Pearl Bailey also did not take kindly to people imposing a life-style upon her. Her ideal was that of a community in which color was insignificant. For Bailey, the autobiographical genre offered a means of expressing her beliefs and explaining the background of their development. She is against labels, especially racial labels, for they are limiting and often based on incorrect stereotypes. Events in her life, she believes, owed to a predestined law, not to her blackness. Bailey plays down her color, though never completely ignoring it:

In reading a lot of books lately, the lives of this or that one, I notice they say things happened "because of" race, religion, or creed. Perhaps this is so, but wearing no label, being of the people, for the people, all under the judgment of God, I can only feel that what has happened to me has been, and will be, because it's my destiny—as your life is yours. (Prologue)

Life, she feels, is much more than her blackness; her humanness is the key to self-realization. A person should be judged on her personal merits and personality rather than prejudged because of color.

Nikki Giovanni expresses some impatience over the discovery of one's blackness: "I've always known I was colored. When I was a Negro I knew I was colored; now that I'm Black I know which color it is. Any identity crises I may have had never centered on race" (p. 24). Giovanni confronted color and knew she was black. She recalls somewhat sarcastically her response to the question of how an African-American deals with it.

> It's great when you near your quarter-century mark and someone says, "I want an experience on how you came to grips with being colored." The most logical answer is, "I came to grips with Blackdom when I grabbed my mama." . . . If your parents are colored we have found—statistically—the chances are quite high that so are you. If your parents are mixed the chances are even higher that you'll grow up to be a Nigger. (pp. 24–25)

Acknowledgment of one's blackness, however, did not bring freedom for Giovanni. She is, she asserts, black, but she is not free. In opposition to Bailey's belief, Giovanni recognizes certain inherent limitations and predetermined characteristics in the state of being black.

The black self-statements expressed in the autobiographical form offer valuable insight into the thoughts black women have about themselves. Autobiography offers each writer the challenge of honestly and thoroughly looking to herself for an evaluation. The evaluations of blackness lack uniformity: for Guffy the magnitude of its importance was so profound that it imprisoned her; for Brehan it is an insignificant but recognizable characteristic; for Hurston it should not be the totality of one's concern and interest; for Bailey the characteristic of being human outweighs one's race; and for Giovanni blackness was reality— a way of life. The conciseness of their statements enhances the depth of their self-understanding and their method of self-evaluation—the autobiographical form.

Black Pride

Somehow, Gwendolyn Brooks does not have to wrestle with the issue of freedom as Giovanni does; she is content within her black self. She explains:

When I was a child, it did not occur to me, even once, that the black in which I was encased (I called it brown in those days) would be considered, one day, beautiful. Considered beautiful and called beautiful by great groups.

I had always considered it beautiful. I would stick out my arm, examine it, and smile. Charming! And convenient, for mud on my leg was not as annunciatory as was mud on the leg of light Rose Hurd.

Charm—and efficiency. (p. 37)

As a child, she accepted her blackness, not having learned about the prison to which Guffy referred. Later, however, Brooks speaks of her growing knowledge of the implications of being black in a racially oriented society. She was initiated into the realities of black existence by her schoolmates who implemented shade prejudice in their selection of friends:

. . . a little girl must be Bright (of skin). It was better if your hair was curly, too—or at least Good Grade (Good Grade implied, usually, no involvement with the Hot Comb)—but Bright you marvelously *needed* to be. Exceptions? A few. Wealth was an escape passport. (p. 37)

In spite of her exposure to shade prejudice, Brooks's self-contentment grows and thrives as her knowledge of being black in white America develops:

Until 1967 my own blackness did not confront me with a shrill spelling of itself. I knew that I was what most people were calling "a Negro"; I called myself that, although always the word felt awkwardly on a poet's ear; I had never liked the sound of it. (Caucasian has an ugly sound, too, while the name Indian is beautiful to look at and to hear.) *And* I knew that people of my coloration and distinctive history had been bolted to trees and sliced or burned or shredded; knocked to the back of the line; provided with separate toilets, schools, and neighborhoods; denied, when possible, voting rights; hounded, hooted at, or shunned, or patronizingly patted (often the patting-hand was, I knew, surreptitiously wiped after the kindness, so that unspeakable contamination might be avoided). America's social climate, it seemed, was trying to tell me something. It was trying

> to tell me something Websterian. Yet, although almost secretly, I had always felt that to be black was good. (pp. 83–84)

Though comprehending the mistreatment to which black people are subjected, Brooks's belief in the value of blackness was not shaken. Her pride came from within.

Gwendolyn Brooks's viewpoint was not identically shared by Lorraine Hansberry. Hansberry's parents and various racial incidents encouraged and emphasized the need for her to be knowledgeable of the realities of life. She considers the element of blackness a primary factor contributing to the shaping of her person and her destiny:

> We were also vaguely taught certain vague absolutes: that we were better than no one but infinitely superior to everyone; that we were the products of the proudest and most mistreated of the races of man; that there was nothing enormously difficult about life; that one *succeeded* as a matter of course. (p. 48)

Though Hansberry knew about black conditions, she would not let them bind her to any lack of ambition or success. Nurtured on race pride, confident of self, she was sure that her blackness would not thwart her, that she would excel.

Her pride in her African ancestry reflected such self-confidence. She often spoke, through her characters, about Africa. Thus, she describes one of her characters, Candace:

> As for the African part, the greater part, she spent hours of her younger years poring over maps of the African continent, postulating and fantasizing: *Ibo, Mandingo, Hausa, Yoruba, Ashanti, Dahomean.* Who, who were they! In her emotions she was sprung from the Southern Zulu and the Central Pygmy, the Eastern Watusi and the treacherous slavetrading Western Ashanti themselves. She was Kikuyu and Masai, ancient cousins of hers had made the exquisite forged sculpture at Benin, while surely even more ancient relatives sat upon the throne at Abu Simbel watching over the Nile. (p. 75)

Hansberry was proud of her black self and conscious of her connections, extending back through time and space, with the continent of Africa. Her realization of the cultural heritage of which she was a part allowed her to develop a positive self-concept as an African-American woman.

Helen Jackson Lee gained her conception of black pride from watching those people who displayed it the most. As she observed the proudest people, she concluded that one's pride was in proportion to one's color:

> Racial pride. What did it mean to be a child growing up in Virginia? I perceived it this way: Be proud you're a Negro, but let your pride be in direct proportion to the color of your skin. The whiter your skin, the more reason to be proud. If your skin was inky black, you felt ashamed of your color. If you happened to be female and black too, God help you. A black woman saw a hard time. (p. 29)

Lee came to this understanding from listening to her mother and her friends discuss color; they laughed about people of darker hues. She could feel her unfavorable comparison with her younger sister, who was of "fair skin." Lee's brother teased her about her color, saying, "You're adopted. Mama found you on a dump!" (p. 36). Quite often, such attitudes toward shade were disastrous to the positive development of self.

Among the aspects of self the autobiographical genre allows its writers to express is black pride. For many of them, black pride is derived from skin color, endurance of oppression, an inner, deep feeling of worth, and/or ancestral background. For some, it is a natural feeling felt first during childhood. For others, it grows and develops with the growth of self-knowledge and conscious awareness. Once felt, its significance is ever present in their lives and thoughts.

Self-Hatred

As a consequence of lacking power, of being victims of racism, and of the failure to develop a positive sense of self, African-American women, however, often suffer psychologically and spiritually from self-hatred. The degrees of self-hatred surface, often agonizingly, as in a line of Imamu Baraka's poem, "An Agony. As now"—"I am inside someone who hates me."[8]

In *Black Rage*, William Grier and Price Cobb attribute this self-hatred and self-doubt to the fact that black women are always judged by white standards, with blond, blue-eyed, white-skinned women of regular features the ideal; consequently, low self-esteem among African-American women is quite understandable. Black women have been "depreciated by [their] own kind, judged grotesque by [their] society, and valued only as a sexually convenient laboring animal."[9]

Given the color prejudice of blacks and the racism of whites, African-American women understandably question their own self-worth at times. Of all those here considered, Maya Angelou expresses the most severe self-hatred derived from her appearance. Beaten down by massive self-loathing and self-shame, she felt her appearance was too offensive to merit any kind of true affection from others. Hence, she devoted much of *I Know Why the Caged Bird Sings* to explaining her internal struggles. Angelou frequently imagined her self as another, for she "was sucking in air to breathe out shame" (p. 1) because of her "shit color" (p. 17). Naively, she imagined that a simple dress would alter her being: "I was going to look like one of the sweet little white girls who were everybody's dream of what was right with the world" (p. 1).

At an early age, Angelou recognized her hatred of self and allowed it to grow in the southern climate. She explains: "If growing up is painful for the Southern Black girl, being aware of her displacement is the rust on the razor that threatens the throat. It is an unnecessary insult" (p. 3).

Angelou's fantasies, dreams, and prayers allowed her to pretend that her black state was unreal and momentary. Her wishes confused her sense of reality, and she longed to be white and so fantasized:

> Wouldn't they be surprised when one day I woke out of my black ugly dream, and my real hair, which was long and blond, would take the place of the kinky mass that Momma wouldn't let me straighten? My light-blue eyes were going to hypnotize them, after all the things they said about "my daddy must of been a Chinaman" (I thought they meant made out of china, like a cup) because my eyes were so small and squinty. Then they would understand why I had never picked up a Southern accent, or spoke the common slang, and why I had to

be forced to eat pigs' tails and snouts. Because I was really
white. . . . (p. 2)

Angelou's conception of self caused her to be self-limiting and to lack
self-assertion and self-acceptance.

Anne Moody's bewilderment and anger was the result of shade
prejudice in her family regarding skin color. Because her mother as
well as Anne and her siblings were "a few shades darker," the mulatto
family her mother married into refused even to associate with them.
Moody found herself competing fiercely with the mulatto girls of her
age and ended up hating her stepfather. In this same vein, a friend
warned her not to go to Tougaloo College, a black college, because it
was "not for people of my color"; she was "too black," her friend told
her, and, moreover, did not meet the second requirement; she did
not have a rich father (p. 239).

Although Angela Davis claims that she had early decided never to
harbor a desire to be white, she admitted to ambivalence about the
white world:

> My childhood friends and I were bound to develop ambivalent atti-
> tudes toward the white world. On the one hand there was our in-
> stinctive aversion toward those who prevented us from realizing our
> grandest as well as our most trivial wishes. On the other, there was
> the equally instinctive jealousy which came from knowing that they
> had access to all the pleasurable things we wanted. (p. 85)

Frustrated and angry by being so confined, she imagined a fantastic
plan, in which she slipped on a mask of a white face and went where
she wanted to go: "After thoroughly enjoying the activity, I would
make a dramatic, grandstand appearance before the white racists and
with a sweeping gesture, rip off the white face, laugh wildly and call
them all fools" (p. 85). Even this innocent fantasy of her early days
suggests dissatisfaction with her self and her world; and also a certain
wisdom. Davis understood that her blackness confined and bound her
life.

Though Nikki Giovanni was aware of these boundaries, she claims
to place no value on whiteness. Indeed, she denied any desire to work

out relations with whites, or to confront them—as so many black people had done: "There weren't any times I remember wanting to eat in a restaurant or go to a school that I was blocked from because of color" (p. 33). She had had friends, she says, who participated in the sit-ins, and she recognizes that their efforts produced what few privileges blacks possess; but she would never have begged for such pseudo-equality.

Double Jeopardy: Black and Female

Self-hatred and self-doubt resulted from racial oppression. Coupled with the state of being female, this resulted in double jeopardy. Since the slave era, black male chauvinism vis-à-vis black females has been common—much as it has existed among whites. Consequently, many black women believe that sexual identity should receive as much importance as women's racial identity. The black female found that her male counterpart, who was equally oppressed and exploited, attempted to place certain restrictions and limitations on her actions, aspirations, and activities.

Angela Davis was frequently exposed to sexism in the political organizations to which she belonged. It was, she states, "a situation which was to become a constant problem in my political life," and she was often criticized for doing "'a man's job.'" Men's reactions to her participation were naively hostile: "Women should not play leadership roles, they insisted. A woman was supposed to 'inspire' her man and educate his children. The irony of their complaint was that much of what I was doing had fallen to me by default." Davis admits: "I became acquainted very early with the widespread presence of an unfortunate syndrome among some Black male activists—namely to confuse their political activity with an assertion of their maleness" (p. 159). As a result, "all the myths about Black women surfaced" (p. 180). Black women were accused of being too domineering; of seeking to control everything, including men; of desiring to rob black males of their manhood; of aiding and abetting the enemy, who wanted to see black men weak and unable to hold their own.

Nikki Giovanni feels that part of the problem is that black men falsely perceive both black women and themselves. As a result, black men define black women "in terms of white women because they frequently think of themselves in terms of white men. But if they ever would decide to define a Black man in Black terms I think they would have different expectations of us as women" (p. 145). Redefining the black female self in black terms from a black perspective is essential.

The identity crisis resulting from centuries of oppression and dehumanization affects black women as well as black men. Shirley Chisholm emphasizes that more obstacles were placed before her because she was a woman than because she was black. There were many drawbacks to being a woman in America, she recognizes, especially in politics. She recalls her fight to make both sexes aware of women's political contributions: "Discrimination against women in politics is particularly unjust, because no political organization I have seen could function without women. They do the work that men won't do" (p. 76). Though confronted by the sexism of black men, she never struck back at these men who argued against her because "I understood too well their reasons for lashing out at black women; in a society that denied them real manhood, I was threatening their shaky self-esteem still more" (p. 53). But such awareness did not prevent her from excelling in the political arena.

Chisholm was also confronted by the sexist beliefs of white males. She admits that "there is as much—it could be even more—panic among white men confronted by an able, determined female who refuses to play the sex role they think is fitting" (p. 54). She refers to Betty Friedan's coinage, "Sexism has no color line." And, though fully aware of the black experience in America, she concludes, "This society is as antiwoman as it is antiblack" (p. 168).

These African-American women have chosen to use the autobiographical genre as their resource for self-analysis. They have taken an established, historical art form as a means of self-expression and suited it to their needs for self-evaluation. In light of the common characteristics of these selves—black and female—the American autobiographical tradition has been given a new dimension.

Autobiography has proved to be a conscious, deliberate method of identifying and revealing the black female self. The process of these women's self-analyses gives rise to the themes of identity, assigning value to this identity, and the double jeopardy of being both black and female in America.

These women have assumed the difficult task of self-portraiture. The complete revelation of self, they learn, requires the realization and acceptance of the ever-present process of growth, development, and change. During the period of writing, the women incorporate themselves in the present, in the past, perhaps in the future, and frequently in the extended past. There is a need to unify their public or social image with their private or personal image in order to present an all-inclusive, true picture. Thus, this task also allows them to consider their sexual identity along with their racial identity.

The fulfillment of the task these women assume provides us with their unique contribution to the autobiographical genre, for the black female self is unique. The combination of their common characteristics—black and female—produces a self that has experiences never shared identically by another self. For this reason, evaluation of this self is most accurate, honest, and clear when assumed by this self. The world described in these women's autobiographies reveals a great deal about the writers' perceived place in it. The dimension their insights add to the American autobiographical genre is significant. Their works contain their cultural heritage, frequently extending back to Africa. That the women represent a variety of professions and lifestyles enhances the dimensions of their insights.

Finally, their contribution of self-analysis to the genre is a declaration that they mattered in their immediate environment, in society, and in the world. In fact, participation in the autobiographical tradition is a declaration of selfhood—a complex, multidimensional, changing selfhood. Such a declaration by these African-American autobiographical writers is a positive step toward bonding the black and female self in America.

9.

Gertrude Stein and the Problems of Autobiography

JAMES E. BRESLIN

When *The Autobiography of Alice B. Toklas* was published in 1933, the book soon became, as Gertrude Stein both hoped and feared, a critical and popular success. Stein earned celebrity and a substantial amount of money, both of which depressed her. *The Autobiography's* subsequent literary reputation might have cheered her up, however, for Stein's critics—with the notable exception of her best critic, Richard Bridgman—have generally either ignored or rejected *The Autobiography*.[1] B. L. Reid dismissed it as "chitchat," and many readers find it merely anecdotal and gossipy.[2] Certainly, readers who approach it with expectations shaped by the revival of confessional writing in the 1960s are apt to reject it as too reserved. Stein herself had somewhat different misgivings about the book, stating in *Everybody's Autobiography* (1937) that the earlier work had dealt with what had happened instead of "what is happening."[3] Yet *The Autobiography's* charming, playful, anecdotal surface has distracted its readers from its real complexity; and it provides not—as Stein seems to have thought—a mere submission to the conventions of autobiography but an intense and creative struggle with them.

In many ways the autobiographical act is one at odds with, even a betrayal of, Gertrude Stein's aesthetic principles. Her essay "What Are Master-pieces and Why Are There So Few of Them" offers a concise statement of these principles. "The minute your memory functions while you are doing anything it may be very popular but actually

149

it is dull," Stein warns; her desire to live and write in a continuous present thus turns her against the necessarily retrospective act of autobiography.[4] But Stein's opposition to the conventions of her genre runs even deeper than this, because her commitment to a continuous present forces her to reject the notion of identity altogether. "Identity is recognition," she writes; "I am I because my little dog knows me" (pp. 148–49). Identity, an artificial construction based on the perception of certain fixed traits that allow my little dog or anyone else to imagine that they know me, stresses repetition, which is, according to Stein, antithetical to creativity. Identity "destroys creation" (p. 149)— as does memory; both, carrying the past over into the present and structuring by repetition, are ways we have of familiarizing the strangeness, the mysterious being, of others. Masterpieces defamiliarize; they derive from "knowing that there is no identity and producing while identity is not" (p. 153). In part Stein is warning against self-imitation, and she quotes Picasso as saying that he is willing to be influenced by anyone but himself; but she is also stressing that to live in a continuous present, to *be* rather than to *repeat*, one must constantly break down identity. But can there be an *auto*-biography in which "there is no identity"? Or, to put the question somewhat differently: autobiographies are customarily *identified* as acts of *self*-representation, but Stein is challenged to refashion the form to show that she eludes or transcends the category of self or identity.

At the same time her belief in a continuous present sets Stein against the kind of narrative that we are accustomed (again) to find in auto-*bio*-graphy. "What is the use of being a boy if you are going to grow up to be a man?" she asks in "What Are Master-pieces" (p. 153). Like remembering and identifying, narrating—telling, say, the story of a girl becoming a woman—such narrating represents a linear sequence of time, not an ongoing present. In addition, remembering, identifying, and narrating all view things in relation to other things (e.g., girl in relation to woman) instead of viewing a thing as what Stein calls an "entity" (p. 151)—a thing existent in and for itself. A masterpiece, transcending linear time and recognizable identity, is itself an "entity," not, as Eliot had said, a revision of the literary tradition, but an absolute act of creation. The fact that the early works of cubism derive from such absolute acts of creation explains why, as we are told in *The Autobiography*, they are so strange—almost physically painful to look at—and yet must be looked at intently: the viewer must struggle to get beyond mere recognition, the comfortably familiar. But autobiographies are hardly absolute acts of creation; they are historical, referring to persons and events that clearly existed out there, in reality, prior to their representation in language. Finally, Stein holds that any concession to—or even consciousness of—an audience undermines creativity; as soon as a writer begins to think of him/herself in relation to an audience, he or she "writes what the other person is to hear and so entity does not exist there are two present instead of one and so once again creation breaks down" (p. 150). But if we now find it problematic to think of even a lyric poem as autotelic, how can we imagine an autotelic autobiography? Can Stein create an autobiography without identity, memory, linear time? And if she did, could we bear to read it? In some ways *Everybody's Autobiography*, dealing with "what is happening" instead of what had happened, comes closer to these aims; but what makes *The Autobiography of Alice B. Toklas* so interesting is that it admits the conventions of memory, identity, chronological time—in order to fight against and ultimately to transcend their deadening effects.

When she was asked to write her autobiography, Stein replied, "Not possibly,"[5] and it is easier to imagine her writing an essay called "What Are Autobiographies and Why Are None of Them Master-pieces" than it is to imagine her writing her own autobiography. Of course, she did not write her own autobiography; she wrote *The Autobiography of Alice B. Toklas*. Or did she? Some writers have speculated that Alice B. Toklas wrote her own autobiography or at least substantial parts of it.[6] But perhaps the most important point about this debate is that it seems to have been generated not just by an extraliterary curiosity about the book's composition, but by an actual literary effect the book has on readers—namely, the effect of raising questions about just whose book it is. I will return to this issue. For the moment, assuming (as I have been) Stein to be the book's author, I want to suggest how she took up the formal challege of autobiography by recalling a young man named Andrew Green, who appears briefly in Chapter 3 of *The*

Autobiography. Andrew Green "hated everything modern." Once while staying at 27 rue de Fleurus for a month he covered "all the pictures with cashmere shawls"; he "could not bear" to look at the strange, frightening paintings. Significantly, "he had a prodigious *memory* and could recite all of Milton's Paradise Lost by heart" (my emphasis). "He adored as he said a simple centre and a continuous design" (p. 47). Green *has* an identity, so much so that his character can be fixed in a single, brief paragraph. Gertrude Stein does not have an identity; in attempting to represent her "self" she created in *The Autobiography of Alice B. Toklas* a book with an elusive center and a discontinuous design.

Even the title page of the current Vintage edition—*The Autobiography of Alice B. Toklas* by Gertrude Stein—is enough to suggest that the center of the ensuing text may be difficult to locate. The original Harcourt edition made the same point in a more subtle way: both the cover and the title page print only a title—*The Autobiography of Alice B. Toklas*—but no author's name is given. The frontispiece (facing the title page), however, is a Man Ray photograph which shows Stein in the right foreground, seated at a table, but with her back to the camera and in dark shadow; Alice B. Toklas stands in the left background, but she stands in light and framed by a doorway. The photograph, with its obscure foreground and distinct background, has no clear primary subject—like the book that follows; the seated Stein, however, is writing, and the possibility is raised that *she* may be the author of the book, an uncertainty not resolved for the reader of this edition until its final page—when "Toklas" tells us that Stein has in fact written *The Autobiography.* Moreover, the book's style blends the domestic particularity, whimsical humor, and ironic precision of Toklas with some of the leading features of Stein's writing—e.g., stylized repetition, digression, a language that continually points up its own artifice. The reader is not certain who it is he is listening to; nor is he meant to be. Richard Bridgman has shown that "Stanzas in Mediation," written at the same time as *The Autobiography,* is at least partly about writing *The Autobiography,* and the poem strongly suggests that our uncertainties were an intended effect: "This is her autobiography one of two / But which it is no one . . . can know."[7]

But most readers are more like Andrew Green than Gertrude Stein; they don't like to dwell in uncertainties. And so most discussions of *The Autobiography* begin by assuming the character of Stein to be its easily identifiable center, and they proceed to discuss this character as if it were not mediated for the reader by a perspective that is to *some* degree external to it. Yet, even if we proceed along these lines, the character of Stein turns out to be an elusive and enigmatic "center." Toklas tells us that Stein, in her writing, sought to give "the inside as seen from the outside" (p. 156); that is one reason she creates herself through the external perspective of Toklas. What she means by "the inside" can be clarified through *The Autobiography*'s account of Picasso's famous portrait of Stein; it was with this painting, we are told, that Picasso "passed from the Harlequin, the *charming* early Italian period to the *intensive struggle* which was to end in cubism" (p. 54; my emphasis). Stein emphasizes the "intensive struggle" that went into the painting of the portrait itself. During the winter of 1907 Stein patiently posed for Picasso some eighty or ninety times, but then he abruptly "painted out the whole head." "I can't see you any longer when I look, he said irritably" (p. 53). At this point both Stein and Picasso left Paris for the summer, but the day he returned "Picasso sat down and out of his head painted the head in without having seen Gertrude Stein again" (p. 57). In the enigmatic sentence, "I can't see you any longer when I look," what is the referent of "you"? On the one hand, it is not the external, literal Stein, recognizable to her little dog or a realistic novelist. That is why, when Stein later cuts her hair short, Picasso, at first disturbed, can conclude that "all the same it is all there." He was not striving for a realistic mimesis, as Stein stresses in her account of Picasso's difficulties with what turned out to be the least realistic feature of the portrait, the face. On the other hand, Picasso was not trying to evoke the inner, subconscious depths of Stein, of the sort that might fascinate a psychological novelist; in fact, Toklas later claims that Stein had no subconscious (p. 79).

In the painting itself Stein's body is solid, massive, weighty, sculptured; the simple, severe lines of the eyebrows, nose and mouth, the slightly uneven eyes create a stylized, masklike face. She inhabits an abstract space, her eyes conveying an almost fierce attentiveness, but she is calm, at rest, even serene. Picasso's Stein seems a regal, perhaps deific, figure, but the earth colors of her dress, blending with the tan background, modify the austerity of the face, the monumentality of the body, to create warmth and humanize Stein. The portrait is thus an instance of what Stein herself called "elemental abstraction" (p. 64); the "you" painted by Picasso is, therefore, not a personality, a recognizable identity, but an entity—Stein's being, awesome, serene, strange, mysterious yet human. Like Picasso's portrait, *The Autobiography* gives the inside by way of the outside; it plays down psychology and sticks to the surface, recording externals (objects, acts, dialogues) in a way that clearly manifests deliberate and idiosyncratic acts of selection and stylization. Such admitted artifice annoys many readers who, with simpler models of self and autobiography, demand a fuller intimacy and deeper psychology of their autobiographers. But Stein's stylization of the surface reveals the "you" that Picasso, having looked so long and intently, could no longer see when he looked. *The Autobiography*, in short, gives us Gertrude Stein being.

To envision *this* Stein required an "intensive struggle" and at many points Picasso was urged by friends—among them Andrew Green—to stop with the "beauty" of what he had so far accomplished, but Picasso, turning his back on his audience, went on. In this way, renouncing a "charming" for a more severe and difficult work, Picasso produced a masterpiece. Compare Picasso's heroic struggles with the facility of a Vallaton:

> When he painted a portrait he made a crayon sketch and then began painting at the top of the canvas straight across. Gertrude Stein always said it was like pulling down a curtain as slowly moving as one of his swiss glaciers. Slowly he pulled the curtain down and by the time he was at the bottom of the canvas, there you were. The whole operation took about two weeks and then he gave the canvas to you. First however he exhibited it in the autumn salon and it had considerable notice and everybody was pleased. (p. 51)

Vallaton's scrupulously predetermined works are the comic opposites of Picasso's adventurous and difficult acts of discovery. Vallaton's paintings pleased everybody whereas at first only "the painter and the painted" admired Picasso's portrait of Stein (p. 6). Creative works thus demand an intensive struggle from both creator and audience. "The pictures were so strange that one quite instinctively looked at anything rather than at them just at first," Toklas recalls of her first evening in Stein's atelier (p. 9), and even in recollection, some twenty-five years later, this difficulty is reexperienced: Toklas comes to describe the paintings (about which the reader is very eager to hear) only slowly, almost resistingly, after several digressions. Gertrude Stein can rest her head against a rock and stare at the Italian noonday sun; but like a masterpiece or the sun, Stein herself is hard to look at directly—another reason for the mediation of Toklas—and even Toklas approaches her, too, very slowly. Stein is first mentioned on page 5 where Toklas reports of their first meeting only that "I was impressed by the coral brooch she wore and her voice," and that "a bell within me rang" certifying that Stein was a genius. The reader expects the first meeting between the two women to be related with ample circumstantial and emotional detail; instead, only two rather oddly selected details are given. Then a long leap is made to a perception of Stein's genius, though the playful tone makes it hard for us to be sure exactly how seriously we are to take this claim. The scene is deliberately simplified; circumstantial and psychological detail are eliminated—to foreground the powerful, strange presence of Stein and the intuitive powers of Toklas.

Stein is next glimpsed obliquely, through objects associated with her—again, as if her presence were too powerful to be looked at directly. Toklas remembers from her first visit to the atelier "a large table on which were horseshoe nails and pebbles and little pipe cigarette holders" which she later found "to be accumulations from the pockets of Picasso and Gertrude Stein" (p. 9). Without any clear associational values, these objects at once invite and frustrate psychological speculation, as the stylized surface of *The Autobiography* so often does; we are tempted to "identify" Stein but are shown that we can't. Resisting metaphorization, these simple objects nevertheless provide humanizing detail (like the earth colors of Picasso's portrait) before the mythologizing of Stein that follows just a few sentences later.

> The chairs in the room were also all italian renaissance, not very comfortable for short-legged people and one got the habit of sitting on one's legs. Miss Stein sat near the stove in a lovely high-backed one and she peacefully let her legs hang, which was a matter of habit, and when any one of the many visitors came to ask her a question she lifted herself up out of the chair and usually replied in french, not just now. (p. 9)

In this Gertrude Stein—sitting "peacefully" in a high, hard, uncomfortable chair, dispensing regal gestures of denial—the reader confronts a presence of profound, contemplative calm, a figure very like the one in Picasso's portrait. This first image points toward the Stein who, later, finds it restful to stare at the mid-day sun or at those disquieting paintings that Andrew Green covered with cashmere shawls; it also points toward the later mysterious, sibylline Stein who makes enigmatic pronouncements, who lives in a world of "hidden meanings" (p. 15), and who does not explain things to the reader or even to Toklas, leaving the adventure of discovery to us; it is this Stein who dismisses Pound as the "village explainer" (p. 200). But in this first representation of Stein, as throughout *The Autobiography*, the external perspective of Toklas, sticking to the observable surface, suggests the inside while leaving it mysterious. As a result, Stein is not created as a realistic, psychologically complex character; she is, rather, an abstraction, a deliberate simplification—a mythical figure whose peaceful self-sufficiency allows her to transcend external circumstances.

The *Autobiography* of Benjamin Franklin records the attempt to create an identity through acts of will; *The Education of Henry Adams* records the breakdown of a similar attempt and the dissolution of the very idea of identity. *The Autobiography of Alice B. Toklas* takes the process one step further; the book shows us not someone striving to create a self, but someone who *exists* calmly in a world without any external orders. Again and again the book shows us Stein existing "peacefully" under circumstances that are often far more stressful than uncomfortable chairs. Even Picasso, the character closest to her equal, is "fussed" when he arrives late for a Stein dinner party, looks "sheep-ish" when he wrests his piece of bread back from Stein, who has acci-dentally picked it up, or he becomes embarrassed when Stein men-tions the possibility of his seeing Fernande after they have temporarily separated. Stein, on the other hand, seems to possess an inner stillness that allows her to respond to external pressures with serenity, some-times even with good humor. When the First World War starts while she is visiting London, Stein is concerned but not alarmed about the fate of her writings, all copies of which are back in Paris. Later, after her return to Paris, during an air raid, she calmly quiets an Alice B. Toklas who is so frightened her knees are literally knocking together; and in *The Autobiography*'s final chapter Stein enters the confused and diminished Paris of the postwar era with the same equanimity she had shown during the many crises of the war. Most impressive, how-ever, is the cheerful confidence with which she meets the frugality, frequent disorder, and the public antagonism of the early years of her career. Stein remains steadfastly committed to her work, in spite of her difficulties in finding publication and of journalistic ridicule when her writing does appear. When *Three Lives* is privately printed, her publisher sends a young man to 27 rue de Fleurus, who questions her knowledge of English; Stein laughs—as she often does at moments when we expect her to be angry or embittered—and her response is contrasted with that of Matisse, two pages earlier, whose feelings are "frightfully" hurt by newspaper ridicule of his art school.

Yet the Stein of *The Autobiography* is by no means as easy to pin down as this discussion of her so far implies; the book, rather, frus-trates any attempt to fix Stein in a simple identity. In *Everybody's Autobiography* Stein admires paintings which move rather than being about movement and which seem to come out of the "prison" of their frames—as if the subject were alive, truly existing (*EA*, p. 312). Stein's own aesthetic theory, as we have seen, made her acutely aware that by attempting to incarnate her being in language in an autobiography, she was running the risk of merely fixing, of limiting and deadening, herself. But the pressures of autobiography, among them the pressure of language itself, constitute another set of external circumstances to which Stein calmly responds with a playful sense of adventure. The result is that *The Autobiography of Alice B. Toklas* presents a Gertrude Stein who keeps stepping out of the frame, as if she were alive, truly existing. The "psychology" of her character may be a simplified one, but a reader who tries to delineate this character in a careful way finds him/herself speaking in contradictions; and these very contradictions are what make the character of Stein remain mysterious, elusive—alive.

Gertrude Stein liked to sit and pose for Picasso and other artists, but she also liked the long walks home afterwards through the darkening Paris streets. Stillness and motion are one set of contraries that create the character of Gertrude Stein. Andrew Green, resisting the challenge of modernity, of the moment, remains anxiously fixed and static—neither at rest nor in motion. But alongside the oracular Stein who can sit peacefully in a hard, high-backed chair, we must place the Stein who, in a recurring phrase, "goes on." "Keep your mind open," William James had told her at Radcliffe (p. 78), and the willingness to move into new experience—or "liveliness"—becomes a standard against which all characters are measured in *The Autobiography*. Fernande feels "heavy in hand" (p. 14) and seems "indolent" (p. 19); Matisse is "very alert though slightly heavy" and, later, virile but without "life" (p. 37). In contrast with both of these Picasso is "quick moving but not restless" (p. 12). Stein herself is lively and adventurous, not heavy or indolent; she may move slowly, but she moves forward—though not restlessly. Not long after Gertrude Stein and her brother arrive in Paris, they begin to buy Cézannes, small ones at first. But "having gone so far," they "decided to go further, they decided to buy a big Cézanne and then they would stop" (p. 33). But even then they go on and later Stein—unlike her brother, another casualty to modernity—goes on to Picasso. This commitment to process explains why Stein "loves objects that are breakable": "she says she likes what she has and she likes the adventure of a new one" (p. 88). In fact, so committed is Stein to ongoing movement that when she is driving her car "she goes forward admirably, she does not go backward successfully."

But even this account of the contradictions in Stein's character simplifies it, for each side of the rest/motion opposition generates, in turn, its own oppositions. Stein may be calmly self-possessed, but she also has an "explosive temper" (p. 11); she enjoys the novelty of fresh experience, yet she is upset if asked to do something suddenly (p. 221). The important point, however, is that these various features are not presented as the odd twists and turns within a complex yet ultimately unified character; they are the unresolved contradictions of Gertrude Stein's being. She resists all our attempts to frame her as surely as that odd assortment of objects from the pockets of Picasso and Stein resist our efforts to find meaning in them: they just *are*.

Contradictions similarly proliferate when we examine the book's theories about and actual practice of writing. At times Stein speaks of her own work as if it were based on a very simple model of art as representation. Real life sources are given for characters in her fiction; Picasso's cubism is given a realistic basis in Spanish landscape and architecture (p. 90); and Stein speaks of art as the "exact reproduction of inner or outer reality" (p. 211). Yet in the same paragraph Stein asserts that "events" ought not to be "the material of poetry and prose"; her writing is often described as the making of sentences, as if it were more construction than representation; and she elsewhere affirms distortion and abstraction in art. Anyone who reads *The Autobiography* looking for a "key" to Stein's fictional works—and many do, as Stein knew they would—will be just as frustrated as the one who reads it looking for the "key" to Stein's private psychology. "Observation and construction make imagination," Stein says (p. 76), as if she were demystifying the imagination, making it a matter of perception and craft, but Stein, of course, *goes on*: "Observation and construction make imagination, that is granting the possession of imagination," and imagination and Stein herself remain playfully mystified. Oracular and witty, Stein is a sibylline presence, no village or even Parisian explainer.

The oppositions in Stein's "theorizing" reappear in the writing of the book itself, which continually offers contradictory clues about what *kind* of book it is. Its anecdotal manner, its preoccupation with recognizable, real figures, its concern with "the heroic age of cubism" give it the quality of a memoir, as if it were presenting a true historical record. Yet it is *The Autobiography* **of** *Alice B. Toklas*—by Gertrude

Stein: the book is marked at once as an autobiography and a fiction (since it is the autobiography of someone other than the author). An ingenuous sentence at the end tantalizes us in the same way: "I am going to write [the autobiography] for you," Stein tells Toklas. "I am going to write it as simply as Defoe did the autobiography of Robinson Crusoe." But how simply was that? Not even this sentence is very simple; it is one written by the (likely) actual author, Stein, imputed to the fictive author, Toklas, who is reporting something said by the character Stein to the character/author Toklas; the sentence, moreover, compares the autobiography of a fictional character (Robinson Crusoe) with that of a character who was real, at least until Stein started writing her autobiography for her. Throughout, *The Autobiography*'s whimsical, self-interrupting, repetitious, stylized prose marks it as a piece of admitted and self-conscious artifice. The book is an historical memoir; the book is a fictional construct.

To put it another way, *The Autobiography* continually points up the disparity between actuality and its representation, but it does so without irony, without lamenting the insufficiency of either reality or of literary fictions. The book's narrative method simultaneously acknowledges chronological time and the power of writing to play freely with that time; again Stein does not privilege either one over the other. "Moving is in all directions," Stein writes in *Narration*.[8] Just the chapter titles in *The Autobiography*—"Before I Came to Paris," "My Arrival in Paris," "Gertrude Stein in Paris—1903–1907," "Gertrude Stein Before She Came to Paris," "1907–1914," "The War," and "After the War—1919–1932"—are enough to suggest that the book both establishes and breaks a forward movement toward the time of its composition. Yet this overall movement is further complicated by the book's local texture—partly by its numerous portraits, which halt temporal progression, and partly by Toklas's wandering style of narration, its constant excursions backward and forward in time. For it is not accurate to speak, as I just did, of the book's forward movement toward the time of its composition, because we listen to Toklas in the *act* of recollection; and Toklas, no Vallaton proceeding along predesigned lines, moves by playful, free association—thereby liberating herself from chronological order while still accepting the reality of chronological time. Another temporal dimension of *The Autobiography* is thus the continuous present of its telling. The book's multivalence, its moving in all directions, can also be seen in its ending. In the foreground of the final chapter we have Toklas writing in the present; she is writing about "After the War—1919–1932," and by looking backward to this period she carries the book's narrative forward into the postwar era and acknowledges the reality of historical time. One feature of this period that is emphasized is Stein's increasing literary success, which might seem to provide the book with a happy conclusion until we remember that, for Stein, recognition is as much reason for self-doubt and suspicion as it is for gratification, and Toklas equally emphasizes the postwar decline from "the heroic age of cubism." At the same time Stein, fixated neither by success nor by nostalgia for an heroic past, is shown searching for the source of a new creative idea she believes has entered painting; the source may be the work of Francis Rose, but this is not certain. With "her never-failing curiosity" (p. 250) the adventuresome Stein remains in a continuous present, an entity. At *The Autobiography*'s close, the narrative catches up with itself or at least with its beginning, as we learn of the genesis of the book and that Stein is its author. In the original edition this final page of the text was followed by a photograph of the first page of the manuscript. *The Autobiography* ends by folding back on itself; and a reader is invited to re-read the book in light of the revelation that Stein is its author. Lest this revelation make the reader too comfortable, he or she is also, as we have seen, assured of the book's Defoe-like simplicity in a way that warns of its complexity and deviousness. At the end *The Autobiography* circles back on itself as if it were an autonomous verbal reality. Yet the book's conclusion also reveals Stein to be on a quest that is not completed; the book's ending is also open. The end of the book closes off and frames a life at the same time that it breaks out of its frame, its artificial closure, to affirm the ongoing process of the author's life. At its close, as throughout *The Autobiography*, moving is in all directions.

Gertrude Stein complained to Matisse that "there is nothing within you that fights itself" (p. 65); that is why he lacks life. Through its contradictions *The Autobiography of Alice B. Toklas* fights itself and so achieves creative life. The problems of the book—many of which are versions of the problem of referentiality, the relation of the work to external reality—are the problems and contradictions of autobiography itself, problems that make the genre such a difficult one for both theoretical and practical criticism. How can we deal with the tension between historical truthfulness and aesthetic design in autobiography? Or with the splitting of the author into character and writer? Or with the difficulties of ending an autobiography, given that the author's life is likely to go on? Stein deliberately raises and foregrounds these difficult questions, not in order to solve or answer them, but to play with them and to make the ways in which the genre fights itself into her book's energizing principles. Her relation to autobiography parallels what she says the relation of a genius to time must be: he or she must "accept it and deny it by creating it" (*EA*, p. 281). By renouncing a simple center and a continuous design, by exploring the formal dilemmas of the genre, Gertrude Stein at once accepted, denied, and created autobiography.

10.

Lillian Hellman and the Strategy of the "Other"

MARCUS K. BILLSON AND SIDONIE A. SMITH

For years critics of self-narrative have defined the memoir in terms of the autobiography.[1] They claim the autobiography narrates the story of a person's unfolding sense of identity, the tale of becoming in the world; the account usually involves considerable self-analysis on the part of the author. The memoir, on the other hand, focuses not on the narrating self, but rather on the outer world of people and events: the memoir writer's intention is not self-examination. Critics who describe the differences in the forms in this way fail to realize that the memorialist's vision of the outer world is as much a projection and refraction of the self as the autobiographer's. The manifest content of the memoir may be different, but the latent content is likewise self-revelation.[2]

Nowhere, perhaps, is this latent self-revelation more intriguing than in Lillian Hellman's memoirs, *An Unfinished Woman* and *Pentimento*. By eschewing conventional autobiography and focusing on the people and the historical circumstances of her past, Hellman invites the reader into a world of "others" who, as they come together in her memory, become significant in the articulation of her "self."[3] They are mirrors in front of which Hellman's self tries to create its own reality ("presence").

In preparing *An Unfinished Woman* for publication, Hellman drew upon previously published work, returned to early diaries, wrote new material. Hence, *An Unfinished Woman* has a disjointed quality to it.

Within the work there are several disparate forms of narrative presentation: the chronological opening; the diaries of her trips to Spain and Russia; the three portraits that conclude the book. *Pentimento*'s form is more consistent because it is primarily composed of portraits; but there is still disjunction in that none of the portraits seem to cohere together: they remain distinct dramas. Throughout the apparent discontinuity in both works, however, the strategy of the "other" persists, demonstrating its versatility in permitting Hellman her problematic goals: to avoid self-indulgence while committing to paper experiences that are uniquely hers and to sustain a fragile balance between the imperatives of the self and the integrity of the "other." We would like to examine the ways in which the strategy of the "other" manifests itself in the disparate forms of narrative presentation mentioned above.

I

Through the first six chapters of *An Unfinished Woman*, Hellman follows the chronological narrative we associate with autobiography. The opening chapter introduces her mother's wealthy family and her father's unconventional one. Hellman describes the origins of her character in the constellation of others that peopled her childhood. She specifies her mother's relatives as those against whom she rebels, not only because they are avaricious, pretentious, and self-satisfied, but also because—ironically—they are appealing with their money and the power it bestows. Simultaneously, she identifies those others to whom she is drawn—her father's relatives, whom she associates with generosity, wit, freedom, and genuine eccentricity. These two worlds of "others" become symbolized in the two geographical worlds of her childhood: she lives half the year with her mother's family in New York and half the year with her father's sisters in New Orleans.

Her position "between" is an uncomfortable one. Northerner and Southerner, she is both and yet not quite either. This dilemma is further constituted in her nuclear family by her position as an only child manipulated by parents whose relationship is one of unexpressed dissatisfaction beneath a veneer of tolerance. She comes to rebel against aspects of both parents: the weakness, passivity, and credulity of her mother and the authority of her father. This rebellion becomes a life-long struggle against weakness in herself and authority in others. Hence, rebelliousness accounts for much of the energy of her narrative and for the persistent self-criticism throughout her memoirs.

Particularly galling to Hellman is the complacency of self-satisfaction. From her mother's relatives to Hemingway, from the Moscow major to Lady Asquith, Hellman sees self-satisfaction short-circuiting the human ability to learn from life spontaneously. The fixity of self-satisfaction precludes authenticity, for pleasure with the self—that is, the absence of rebellion—means that one no longer interacts with the world, one merely inhabits it, projecting one's self at others' expense.

The chronological presentation continues through the second chapter of *An Unfinished Woman* as Hellman summons up two crucial childhood memories: (1) her learning of her father's infidelity to her mother, and (2) her running away from home. The first incident occurs in her "first and most beloved home"—the fig tree in front of her aunts' house in New Orleans.[4] This tree is a kind of surrogate school where she spends her days playing hooky, reading, and watching life pass below her. There, in the privacy of self-imposed isolation, the knowledge she gains is the deeper understanding of life itself.

It is in the fig tree that she learns the ambivalence of all desire: "it was in the fig tree . . . that I was first puzzled by the conflict which would haunt me, harm me, and benefit me the rest of my life: simply, the stubborn, relentless, driving desire to be alone as it came into conflict with the desire not to be alone when I wanted not to be" (*UW*, p. 9). This desire for aloneness shows the necessity of the "other," for to be "alone" is to posit an "other" away from whom one wishes to be. In positing an "other," one loses one's ability to control the "other's" relations to the self. Thus, the issue is not merely solitude versus sociability, but the conflict that shapes much of Hellman's life, the struggle for independence in the midst of an inexorable, existential dependence. The struggle involves an implacable alienation both from the self and from the "other." The self is alone and independent insofar as it is not "other"; yet by the same token, as "not other" the self is specified and defined not from an inner-derived subjectivity, but from its relation, albeit negative, to the "other." In this way, the self is subjectively alienated. The quest for independence which starts so early and pervades all the memoirs is consequently thwarted from the beginning.

The most dramatic knowledge Hellman gains in the fig tree is sexual. Inevitably, the fig tree through its archetypal associations with genitalia becomes the site in which she discovers a frustrating pattern of sexuality, for there the anguish of learning of her father's infidelity with a woman in her aunts' boarding house causes her to throw herself to the ground in an action of double-edged rebellion against the paradigm of the sexually aggressive, unfaithful male and the passive, helpless female. The rebellious act is ultimately self-destructive, or at least self-injurious: she breaks her nose in the fall. The price of rebellion is high, as it continues to be throughout her life.

The second experience is also a psycho-sexual one. She runs away from home to protest her father's questions about a lock of hair she has put inside a new watch. The two nights and days she spends roaming through New Orleans become a sexual odyssey, a rite of passage from childhood to maturity, whose incidents are no less metaphorical because they are real. The first night she spends in a huge doll house on the grounds of a local mansion; however, she can no longer find protection in this structure of childhood, so she must wander on, frightened away by nightmares. The second day, she discovers she has begun to menstruate. The evidence of her sexuality is frightening; in response Hellman enacts a drama which attempts to allay the fears and risks inherent in her new womanhood. She seeks refuge in a black boarding house. When the suspicious landlady questions her, Hellman tells the following lies: she claims that her mother is a widow, working across the river, who has asked the young Lillian to wait for her in this house; Hellman also explains that she is related to Sophronia (her former black nurse) who is known in the neighborhood. In this way, the adolescent symbolically kills off her father. This gesture is as violent as the gesture of the fig tree incident, but here, in the form of a lie, the violence is turned away from herself. She tries to master her father and his male authority. Such mastery is particularly necessary at this moment: Hellman has just become unquestionably woman and must rebel against the "other" who is unquestionably man.

The recourse to the black neighborhood and the identification with Sophronia suggest the degree to which Hellman fears an inevitable identification with white womanhood embodied in her own passive mother. The adolescent's psychological dependence on Sophronia manifests itself in times of crisis, when she seeks out the woman who "was the first and most certain love of my life" (*UW*, p. 11). Indeed, Sophronia becomes her surrogate mother, "the one and certain anchor so needed for the young years" (*UW*, p. 11), who exudes an aura of independence, strength, integrity, wholeness of being that the child desires so much and that she fails to sense in her own mother. Sophronia becomes the standard against which all "others" are judged, including herself: "Oh, Sophronia, it's you I want back always. It's by you I still so often measure, guess, transmute, translate, and act" (*UW*, pp. 206–07). But economic circumstances have necessitated that this surrogate mother be taken away from the child too soon.

Sophronia becomes the locus of a sense of loss and of unfulfilled desire. This earliest embodiment of the self-sufficient female, the desired "other," remains beyond Hellman's grasp. All through her life, then, she will seek out, admire, and look for guidance from those women she identifies as self-sufficient: Sophronia, Bethe, Julia, Helen. Hellman's search for surrogate mothers involves a desire for identification with a female model who contains the inner conviction and calm Hellman knows she lacks herself. The search also insures the experience of unfulfilled desire. Sophronia and Helen choose to maintain a reserve with Hellman, a psychological distance prompted by their difference of race. Bethe and Julia die.

For the child, rebellion has a definite target: parents. In young adulthood, the object of Hellman's rebellion is much less readily identifiable; and when the entity against which Hellman feels compelled to rebel is elusive, then so is her sense of her own identity. *An Unfinished Woman* goes on to narrate Hellman's early adult years—her first experiences with love, with a career, and with marriage. The nature of her frustration at the inconclusiveness of these experiences is clearly captured in the restlessness of her description of herself at twenty: "I knew that the seeds of the rebellion were scattered and aimless in a nature that was wild to be finished with something-or-other and to find something-else-or-other, and I had sense enough to know that I was overproud, oversensitive, overdaring because I was shy and frightened" (*UW*, p. 26). In the last half of this passage, Hellman portrays herself as the "other" would see her, through adjectives describing an outward behavior that is intended to screen the insecurity she actually feels. But the "other" is a mirror whose reflections of her outward behavior point to and away from the fear and shyness she wishes to hide.

Like a passenger on a milk run, Hellman passes through the "something-or-others," looking for meaning. She tries an affair to test romantic illusions, but the affair leads only to nastiness—and later to an abortion. She gets an exciting job in publishing at Liveright's, but it ends with the recognition of the vacuity underneath the glamour. She lives for a time in Europe and ends up feeling "bewildered," "restless" (*UW*, pp. 43–44). A job in Hollywood brings on incapacitating phobias as she drives home at night. Her marriage to Arthur Kober ends in divorce. All these experiences capture the woman rebelling against sentimentality, love, motherhood, and traditional marriage. Defined by the forces against which she rebels, by what she doesn't desire, she finds herself restive and dissatisfied. Within the rebellion, there is no identification. On looking back with the advantage of hindsight, she observes about these years: "I needed a teacher, a cool teacher, who would not be impressed or disturbed by a strange and difficult girl" (*UW*, p. 44).

The autobiographical discourse ends in Chapter 6, when she meets her "cool teacher," Dashiell Hammett, the most important "significant other" in Hellman's life. From then on her life is always shared in one way or another with others. Dash's presence pervades all her memoirs, even though only one chapter in *An Unfinished Woman* is devoted exclusively to him. In fact, Hellman is so silent about him that one must learn to read these silences as if they were blank spaces between words, giving meaning and form to what they separate. She portrays Hammett as the teacher who shows her a form of political independence and a defiance of social conventions and pretensions and who forces her to exert herself in ways she did not imagine were possible. He helps her to shape the focus of her rebellion and thereby to shape herself. He encourages her artistic productivity: she begins to write plays.[5]

Hellman's identification with and dependence on Dashiell Hammett ironically mediate a more basic desire for independence and self-reliance. This paradox suggests why over the years their relationship is characterized by movements away from and toward each other. These movements and Hellman's reticence about the complex relationship in the memoirs enable her to affirm her separateness from Hammett to the reader at the same time that they point as a resistance to her continuing dependence on him. In the relationship, Hellman is embroiled in the struggle for independence in the face of a fundamental dependence, that unresolved ambivalence she experienced in the fig tree as a child.

II

In order to show Hellman's narrative strategy's effectiveness in and adaptability to the various forms of narrative presentation she employs, we turn now to a consideration of the diary form. A large portion of *An Unfinished Woman* is made up of passages from diaries written while on trips to Spain during the Spanish Civil War and to Russia during World War II. Another trip to Russia in 1967, twenty-two years after the first, is also partially chronicled in diary form. The diary entries have to do with the people Hellman meets and the historic events she witnesses. These documentaries of her trips narrate tales of privation, ineptitude, dignity, and hope in the struggles against Fascism. Beneath the surface, however, is a narrative as self-revealing as the earlier, more explicitly autobiographical portions. The clear, obdurate prose relates an extraordinary self-awareness and often an ironic toying with and understating of her own identity. Hellman rebels against herself as much as anyone, mocking her stance as a political rebel in relation to the "significant others" around her.

For instance, while in Spain, as she visits a field hospital and sees men whose idealism has led them to war, she becomes acutely aware of the nature of her own idealism and measures it against this "other" reality. Gustav Regler has introduced her to the hospital staff in an after-dinner meeting. She comments wryly, "he made me and my visit too important" (*UW*, p. 77). Two Spaniards in turn speak about the urgency of American aid to their cause and ask Hellman to inform President Roosevelt of their plight immediately. "I said that wasn't the way things worked, it didn't matter what people like me said or thought. They were silent for a second and then a woman applauded politely and everybody went off to bed" (*UW*, p. 77). Hellman's modesty is an honest assessment of her influence. The memory of the one woman clapping is a self-mocking comment on the disappointment of the audience. The scene captures concisely the feelings of frustration and futility Hellman experiences in Spain; she does not like her role of observer even though she is painfully aware she can do no more.

That night in the hospital she shares a room with the Czech wife of a Yugoslav officer. Since Hellman has just returned from a visit to Prague, she tells the woman "about the famous doctor and his wife with whom I stayed, their friends . . . and my shock when they spoke of Hitler's domination of Czechoslovakia as almost certain, and seemed so resigned and passive in the face of it" (*UW*, p. 77). Not until the single candle has burned itself out does the Czech woman respond. She asks what "friends" Hellman had met. When Hellman tells her of two brothers who owned a newspaper, a shot of anger and indignation comes out of the darkness. "The brothers are related to me. Liberal pigs. Pigs. They will kill all the rest of us with their nothing-to-be-done-about-it stuff. They will save themselves when the time comes, the dirty pigs" (*UW*, p. 78). Hellman makes no answer except to say to the reader, "I didn't sleep much that night thinking about what she said . . . " (*UW*, p. 78). The Czech woman's condemnation is an ironic disclosure of the distance between the two women: the Czech woman's political convictions are far more rigorous than Hellman's own political naïveté. Hellman had thought nothing of being the guest of people whom the Czech woman regards as "pigs." The force of this woman's *engagement* uncovers the superficiality and the easy safeness of Hellman's own.

The next morning Hellman tours the wards to visit the sick. An American boy with serious injuries screams and writhes in pain. Just as Hellman has carefully set the scene and culled the reader's sympathy, she deliberately undoes all that she has accomplished. The political attaché accompanying her observes, "the kid's a hypochondriac" (*UW*, p. 79). The previous night she had meditated on the nobility of the fighters in this war; now she undercuts those sentiments. Hellman shows her preconceptions about the efficacy of her activity in Spain, about her evaluation of her Czech friends in Prague, and about her simple sympathy for the wounded American to be in each case not quite accurate and perceptive enough. The situations are far more complex than she had imagined, and each subverts the possibility for any certainty or complacency.

In re-reading the diaries from this time, Hellman recognizes that the Spanish experience had been "a minute-to-minute confrontation" with herself, a "struggle with what courage . . . against discomfort" she possessed (*UW*, p. 99). The significance of the diary experience is that it forces the now older woman to understand the limits of her own political commitment. She realizes she had not been a revolutionary: "It saddens me now to admit that my political convictions were never very radical, in the true, best, serious sense. Rebels seldom make good revolutionaries, perhaps because organized action, even union with other people, is not possible for them" (*UW*, p. 101).

Hellman's trip to Russia in 1944 is an interesting glimpse into that country at a time when there were few foreign observers and even fewer who could appreciate what they saw. Certain passages from the diaries of this time are clearly self-revelatory: the Russian army's invitation to observe its offensive against the Germans all the way to Berlin causes Hellman to appraise her "nature," which does not allow her to make the trip. But unlike the diaries from the Spanish experience, the ones from the Russian trip of 1944 are interesting to Hellman for what they fail to record. She finds she "kept diaries of greater detail and length than I have ever done before or since, but when I read them last year, and again last week, they did not include what had been most important to me, or what the passing years have made important" (*UW*, p. 111). Thus, the entries are supplemented by material from Hellman's memory as she writes the memoir. This sifting of the past through the sieve of the present is an epistemological act— an intentional search for knowledge.

Some self-illuminating moments come unexpectedly out of her

memory, their meaning seemingly hidden in the unknown workings of the psyche. Again, it is a hospital scene:

> But the most important few hours are not even recorded in the diaries. I had gone to a hospital for the severely wounded and was making the handshaking, false-smile clown-sounds that healthy people make when they are faced with the permanently injured, when suddenly a man came into the room. I think he was in his late twenties, I think he was blond, I think he was tall and thin. But I know that most of his face had been shot off. He had one eye, the left side of a piece of a nose and no bottom lip. He tried to smile at me. It was in the next few hours that I felt a kind of exaltation I had never known before. (*UW*, p. 113)

A close examination of the text reveals a subtle process of mirroring at work, a moment of recognition of identity and subsequent reversal that contains all the joy of the birth of tragedy.[6] Her own description of herself—giving handshakes, smiling falsely, making clown-sounds—underscores her displacement as a healthy person among "the permanently injured" who "face" her. There is an element of the passive here, which is indeed ironic, for one cannot be "faced with" another without "facing" also. Then into the room enters a "face," for that is what she is certain of seeing after all these years. He is a kind of opposing *Dopplegänger*—male while she is female; in his late twenties, she in her late thirties; he is tall, she is short; both are blond, and both are attempting to smile. For a moment his face displaces her face, all faces, in fact. In the displacement and its resultant distortion, no less symbolic for its topography on a real face, Hellman sees herself in this "other," not only in the heroism of the grotesque disfigurement, but also in this half-a-face, which is what her "clownish" face was. From different directions, and in different ways, two people in a contiguous way mirror each other. His face occasions a great exaltation coming from a moment of kinship and identity. Yet, the identity is made possible only through differences.

Hellman's identification with the Russians is no less authentic for its being the result of a sense of difference. Observing herself in the mirror of the Russians allows her to recognize clearly her own limitations: Tanya "said it was Russian of me, not to care about money. I said I did care about money, cared so much, in fact, that I pretended not to care, and maybe that was the reason I had always been so attracted by Russians, who are nonsavers, noncomputers, generous about sharing and giving, no middle-class calculations about what you take or give back" (*UW*, p. 152). Moreover, the Russian "mirror" forces her to confront the fact that in 1966 she is no longer the woman who can withstand the hardships of the 1944 trip. As the plane lands in Moscow, this recognition brings tears that "had to do with age and the woman who could survive hardships then and knew she couldn't anymore" (*UW*, p. 144). The gap in time since the last visit to Russia becomes a metaphor for the gap of time in her memory: " . . . I knew that I had taken a whole period of my life and thrown it somewhere, always intending to call for it again, but now that it came time to call, I couldn't remember where I had left it" (*UW*, p. 146). That gap has direct relationship to Russia because it is the gap that has to do with the McCarthy era and all the hardship it is identified with: the trial and jailing of Hammett; her appearance before the House Un-American Activities Committee; the loss of her farm. Just as her Russian friend Raya has difficulty telling her about the postwar Stalin years, Hellman has trouble telling Raya about the intervening years of McCarthyism, because those years have significantly changed her, and she has yet to assess that change. The Russian trip forces her to evaluate the passing of an earlier self as it is mirrored in her Russian friends, Raya and Captain K. Thus, both Russia and Spain act as foils to the self, highlighting the self's strengths and weaknesses, calling attention to its valorizations, to its lacks, and to its being "unfinished."

III

"Pentimento," the title of the second memoir, suggests a visual, painterly metaphor for the working of time. Through the layers of paint covering a canvas, the accretions and encrustations of time, the original outlines of an underlying subject or sketch come to be perceived. The perception of the original painting, the process of its slowly revealing itself through the more recent layers of paint, is what is meant by the term *pentimento*, which in Italian carries a flavor of regret and nostalgic sadness. The Italian term accurately describes

Hellman's moving backward and forward through the layers of time, uncovering those traces of meaning she finds in portraits of relatives and loved ones: "what was there for me once, what is there for me now."[7] These portraits and vignettes (three of which conclude *An Unfinished Woman*) seem to possess a self-sufficiency, but the connection between them is subtly held by the consciousness of the narrator who relates them. We find that Hellman, the talented dramatist, captures her own life in these quiet, yet intense dramas of other people's lives.

In each portrait, Hellman divides her life into segments whose principle of organization lies in a subject outside herself. The selection of a subject is dictated neither by an obvious psychology nor an obvious autobiographical importance. The recall is often arduous: as Hellman continually tells the reader, she must consult diaries for memories worthy of notation. The process of recall and reordering is therefore a conscious one, a fully aesthetic endeavor. She structures the variegation of her life into accessible and meaningful channels. Each portrait, then, becomes a kind of self-portrait.[8]

The choice of Bethe in the opening portrait of *Pentimento* is interesting, for unlike other memorialists Hellman oftentimes chooses the unknown, the little people of the world who in no way have shaped the history of her time. Bethe is a poor immigrant cousin sent to the United States by her grandfather's family to make a match with another cousin. She marries Styrie Bowman and in six months her cousin walks out on her. She then becomes involved with a member of the Italian Mafia in New Orleans. When Bethe's lover, Arneggio, is killed in a gangland slaying, Bethe disappears for several years. Later, with the help of her aunts, Hellman finds Bethe living with a nondescript plumber in a run-down shanty. A couple of years after that, Bethe dies of pneumonia. Her drama is that of an older woman's influence on a young female adolescent. She enters Hellman's life at the moment when the young Lillian becomes aware of romantic love. In her portrait of this "significant other," Hellman has captured through a series of skillfully concise scenes the evolution of her own concept of love. The older writer retrieves knowledge only dimly perceived by the adolescent. Thus, Hellman is saying that knowledge about one's self can only be appreciated after experience has given it value.

The first important encounter with Bethe occurs when Hellman is thirteen and finds Bethe in a strange Italian delicatessen after the disappearance of Bethe's husband. The immigrant cousin says to the young Lillian: "'No longer am I German. No longer the Bowmans. Now I am woman and woman does not need help'" (*P*, p. 18). The child's response is to realize that something has happened to Bethe that she doesn't understand; the adult's response, as Hellman is to describe it later, is jealousy. What Bethe has said is that she has not inherited an identity; she is her own independent person who chooses to act the way she wants and not the way others expect her to act.

The next significant meeting with Bethe occurs when Hellman finds her in church one Sunday. As this is unusual for Bethe, the young Lillian accuses Bethe (who would be Jewish) of lying about her religion because her new man has told her to do so. In response Bethe invites Lillian to eat with her in an Italian restaurant, an odd overture for this woman of great reserve. In the restaurant, the food is terrible, but a drama of intense love unfolds. The child-adolescent becomes aware that the man with whom Bethe sat in church is now a few tables away in the same restaurant. Hellman watches mutely as a mating dance of quiet, powerful gestures takes place between Bethe and this man. The wild, brute, overpowering strength of passion reveals itself before the terrified eyes of the young Lillian:

He was sitting alone at a table, staring at a wall, as if to keep his face from us. I asked Bethe for a glass of water and found her staring at the man, her lips compressed as if to hold the mouth from doing something else, her shoulders rigid against the chair. The man turned from the wall, the eyes dropped to the table, and then the head went up suddenly and stared at Bethe until the lips took on the look of her lips and the shoulders went back against the chair with the same sharp intake of muscles. Before any gesture was made, I knew I was seeing what I had never seen before and, since like most only children, all that I saw related to me, I felt a sharp pain as if I were alone in the world and always would be. As she raised her hand to her mouth and then turned the palm toward him, I pushed the heavy paste stuff in front of me so far across the table that it turned and was on the tablecloth. She did not see what I had done because she was waiting for him as he rose from his chair. She went to meet

him. When they reached each other, his hand went down her arm
and she closed her eyes. (*P*, p. 22)

In this moment, the young adolescent has intuited the rhythms of
physical love re-enacted metaphorically before her. The abrupt rise of
Arneggio's head parallels the swift erection of something (the virginal
Hellman does not exactly know what; the mature woman does) directed at the "lips" of Bethe until to the young Hellman both sets of
lips become one. Arneggio's back muscles parrot the instinctive "intake" of Bethe's penetration, and then, even the virgin can no longer
doubt that she is witnessing something she has never "seen before."
At this crucial moment, young Lillian superimposes herself on Bethe,
identifies with her so that it is Hellman who has been penetrated, and
living through the "other," she experiences the "sharp pain" of penetration as the inevitable violation of independence. But just as she
identifies with Bethe, she also knows that she is different from her and
the "sharp pain" comes from fear of union, which to her virginal mind
can only appear as a process of alienation from her nonsexual self.
Then, too, the mature narrator remembering sees the "pain" of
Bethe's union as excluding her, casting her forth into an "aloneness."
That Hellman will remain "alone" in each of her own unions (that is,
in different ways with Arthur Kober and Dashiell Hammett) is, of
course, one of the primary realizations the later Hellman understands
from her mirror image Bethe.

Present in the "Bethe" portrait is the juxtaposition of an idealistic,
romantic, ultimately illicit love against a prosaic, unattractive concept
of marriage embodied in her mother and father's relationship. In their
marriage, there is no communication, no intimate gestures so expressive of a passionate union—only nagging, attack, routine. The older
Hellman recognizes that at this moment the younger Lillian understood the difference between these two kinds of union. This recognition comes at precisely the time Hellman is becoming a difficult and
rebellious teenager. Thus, when Arneggio's mobland murder thrusts
Bethe's name into the New Orleans newspapers, Hellman takes sides
with Bethe and "love" against the conventional attitudes of her family.
Hellman discovers for herself the implications of the term common-

law husband which a friend informs her means that Bethe is a whore. In response, the adolescent Lillian shouts back: "'Does love need a minister, a rabbi, a priest? Is divine love between man and woman based on permission of a decadent society?'" (*P*, p. 27). Here during the transitional, formative stage of adolescence, Hellman, with a heroism and rebellion mirroring Bethe's, clarifies her values and adopts a congruent posture of commitment to them. She realizes the difference between love and marriage, the conflict between personal codes of relationships and conventional, institutionalized codes; she understands Bethe's gesture of defiance in the face of society. Therefore, when young Hellman is taken to the police station to be questioned after she has tried to see Bethe at the delicatessen where Arneggio has been murdered, she admits to the police that she had gone to the shop because of "love" (*P*, p. 32). In the utterance of that word is something profound for the girl: "I had already come near a truth I couldn't name, so close to it, so convinced that something was being pushed up from the bottom of me, that I began to tremble with an anxiety I had never felt before" (*P*, pp. 31–32). Indeed, the whole experience with Bethe is associated with a drive beyond language to embody "a truth I couldn't name," but repressed, until the mature author can understand, forgive, and accept the complexity of love.

Hellman tells the reader that from age fourteen to twenty-five, she had no news of Bethe, but that she thought of her often, especially on her own wedding day. The mature narrator now realizes why the recollection caused her to change from her bright wedding dress to a dull gray chiffon. Hellman had psychologically associated marriage with a conventional, dull experience. The next time she thinks of Bethe is the first afternoon she sleeps with Hammett, who is to become her passionate lover and common-law husband.

Later, after a decision to divorce her husband and to live openly with Hammett, Hellman returns to New Orleans to inform her aunts. During her stay she rediscovers Bethe, who is still the handsome earth mother and who now lives in isolated poverty, struggling, but resilient. The morning she visits Bethe alone, she makes a journey into her past, present, and future directly confronting the life style she has chosen. Momentarily Hellman becomes lost on the way—perhaps a resistance to that confrontation—but she emerges at the right place and finds Bethe as the earth mother, characteristically naked in the proportions of an heroic nudity:

> She was naked and I stopped to admire the proportions of the figure: the large hips, the great breasts, the tumbled auburn hair that came from the beautiful side of my father's family and, so I thought that day, had been lost in America. She must have heard the sound of the wet, ugly soil beneath me, because she turned, put her hands over her breasts, then moved them down to cover her vagina, then took them away to move the hair from her face. (*P*, p. 37)

Again Bethe's gestures are beautifully expressive of a concealment and revelation that promote the excitement of sexuality. Hellman shouts out: "'It was you who did it. I would not have found it without you. Now what good is it, tell me that?'" (*P*, p. 37). In this half-accusing, half-thankful admission, Hellman the woman recognizes her model, the real sexual teacher of her adolescence, who taught her the depth and risk of love, which is passionate, personal, unconventional, and ultimately lonely. Hellman the woman recognizes that the morality of her love for Hammett is immoral by conventional standards; at the same time she sees in herself, as she saw in Bethe, an inability to give in to conventional standards and thus live the easy, but stifled life. Such recognition of model and mirror, of love and its commitments and sacrifices, brings with it its own anxieties, insecurities, pain.

IV

We do not maintain that these forms of narrative presentation exhaust the possibilities of discourse within Hellman's memoirs. The forms we have discussed are, however, the most frequent, and, we think, the most important. We have wanted to suggest how Hellman, regardless of form, pursues an effective rendering of the self through the "other." That we have not discussed *Scoundrel Time*, the last of Hellman's memoirs, published in 1976, results from our opinion that the critical problems posed by the strategy of the "other" in this work require a study in themselves. In her recollection of the McCarthy era, Hellman must deal with the reverberations of her public image, an image that is in itself an "other." She has done this before but with this difference: she never had to justify this "other" against the pressure of a world so unceasingly bent on punishing her for her rebellion. In *Scoundrel Time* the mirroring function of the "other" becomes opaque, as Hellman defends herself against what she considers the perverse, unjust distortions of the mirror. In this work, the parallax perspective of the persecuted playwright and the reminiscing memorialist is not always able to distinguish distortion from reflection or the degree to which either emanates from the self or the world.

Be that as it may, the strategy of the "other" serves Hellman well in both *An Unfinished Woman* and *Pentimento*: (1) it allows her to explore the self from the distance of the "other"; (2) it permits her to see the self, not as a confining ego, but as the sum of all past experiences; (3) it enables her to confront the unfulfilled desires of her life through the process of conscious recall; and (4) it provides her with yet another means to create drama, for in the conflict between the self and the "other" is the stuff out of which all drama is made.

In conclusion, the strategy of the "other" that pervades Hellman's memoirs proposes a dialectic between the memorialist and time—past and present. All three titles of the memoirs implicate demon time: *An Unfinished Woman* suggests time's irresolution; *Pentimento*, time's obfuscation; and *Scoundrel Time*, time's rapacity. To prevent some of time's depredations, Hellman writes her memoirs. The synthesis that results from the dialectic, that is, the repossession of the past in the articulation of the "other," becomes an act of renewal in the midst of a sense of loss. And yet, the canvas of the past, that metaphor so dear to Hellman, is never quite restored nor completely painted over, the disclosures and revelations left open to the reader to whom Hellman appeals as the last arbiter of meaning, the final and silent "other."

11.

The Metaphysics of Matrilinearism in Women's Autobiography: Studies of Mead's *Blackberry Winter*, Hellman's *Pentimento*, Angelou's *I Know Why the Caged Bird Sings*, and Kingston's *The Woman Warrior*

STEPHANIE A. DEMETRAKOPOULOS

Women derive a sense of feminine godhead from their biological connections with one another. This essay attempts to reestablish the sacrality of feminine experience and also to re-mythologize all human experience by treating the development, characterization, and significance of the matriarchal realm in female autobiography.

Some essential definitions are necessary before beginning. In this paper "matriarchal realm" or "matriarchate" means the home in which a child grows up, its management and domination by the mother and by feminine values of nurturing, relatedness, process. Though fathers influence this realm, theirs is an intrusive influence and the child is chiefly shaped, especially in the earlier years, by the mother. Throughout a child's life in the home, the mother's influence is stronger for a daughter than for a son. "Matrilineal consciousness" refers to the mother/daughter patterning of generations that only woman directly experiences. This may be an intra-psychic phenomenon even more than an extra-psychic experience. C. Kerényi calls this the "archetype of feminine destiny," and Carl G. Jung defines it this way:

> The conscious experience of these ties produces the feeling that her life is spread out over generations—the first step towards the immediate experience and conviction of being outside time, which brings with it a feeling of immortality. The individual's life is elevated into a type, indeed it becomes the archetype of woman's fate in general. This leads to restoration or *apocatastasis* of the lives of her ancestors, who now, through the bridge of the momentary individual, pass down into generations of the Future. An experience of this kind [a numinous sense of the mother/daughter chain of being] gives the individual a place and a meaning in the life of the generations, so that all unnecessary obstacles are cleared out of the way of the life-stream that is to flow through her. At the same time the individual is rescued from her isolation and restored to wholeness. All ritual preoccupation with archetypes ultimately has this aim and this result.[1]

Women's autobiographies (especially American ones) recount this Demeter/Kore matrix of being.

Along with a number of other critics, Albert Stone notes that American autobiography is "a democratic literary genre [that] has much closer links to political and historical events than do fiction, poetry, or drama."[2] Certain kinds of autobiographies have flourished and clustered around specific historical events. The large number of American female autobiographies recently published can be connected to a new self-consciousness in women, attributable to the latest feminist movement, which centers in the United States. The collective though sometimes unconscious urge in many of these autobiographies is to give flesh once more to the archetype that the Eleusinian rites embodied. To put it another way, as Stephen Shapiro says, "every autobiography testifies to the power of models and then participates in the cycle of incarnations by becoming a model itself . . . [by] making old myths available in new forms."[3] Some critics of autobiography see their duty as elucidating the author's unintended revelations as well as her/his intended roles and modes; Shapiro too says that discovering the "dark core" of unawareness in each autobiography is the critic's job.[4] My study connects the "dark cores" of several women's autobiographies to reveal an ultimately metaphysical layer of the feminine psyche. Stone further defines autobiographical study as a "natural interdisciplinary study" of history, literature, and psychology.[5] All three disciplines are employed in the critical framework here: the Eleusinian rites of matrilinearism are historically manifest in ancient Greek culture, but are a universal aspect of woman's psyche. These rites surface as psychic necessity in the literature twentieth-century women write to explain their development. This delineation of the matriarchal realm and matrilineal consciousness in so many individual women's autobiographies illustrates a major archetypal constellation of the feminine principle as experienced by women themselves. Before analyzing how women confront this archetype and work through it in their autobiographies, let us consider briefly the reasons for the virtual absence of the matriarchal realm in male autobiography.

Many forces support a young man's separation from his mother and her matriarchal realm that shelters the child but blunts its individual development and autonomy. In most of Western culture, but especially in America with its emphasis on self-reliance and independence, the young man is expected to leave home and forge selfhood apart from his family. As many psychologists point out, male gender consciousness is accomplished by fantasy about and identification with an often absent father, represented by the patriarchal collective outside the home.[6] The boy must reject his mother and her whole realm in order to become an individual. For this reason, it is not surprising that few male autobiographies feature a portrait of the mother; mothers are simply a rather faceless part of the biological matrix necessary to support life as the boy grows. The father's influence seems much more important to the achievement of adulthood and the retrospective, mature sensibility that shapes the autobiography. Certain psychohistorians are challenging this stance and are showing that often the mother, though not acknowledged, was of singular importance to the personality of the male autobiographer.[7] Nevertheless, the struggle to extricate and separate the self from the mother is not a struggle for a man in the way it usually is for a woman. He need not bring the influence of the mother into consciousness to achieve a sense of separate selfhood; he need only identify with the father and move away into male groups.

Thus critics of American autobiography decry the fact that woman has "been rendered irrelevant by American autobiography and revolution. There were no women in Franklin's world of the self-invented self—only the wife as helpmeet in the most practical sense and as a practical object for excess sexual energy. There were no women at all in Thoreau's world. Although there was a feminine principle in Whitman, he hermaphroditically absorbed it as he absorbed Kanada and Missouri and Montana."[8] This absence of women, especially mothers, from male autobiography perhaps reflects an inflated sense of ego consciousness; does the writer unconsciously envision himself as one of Campbell's "Heroes with a Thousand Faces," all of whom seem to grow out of tree roots, need no shaping or nurturing, and seldom seem to feel mortality impinging? The answering of this question can be left to someone more interested in plumbing the curiosities of the masculine psyche. I point out this "feminine vacuum" in male autobiography in order to highlight the complexity and predominance of women's treatment of the matriarchate.

I suggest that the emphasis on their mothers in women's autobiography is due to innate and archetypal aspects of the woman's psyche, celebrated and codified long ago as the Eleusinian Mysteries. The emphasis on the matriarchal realm as the bedrock out of which a woman forges her identity is strongly developed by many kinds of female autobiographies, which fill a vacuum in our collective sense of identity for both men and women. The feminine principle and personality have long been publicly silent, inarticulate; and it is gratifying to see how many men as well as women can respond to, for example, the tough-woman persona of Lillian Hellman's *Pentimento*. But grappling with the forces of the matriarchal realm is far more important to women, who are signing up in droves for courses on women's autobiography and are reading avidly even such long works as Anaïs Nin's epic, seven-volume journals.[9] Woman's mythos is taking shape as women present their lives and persons for public scrutiny. Our uniqueness and meaning is becoming incarnate through the number of female autobiographies now available.

I will center on four autobiographies to demonstrate the importance of feminine archetypes. I begin with Margaret Mead's almost completely positive though split depiction of the archetype of the Great Good Mother. Three much more highly wrought and literary autobiographies will then be studied: Lillian Hellman's *Pentimento*, Maya Angelou's *I Know Why the Caged Bird Sings*, and finally Maxine Hong Kingston's *The Woman Warrior*. In each case I will analyze the imagery and themes with which the writer delineates matriarchate archetypes and then the impact the archetypes have on the way she structures the book, on her implicit assumptions about psychic reality, on the persona/narrator she adopts, and (when the author reveals them) her metaphysics.

Finally, I will sum up the meaning of the Great Good Mother archetype, the Primal Mother who shelters the child forth. For women's experience of this Primal Matriarchal Realm largely determines the extent and the way in which they identify as adults with the matriarchate. This archetype can be and often is split in the actual experience of the girl child, but splits can be positive as in a harmonious extended matriarchate like Margaret Mead's.

In the first chapters of *Blackberry Winter*, Mead presents her mother as an active, intellectual, loving, and strong woman. Her mother maintains an orderly matrix for the family, can instantly find things for her careless husband, and seems mainly to embody the Great Mother as the trustworthy manager of resources. She is an "anchor" (p. 42)[10] for the father and uses this family position of centrality to force him to allow Margaret to go to college. She is so socially responsible that she tends to be "Spartan" (pp. 22, 24), unable to play; and her practicality sometimes dampens the family's spontaneity. But, on the whole, Margaret seems satisfied in a cool way with her mother.

It is in her grandmother that Mead finds a more numinous image of primal and nurturing strength that extends the more limited personage of her mother into a strong, developed, monumentally maternal matriarchate. There is a sense of bulk, of massiveness, of fortress-like centrality about the grandmother that is typical of this archetype.[11] Mead devotes a whole chapter to her as the most "decisive influence in my life" (p. 49). Although her autobiography is journalistic in its stripped down, matter-of-fact, almost Protestant prose, Mead waxes lyrical and even symbolic about her grandmother:

> She sat at the center of our household. Her room—and my mother always saw to it that she had the best room, spacious and sunny, with a fireplace, if possible—was the place to which we immediately went when we came in from playing or home from school. There my father went when he arrived in the house. There we did our lessons on the cherry-wood table with which she had begun housekeeping and which, later, was my dining room table for twenty-five years. There, sitting by the fire, erect and intense, she listened to us and to all of Mother's friends and to our friends. In my early childhood she was also very active—cooking, preserving, growing flowers in the garden, and attentive to all the activities of the country and the farm. . . . Grandma was trustworthy in quite a different way [from Mother]. She meant exactly what she said, always. If you borrowed her scissors, you returned them. . . . She simply commanded respect and obedience by her complete expectation that she would be obeyed. And she never gave silly orders. (pp. 49–50)

Helpful here is the Jungian precept that rooms symbolize parts of the psyche.[12] Notice Mead's development of this place as the most important, central, light-filled, and warm room. This is where their education and family interchanges took place. Everyone went there first upon return to the home. The connection with nature, especially plants, is developed more fully within this chapter and is important in evoking the Lady of the Plants archetype,[13] one aspect of the Primal Good Mother. (A good touchstone for this archetype is Colette's mother, Sido, and her garden.) The importance of this room to the family is underlined by her rhetorical use of the word "there," which she repeats three times. The loving though iron rule of this archetype is reflected in the grandmother's trustworthiness. Mead again emphasizes this stability and inner strength later, saying that when her grandmother became angry she became very still and silent. Her grandmother taught her to cook, kept her at home sometimes for whole years to educate her (she had been a teacher), and was integral to the matrilineal alliance against Mead's father: she always agreed with her daughter-in-law. When her own son threatened to leave the family, Grandma "told him firmly that she would stay with her [the mother] and the children" (p. 55).

Mead reveals how the more permeable ego membrane of the woman can be beneficial to a developing girl if she has good models to internalize. At times Mead says she found it difficult to distinguish between her grandmother's life and her own. Mead heard so many stories about her grandmother's girlhood that she felt as a child she had lived them herself. The stories grandparents tell children may be a very important part of the psychic development of time and ancestral connections; many women autobiographers seem to have internalized such stories as part of their own mythos (Kingston particularly demonstrates the power of the "talk-story" to children). Her grandmother also shaped Mead's attitudes toward being a woman and toward men. "Grandma had no sense at all of ever having been handicapped by being a woman" (p. 52), and she thought that boys were slower to educate and "more vulnerable" (p. 51). Her grandmother embodies pleasant, warm aspects of woman's physicality. Mead's love for her was sensuous and physical in a way that she never depicts with her mother; she "loved the feel of her soft skin" (p. 56). Most important, finally, was that her grandmother had a career of her own: "The two women I knew best were mothers and had professional training. So I had no reason to doubt that brains were suitable for a woman" (p. 56). When her unstable and temperamental father later refuses to educate her (due to his economic insolvency, but he uses sexism as an excuse), it never dents her sense of being bound for a career. He, in fact, incurs what she calls "one of the few fits of feminist rage I have ever had" (p. 90).

Unknowingly, Mead depicts her father in a role reminiscent of the peripheral and castrated priests of Isis. He is seen as intrusive and imperative, interrupting the real business of the household, "my mother's and my grandmother's absorption with the children" (p. 34), and after the mother dies, he can never find anything again. His friends and hobbies are treated by the women as irrelevant and bothersome, and he is called "impatient," "irrational and untrustworthy," "arbitrary," and "rebellious" toward the matriarchal realm about which he gyrates (pp. 34, 38, 40, 41, 44). Her later relationships with men seem to reflect some of this familial pattern. At a time when it was unheard of, she kept her own name when she married. She recalls that a friend in college said her future husband would have to have an Oedipal complex; Mead later remarks on the Oedipal complex of her second husband as he notes the more mature relationship she begins building with the third husband (while still married to the second one). All her husbands (except possibly Gregory Bateson) seem to have been less competent than she, and it is noteworthy how little emotional turmoil she undergoes when breakups come. She also maintains a good relationship with them and their new wives. She does not like to compete with men, nor does she seek power in the form of administrative posts. She is not destructive in any way toward men; she simply does not center her identity around her relationship with them in the way that many women do in our nuclear family oriented culture.

This is not to say that a matriarchate as almost wholly devoid of masculine influence as the Meads' is unequivocally good for everyone. Mead's brother seems to have suffered from some very specific expectations of success that her father projected onto him; Mead escapes this problem because of being a girl and is encouraged by her mother and grandmother to move into whatever realm of life she finds professionally fulfilling. The brother suffered within the family matriarchy in other ways; Mead says she projected all frailty and weakness onto him, keeping images of strength for herself. (Colette's and Angelou's brothers share a similar fate, suggesting that boys can feel painfully ousted in an overly cohesive and exclusive alliance of women.)

There are some negative aspects to her development, though decidedly minor. Because of her constant espousal of roles of strength, warmth, and cheerfulness, she admits early that she represses negative feelings and experiences. This seems to allow a rather long-suffering acceptance of injustices, as with her father and her second husband, who appeared actually cruel in his attitude toward her. Sometimes she seems to see men mainly as Father figures, needed to complete the family constellation. She marries Luther, her first husband, mainly because she wanted to have six children, and she leaves him when she finds she cannot have children. This is a rather callous treatment of him and suggests the facelessness that Psyche imposes on Amor until she finally lights the torch and is forced to see that he, like she, is an individual person.[14] But many first marriages are rather faceless, anonymous affairs. She also has an overdeveloped sense of responsibility, a fear of letting others down; she cannot bear being called "heartless," nor can she withhold support from friends even when it costs her too much. This, of course, is the maternal role becoming so sacrificial that it is self-destructive. Most puzzling of all, perhaps, is her sense of being "expendable" as an anthropologist in the field when she finds she cannot have children. Before that, she agreed with Franz Boas and others that women who can potentially give birth ought not be exposed to dangers. (This perhaps reflects the sense of sacrality that surrounds the Persephone or Kore figure in matrilineal cults—the daughter who can give birth stands for potential fruitfulness and on-goingness. The whole culture rebels for deep and possibly healthy psychic reasons at the sight or thought of a young woman dead on the battlefield.)

But the positive aspects of her identification with the matriarchate far outweigh the negative, and no human being is free from flaws or shortcomings. For one thing, she says she was always glad to be a girl. That is a singular (and, I think, wonderful) statement for a woman to be able to make. She carries with her throughout life a system for relating with groups of people that makes her comfortable and strong. For example, in the apartments she rented as a student, she organized her college friends into kinship systems which she orchestrated; the strength of these bonds is reflected in her lifelong relationships with these women. Her desire to be a mother was apparently completely without the ambivalence that women usually bring to that experience. Her chapter on the child she finally did have, her daughter Cathy, is one of the most joyful celebrations of motherhood I have ever read. She never gives up her career or feels guilt about leaving the child with the very competent and loving nursemaids she always seemed able to find. Because of her sense of strength and self-esteem as a woman, she was apparently able to divorce and remarry without the long periods of depression, anxiety, and lack of productivity that most women go through.

In fact, her early recognition and internalizing of kinship bonds formed the framework for her whole career. She says she always preferred learning in a personal context (as with her grandmother), and she never seemed threatened by another person's prestige or knowledge. Most poignant and sad in this regard is her great depression over the period of time when she tried to get scientists to work together as "a united family" rather than becoming monomaniacally separate as they have become.

Finally, she experiences in her own rather prosaic way a metaphysical sense of the continuity and ongoingness of life through her sense of matrilinearism. Her last chapter (there is an epilogue, but it only "gathers threads") is called "On Being a Grandmother." The lovely pictures of Sevanne Margaret (who fittingly takes her grandmother's name) accompany a text that almost defies complete explication:

> I suddenly realized that through no act of my own I had become biologically related to a new human being . . . how strange it was to be involved at a distance in the birth of a biological descendent. . . . I have always been acutely aware of the way one life touches another. . . . But the idea that as a grandparent one was dealing with action at a distance—that somewhere, miles away, a series of events occurred that changed one's own status forever—I had not thought of that and I found it very odd. (p. 321)

Her syntax is often labored and twisted in this chapter, as she struggles to state the metaphysical truths she has intuited. Here is one of her clearer summations:

> Scientists and philosophers have speculated at length about the sources of man's belief that he is a creature with a future life, or somewhat less commonly, with a life that preceded his life on earth. Speculation may be the only kind of answer that is possible, but I would now add to the speculations that are more familiar another of my own: the extraordinary sense of having been transformed not by any act of one's own but by the act of one's child. (p. 322)

She celebrates at length the way that mothers transcend their "creatureliness" in being able to accept their unknown children, who come to them as strangers (pp. 324–25). In becoming a grandmother, she finds she has acquired a special and perhaps transient sensitivity: "It is as if the child to whom one is bound by greater knowledge and the particularity of love were illuminated and carried a halo of light into any group of children" (p. 327). She says that everyone needs "access both to grandparents and grandchildren in order to be a full human being":

> In the presence of grandparent and grandchild, past and future merge in the present. Looking at a loved child, one cannot say, "We must sacrifice this generation for the next. Many must die now so that later others may live." This is the argument that generations of old men, cut off from children, have used in sending young men out to die in war. (p. 32)

Thus, in coming full circle into the role of Grandmother, which features the mature woman's sense of transcendence and transformation, Mead experiences and embodies the wisdom of the Sophia archetype,[15] as it grows out of the latter stages of the Demeter role.

This archetype of matrilineal foothold, of a four-generation matriarchate, seems the bedrock on which the repose of the narrating, retrospective Mead rests. Her sense of transcendence, yet loving understanding of process, is consolidated by her experience of the last transformations of the Demeter/Persephone myth, in which finally the daughter (Kore or Persephone) gives birth to a child. (This archetype is imaged forth even in the patriarchal religion of Christianity by Leonardo da Vinci's painting of the Virgin Mary sitting upon the lap of her mother and holding the Christ child in her arms.[16] "Kore" often has a baby son too.) This archetype of the endless chain of mothers/daughters underlies a woman's sense of kinship, and Mead demonstrates through her lifelong trust and adherence to this force how it helps the personality "unfold"—a metaphor which reflects the implicit assumption that human personality has its own innate nature which, if allowed to, will blossom and individuate without a great deal of struggle. The very title of her autobiography reflects Mead's sense of the importance of allowing the seasons of life to teach, to impregnate one with a sense of meaning that is at first organic, natural, allied with the unconscious. Mead's life demonstrates that one need not separate from the matriarchate in order to develop, to self-actualize fully; her life proves that a woman can individuate without rejection of the matriarchate. Indeed, rich and full development can come by remaining always rooted into it, if the substratum of the Primal Great Mother was primarily sheltering and, as Mead puts it, "trustworthy." If those women who embody this Great Mother are also fully developed, educated, and career-oriented as her mother and grandmother were, the daughter will naturally individuate and enter the community at large.

Lillian Hellman's life story demonstrates the struggle a creative mind must go through when it is bereft of a strong, warm, and intelligent matriarchate. Even the form of her best autobiography is dialectical, fraught with struggle. *Pentimento* is much more carefully fashioned than *Blackberry Winter*, arranged thematically and tightly so that chapters speak to one another; there is a progressive, chronological development of character traits though most of the stories cross the author's entire life span in time. A more conscious "voice" than Mead, Hellman has taken one aspect of her personality to stand for the whole[17] as narrator, and her persona is usually modeled around the "tough survivor" motif. All the main characters are dead except for the brilliant young black man who has renounced self-development (that is, left his career of research science for a commune) rather than face the struggle with an oppressive society. She identifies with the appallingly relentless life force of the turtle. A close look at the women in her early childhood elucidates this choice of persona.

Although she says that long after her mother's death she realized her mother gave strength to her father, all the references to her mother emphasize passivity and weakness. At fourteen Hellman trades verbal abuse with an aunt while "my gentle mother started to cry" (p. 149). Willy calls her mother "the charming flower under the feet of the family bulls" (p. 47). She is repeatedly shown to be an innocent, pitiful victim within the family, and she cannot ever be counted on to protect Lillian, even to perceive danger. She is like the hapless Birdie in *The Little Foxes*.

A more sinister model of Southern white womanhood, a seductive model of elegant facelessness, appears in the figure of Aunt Lily, a drug-addicted, hypocritically soft-spoken *poseur*, who sleeps with her black chauffeur with the full knowledge of her family. Rather than individuate, she sinks into a stupor from morphine. Aunt Lily stands in many ways for the Devouring Great Mother who attaches herself parasitically to the life force of the young and sucks them dry. Her son, Honey, is a pathetic emblem of how this Devouring Mother swallows her children. Hellman is intrigued by this pathologically feminine weakness and admits that her aunt's elegant dress and stylized (though empty, she later realizes) "culture" and upper-class attitudes fascinated her for years, like, one suspects, the pool in which Narcissus finally drowns. For Aunt Lily clings to the unconscious and manipulates others. Her life is devoid of rationality or meaning, both of which the mature Hellman heroically strives for. But this polar face of womanhood haunts her childhood.

Hellman's spinster aunts seemed to have chosen never to marry rather than to relinquish their independence and selfhood. They are models of strength but also of alienation. They are supportive of the elder Hellman but are unable to supply the warmth and physical affection/sheltering that the child needed. Finally, then, the young Hellman finds the Primal Great Mother in the black women who care for her all her life. While she in many ways gives real life to the characterizations of these women, her own relationship to them partakes of the impersonal: "All my life, beginning at birth, I have taken orders from black women, wanting them and resenting them, being superstitious the few times I disobeyed" (p. 205). For a complete portrait of this archetype as embodied in Sophronia, her childhood nanny, one needs to look at the first parts of *An Unfinished Woman*, in which she turns to two maternal forces when in trouble, Sophronia and the fig tree. Her love for Sophronia contains the ferocity of all Hellman's passions. But in *Pentimento*, she unwittingly gives away her pigeonholing of this archetype when she emphasizes that Caroline Ducky, Aunt Lily's frail, retired servant, dispenses all her irrational yet primitive and true wisdom about human relations from a third floor attic out of which she hardly ever comes. Helen, Hellman's domestic during her adult years, is also depicted as uneducated, frequently difficult, and irrational, even though Hellman works side by side with her in the kitchen. Hellman prides herself on her iron will and often also on her rationality while projecting so much irrational wisdom on these black women, that one often feels she has a Delphic oracle living in her kitchen. They seem like the first stages of the Great Mother—large, mostly torso, often faceless, always eyeless, just a huge sheltering force. Their wisdom seems to come from the depths of their unconscious and bubbles forth sporadically. They also stand for the intuitive forces of the psyche which Hellman often represses in her hard-nosed, almost Calvinistic rationality. Thus they carry a split-off aspect of feminine consciousness for Hellman herself.

Clearly what Hellman needed was a model of escape from the devouring aspects of white womanhood and a much fuller model of development than the black women could give her. She quite consciously develops a model for adventuresome wandering and fulfillment outside the kinship fold in Bethe, a poor cousin who emigrates from Germany and proves an embarrassment to her American relatives.

Bethe stands for the Venus archetype of womanhood but coupled strangely with Artemis qualities.[18] Venus' *raison d'être* is her sexual link to a man, but Artemis is the cold, unrelated wanderer. Bethe is called stupid by Hellman's father, but her strength in following her own impulses and needs searching for a man *she* wants (regardless of how the clan feels) takes her into dangerous criminal realms where she both survives and thrives. She is so stubbornly herself that she becomes an epiphany and a turning point for Hellman; following many side references to her voluptuousness, beautiful thick auburn hair, slow movements as if in a stupor, coupled with a certain expressionlessness, we come to this numinous, Botticellian Venus vision of Bethe:

> I saw Bethe hanging clothes from a line that stretched from a pole to an outhouse. She was naked and I stopped to admire the proportions of the figure: the large hips, the great breasts, the tumbled auburn hair that came from the beautiful side of my father's family and, so I thought that day, had been lost in America. She must have heard the sound of the wet, ugly soil beneath me, because she turned, put her hands over her breasts, then moved them down to cover her vagina, then took them away to move the hair from her face. (p. 37)

When Bethe moves the hair from her face, it is as though she recognizes Hellman as a fellow traveler down the forbidden roads to self-fulfillment. The image of Bethe leaving the duty ties and kinship patterns gives Hellman the permission to leave her innocuous but unloved husband and to enter into the mature, demanding, intense relationship with Dashiell Hammett, which challenges and fulfills her all their life together. She is able to become the "hetaira" or Venus figure to a man through internalizing Bethe and rejecting the passive sexual or sexually rejecting roles of her mother and aunt. Bethe shows her a different face of feminine godhead than Mead's life demonstrates, and these Venus and Artemis archetypes stand Hellman in good stead all her life. It is important to see that Hellman had no developed maternal figure in her life to make the Demeter role compatible with her need to explore and write about the world. The title *Pentimento* suggests internalized images (like Bethe) that emerge from under the canvas of the portrait of the created self. The metaphor contains a lot more struggle, use of will power, and ardor than Mead's more organic vision because Hellman's "natural" young world, her matriarchate, contained no positive images. She had quite literally to look for a Bethe in order to escape to other models.

Hellman's father is important in this release from the negative formative female roles. Mead's father was unfaithful to her mother; but she dismissed this as just the foibles of the irrational male, and his behavior did not seem to touch the family very much. Hellman, on the other hand, in *An Unfinished Woman* throws herself out of the arms of her fig tree and breaks her nose when she first finds out.[19] She remarks on his affairs repeatedly in both autobiographies, and one suspects that in his unfaithfulness she finds permission for her contempt for and psychic unfaithfulness to her white Southern matriarchate. Thus she identifies with her father and undoubtedly found fulfillment through Hammett for her rather undeniable father complex.

Her relationship with Hammett was far more complex than only this father/daughter side, but it elicited one of the less appealing components of the Hellman persona, the "snotty brat" or "cheeky daughter" affectation toward men older than herself. Because she found most if not all of her expression of the feminine principle in her relationship to men as a Venus/mistress figure, she needed them to reify her individuality, her rebelliousness. She usually accomplishes this by forcing a father/daughter relationship to form or constellate through her donning of a little girl persona. In *An Unfinished Woman*, she spits in Hammett's eye and "quotes" him as saying, "That's my girl. Some of the time the kid kicks through" (p. 171). In *Pentimento*, she actually admits that even when she is on the outs with Hammett, she would not have married without his permission! She frequently quotes herself as the cheeky brat to the point that it becomes a little cloying. Her dependence on Hammett's aesthetics was undoubtedly helpful to her as an artist, but when she says, "I was on the eighth version of the play before Hammett gave a nod of approval" and when she admires the "toughness of his criticism, the coldness of his praise" (p. 142), his mentorship becomes too paternalistic.

But in many ways he stands for the coldheartedness she had to adopt toward her past and herself in order to reject mothering, which her own mother was afraid would kill Hellman physically and (this fear was unconscious) psychically. So she projects onto Hammett her own rejection of nurturing, relating deeply in terms of a permanent commitment and expressing warmth and tenderness; he becomes in many ways a perfect "animus" figure in Hellman's autobiographies. Her attributing paternal aspects to him gives him a transcendent and sacred aspect that sanctifies these qualities—she claims he gave her standards toward which to strive. He becomes finally the unfaithful father with whom she couples and moves away from the matriarchate that would envelop and devour her attempts to individuate.

Thus we see the meaning of her persona. Only by delineating herself as different, an outlaw (like Bethe), can she escape; and this does take toughness. She truly is a loner; she had to tear her roots out of the matriarchate of Southern white womanhood, although, curiously enough, she always seems to have a black woman waiting on her. This way, she need not connect *herself* with the Demeter role. Finally, her metaphysics at the end of *Pentimento* are apparent as extensions of her sense of self. What survives is brute life force. Human individuals die and have no meaning except for the artifacts they leave behind and the ways they have (often unknowingly like Bethe) affected another's being. Human individuality must be wrought, indeed rent, out of the life force of nature; great will and strength are required for this, and only a few accomplish it (note the elitism). The rest doze for a lifetime in the inertia of the unconscious. Hellman celebrates the brute determined life force of the turtle and the turtle in her, but ultimately nature is the enemy in her vision, against which humans triumph by surviving it, not by fulfilling it. Julia, Willy, and Helen are swept away, like the sea almost takes Lillian. Her metaphor for her work (and life) is characteristic of Artemis, the huntress who rapes nature: "Hunting in an open field with shot from several guns, following the course but unable to see clearly, recovering the shot hands full, then hands empty from stumbling and spilling" (p. 159). She wrests her work and self from nature, but paradoxically, only because of nature's strong life urge in her. Yet the end of her book seems sad and apocalyptic in that life has, in terms of humanity and the meaning of individuality, no ongoingness. It is not necessary to be a biological mother or grandmother to accomplish this sense of life. Anaïs Nin never had children, but she had spiritual sons and daughters who gathered around her to celebrate the gift of her life, which they internalized for its psychic and spiritual fertility. Thus the devouring faces of Hellman's matriarchate force her to embrace the masculine and American traits of self-reliance and independence carried to a pathological extreme. She lives out only the Artemis and Venus feminine archetypes, coupling with a man who literalizes these psychic needs. She is Kore only to a man and thus loses touch with her feminine roots of ongoingness and continuity. Nevertheless, Hellman's autobiographies are satisfying aesthetically; they have clarity and closure.

Increasingly puzzling and unsettling, the more one tries to work with it, is Maya Angelou's *I Know Why the Caged Bird Sings.* Writing during her thirties, Angelou, of course, has a far less mature point of view than Mead and Hellman, whose autobiographies were written when they were in their sixties, which may be why she never comes to terms with the matriarchal face that her biological mother embodies. She paints it over with a daughterly love that the mother does not deserve and that is singularly unconvincing.

The most positive and convincing face of the matriarchate and the

one that provides the foundation of Angelou's personality is her
father's mother, the grandmother to whom she is strangely and without explanation sent at age three just because the parents are divorced. She calls her Momma, and the first part of the book is a hymn
to her.

Momma's looming, quiescent, brooding qualities make her far more
primal and numinous than Mead's grandmother. Momma's religiosity,
her resting on providence, her inflexibility and conservativism, and
even her irrationality make her into a mindless though practical
mother hen:

> People . . . said she used to be right pretty. I saw only her power
> and strength. She was taller than any woman in my personal world,
> and her hands were so large they could span my head from ear to
> ear. . . . In church when she was called upon to sing, she seemed to
> pull out plugs from behind her jaws and the huge, almost rough
> sound would pour over the listeners and throb in the air. (p. 38)

Everyone in Stamps admired "the worth and majesty of my grandmother" (p. 39). Momma is proud of being black, disapproving even
of Shakespeare since he was white. Her matriarchal realm includes
her son Willy, crippled from birth, whom she continues to protect and
shelter as if he were a child. She rules with deep love and an iron
hand, often from principles she does not bother to explain to Angelou
and her brother Bailey: "Her world was bordered on all sides with
work, duty, religion and 'her place.' I don't think she ever knew that
a deep-brooding love hung over everything she touched" (p. 47). She
stands strong and silent even before the obscenely vicious baiting of
the local white children; Angelou seems in the rest of her narrative to
emulate this strength during such horrors as the rape by Mr. Freeman
and the knifing by her father's mistress.

It is not until the appearance of her father that Angelou questions
the worth of being female, but the father's obvious preference for
Bailey makes her wish to have been a boy. Then she meets her frivolous and beautiful mother who could pass for white and finds that even
as a female, she is inferior to the prevailing cultural standards. The
oppressiveness and lack of maternal love in her mother's Venus-like

role are reflected in the gradual destruction of Bailey as he attempts to internalize his mother's image, to come to terms with her sending them away twice to Momma. The mother's cold yet heated sexuality is apparent throughout. In the matriarchate of her mother, Mr. Freeman (the mother's live-in lover) seems to have all life force suspended, sitting inanimate until the mother appears. He seems to be useful only for sexual purposes, and he uses Angelou as an extension of her mother. Then, in the most shocking callousness one could adopt toward a child, the mother returns her daughter to Momma because Maya is depressed after the rape.[20]

In her own behavior at the end of her book, Angelou splits the feminine archetype of her mother's cold Venus and her grandmother's primal warm sheltering Demeter aspects. She offers herself to a neighborhood boy for her first voluntary sexual experience. This partakes of the anonymity of the temple whore and Venus' use of the male as sexual cohort only. This act also reflects Angelou's inability to feel that a man could find her desirable, even though her mother's third husband, who appears on the scene in Angelou's early teens, has been kind to her. In a psychologically bizarre ending, Angelou finds her adulthood through her acceptance and love of her baby son. Her mother brings him to her bed, and when she awakens, she finds that she has instinctively slept so as not to hurt him. This acting out of her grandmother's qualities of sheltering, warm, fortress-like physicality reflects her comfort with the Demeter archetype, not with the adult woman's Venus or Hera (the wife archetype) couplings with the male. It seems a celebration of womanhood through becoming the Primal Great Good Mother, but skipping all the steps in between of establishing authentic contact with the male world and/or making one's own matriarchal realm. She says she feels close to her own mother at the end, but that too is difficult to believe. Her mother has thoroughly betrayed her, but never does Angelou show us that she or her mother has consciously confronted this rejection. In a way, having the baby can be seen as Angelou's counter-betrayal. At any rate, the emergence of the baby from the womb of this girl-child who has not even been truly sexually awakened in any concrete way seems a tragic way to end the book and begin life as an adult. Birth as self-actualization or gender realization would appear a very limited step toward consciousness; at any rate, I always feel tricked at the book's conclusion. However, perhaps it is psychologically apt and even life-affirming in that Angelou does not lose but consolidates her sense of the strength of her grandmother and all she symbolizes. Like Hellman, she is a survivor *only* through the expression of a positive feminine principle *outside* the nuclear family.

I Know Why the Caged Bird Sings fails precisely because it does not face squarely and reconcile in any way the distorted faces of the matriarchate. Perhaps the tour de force in exploration of the depths, glories, and despair of the matriarchate belongs to Maxine Hong Kingston's *The Woman Warrior: Memoirs of a Girlhood Among Ghosts.* Kingston's own very complex mother, Brave Orchid, bristles with polar faces of the matriarchate. Because her daughter has such a poetic imagination, Brave Orchid need only evoke certain archetypes, which Kingston then mythologizes, or bodies out, into full-fledged personages. The powerful, almost superhuman life force of Brave Orchid permeates this book, demonstrating the Jungian axiom that archetypes operate in polarities. When one extreme is constellated or made flesh (literalized in actual life or vividly and consciously imagined as in Kingston's "myths"), the opposite is automatically invoked and struggles to emerge, to give a completion, a wholeness. Some recent Jungians have wondered what Jung meant when he said that the masculine principle is more concerned with perfection, the feminine principle with completion; Brave Orchid's character demonstrates how women can be more complex than most men because they grow in a nonanalytical "both/and" way that defies and exceeds perfection. The pressure of different roles that conflict with perfection of any one role makes, furthermore, a great deal of woman's individuation intra-psychic (perhaps more necessarily than a man's because of the pressures on her of mothering and wifing); that is, her imagination and fantasy life complete her sense of self.

Brave Orchid gives Kingston the legacy of her aunt, No-Name Woman, whose very existence has been expunged from the family history because she had an illegitimate child. She teaches her that her matrilineal existence is contingent upon complete obedience to the patriarchal Chinese culture. Kingston sees around her the embodiments of these females who surrender selfhood, who do not speak. These images of the matriarchate partake hauntingly of the same oppressions that Hellman's mother and Aunt Lily portray—a cross-cultural phenomenon perhaps best called the Devoured Woman archetype. Again like Hellman, Kingston is terrified by this image; a restless, creative, poetic mind like hers sees the death-in-life reality of this silence. She reacts in violence against this image to which her mother gives verbal assent (while acting out the most ferociously opposite attitudes possible). But Kingston is haunted by the fear that this ghost/shadow model of womanhood will surface in her own self and take over. In an attempt to destroy this shadow reality of the silent, extinguished woman, Kingston dirties her fingernails, swears, and behaves as much like a clumsy boy as possible.

Finally, in an extraordinarily harrowing episode, she attempts to change the essence of the shadow image. The image is, of course, intra-psychic and cannot be destroyed or changed, only assimilated, worked against, or wept over. Yet she attacks the classmate who never speaks in public, intent on literally reforming the very flesh of this girl who is silence incarnate. The setting, an underground lavatory, is sterile, ugly, and labyrinthian and suggests the place where Theseus met the Minotaur or the underground rooms in which Beowulf grapples with Grendel. This motif of a trip to the underworld and confrontation with the shadow is emphasized by Kingston's year-long illness after she attacks the girl. Her attempt to literalize and concretize the psychic dragon or shadow rends her psyche, her being, with its ontological wrongness. We cannot destroy spiritual demons by attacking our physical projections of them. After her own year of silence, Kingston walks outside, leaning on a staff made from the peach tree whose seasons she had watched as she lay ill, learning its lesson of organic, natural change. She tells us that "at school I had to figure out again how to talk" (p. 212).

Kingston's Aunt Moon Orchid provides an adult version of the suppressed undeveloped woman. Moon Orchid has recently come from China, where she had lived, a sort of pensioned-off (but very comfortable) wife of her now-Americanized husband who has remarried bigamously, many years before. Her inability to cope with her own life outside of the protected Chinese aristocracy is devastating; she cannot even fold a towel properly and becomes more childlike than the children, following them around and exclaiming wide-eyed on their activities. She cannot cope at all with her new-found American independence, nor does she wish to resume contact with her husband, although Brave Orchid forces her to confront him. She ends up in an all-women's ward in an asylum, a retreat to a totally female world in which she thinks the pregnant inmates are her daughters. This retreat into a feminine unconscious of insanity is not unlike Hellman's Aunt Lily's drug addiction. Kingston lists other crazy, silent, withdrawn women, but Aunt Moon Orchid is the major paradigm.

To paraphrase Hamlet, Kingston's mother is more than "a sometime paradox." At the same time that she threatens Kingston with this image of the worthless, good-only-for-barter woman, saying that she will sell her if they return to China, that she is worth nothing because she is a girl, Brave Orchid demonstrates and teaches her as a ferocious and compelling Amazon archetype. She also constantly keeps Kingston unsettled, telling her lies or truths, then retracting them—like the story that two of her children were born and died in China before Brave Orchid emigrated, or like the claim that she cut Kingston's frenum as an infant so that she could wield a sharp tongue. Because it is impossible to perceive the true outlines of the mother's life and character, she becomes a more and more powerful figure in her ambiguity, her ruthless life force, and her almost terrifying energy. It is this looming ferocity of her mother that lies behind Kingston's myth of the Woman Warrior, a perhaps seminal feminine fantasy that compensates for the powerlessness of No-Name Woman.

Kingston recreates the Royal Couple archetype, so corroded by her distant, aloof father and her almost savage mother. In her fantasy, she leaves her real parents for fantasy parents who are perfect mentors to her warrior self. Her poetic creation shows how fantasy and dream are as integral to personal development as the most singular episodes or characters in our life. The old couple that train her are perfectly egalitarian, logical, nurturing, and appropriately severe. Before she sets off to war, Kingston the warrior has a mystical vision that seems to lie behind the rest of the book's thrust toward synthesis and wholeness:

> I saw two people made of gold dancing the earth's dances. They turned so perfectly that together they were the axis of the earth's turning. They were light; they were molten, changing gold— Chinese lion dances, African lion dancers in midstep. I heard high Javanese bells deepen in midring to Indian bells, Hindu Indian, American Indian. Before my eyes, gold bells shredded into gold tassles that fanned into two royal capes that softened into lions' fur. Manes grew tall into feathers that shone, became light rays. Then the dancers danced the future—a machine-future—in clothes I had never seen before. I am watching the centuries pass in moments because suddenly I understand time, which is spinning and fixed like the North Star. And I understand how working and hoeing are dancing; how peasant clothes are golden, as king's clothes are golden; how one of the dancers is always a man and the other a woman.
>
> The man and the woman grow bigger and bigger, so bright. All light. They are tall angels in two rows . . . [they are] the old brown man and the old grey woman . . . [afterward] I could stare at ordinary people and see their light and gold. I could see their dance. (pp. 32–33)

The Royal Couple archetype is envisioned by some Jungians as the polarity that most broadly underlies and symbolizes all wholeness;[21] this archetype has always been associated with the royal lion and lioness and with gold. Kingston makes the image fill all space and time with its process of dance; it finally and forever irradiates all reality, revealing the miracle behind the ordinary.

Without the Amazon archetype that her mother taught her in songs and demonstrated in her stories of her life as a medical student and physician, it is doubtful Kingston's powerful imagination would have produced this image of the strong woman who sees visions and goes unafraid. Brave Orchid has also stimulated this archetype by telling of her triumph over the Sitting Ghost, a phantom who haunted her student dormitory and terrified the other medical students. Even as an old and worn woman, Brave Orchid goes on demonstrating a rather fierce restlessness, a need to operate in spheres beyond the traditional

Chinese woman's place. She dyes her hair black and stands in line to labor in the fields even though she does not really need the money, as Kingston points out. She is also unafraid to sally forth into patriarchal realms like her sister's bigamous husband's office. In fact, Brave Orchid comes to embody a harsh and cruel reality that finally eclipses the frail psyche of Moon Orchid, her passive sister. In a way, she drives her sister Moon Orchid insane, first making her leave the safe haven of her daily life in China, and then forcing her to attempt to reclaim her husband. Kingston ends this hilarious yet painful story with Brave Orchid's admonishing her own children to be cruel to any second wife their father takes. The poor father, obviously very peripheral to this ruthlessly matriarchal household, protests he does not want another wife. But the children listen to their mother and think about the destruction of their aunt Moon Orchid: "Brave Orchid's daughters decided fiercely that they would never let men be unfaithful to them. All her children made up their minds to major in science or mathematics" (p. 186).

Thus, the irrational power and strength of Brave Orchid becomes a saving image for Kingston, yet sadly the perverse overbearingness of her mother also stifles her so that she can only survive away from her mother. As an adult, she is sick whenever she visits home. Nevertheless, it is obvious that at some level, probably mainly unconscious, Brave Orchid (who had, after all, experienced her own profession and freedom for years before she joined her husband in America) delegated this daughter to become free, strong, and independent. The story of the cut frenum and the songs of the woman warriors reveal this rather underground message of the possibility of freedom for a woman; and one wonders if the grotesque, even retarded suitors that Brave Orchid invites in and circulates through the house were not intended to repulse Kingston.

This exceedingly rich book lends itself to interminable analysis. The most important point here, however, is that Kingston is given a dazzling array of contradictory faces of the matriarchate. The structure of Kingston's book seems on casual perusal much like Hellman's, until the dialectical aspect of the book is examined; chapters answer one another and voices of Kingston's internalized matriarchate argue with one another within chapters. The final story of the book is a dialogue in which Kingston completes a story of Brave Orchid's with one of her own. This quiet little ending story beautifully and lyrically reconciles the sides of Kingston's matrilineal inheritance. She shares a story with her mother, beginning it with an episode from her mother's girlhood about Kingston's maternal grandmother, who must have been as full of vigor and life as Brave Orchid. Even though her feet were bound, she ruled her family with an iron hand, forcing them all to accompany her for days on end to the theater. She is attacked by bandits but continues to attend the plays. Thus Kingston establishes the strength of her foremothers; some of the women managed to establish rights and dominance in spite of everything. Then Kingston finishes this "talk-story" with musing on the life of a woman who lived among the Barbarians (Americans) but sang songs with such power that they understood the meaning even though the language was unknown to them. These songs, she tells us, translate well, even though the poetess was forced to return to her own people to provide heirs for her own father's clan. Telling and sharing the pain redeems and bestows meaning on the oppressed and struggling matrilineal forces of Kingston's life. For Kingston establishes the true fullness of the Chinese woman. The oppressed wife/mother/slave image constellates at least in the stronger woman the opposite aspect of womanhood, so powerfully embodied in Brave Orchid—the Amazon, Athena, even the paralyzing power of the Medusa. The full tale of her family women is found in their inner myths as well as in the hideous sequence of her No-Name aunt.

In connecting this autobiography to the metaphysical dimensions of Hellman's and Mead's, it is important to remember that the central metaphysical vision in the book is worked toward through the power of the Amazon archetype. The goddess Athena is sometimes considered an embodiment of the Amazon archetype; she is possessed of much wisdom and insight, which, of course, carries over to the Sophia archetype. Jung postulated at the end of his life that all the archetypes blend into one another like the color spectrum, and the feminine archetypes do often seem to lead almost imperceptibly into one another. This is why, lived out as fully as possible, intra- and extra-psychically, different feminine archetypes will often lead to the same kind of wisdom. For Kingston's vision of interconnected, acausal transcendent reality is very much like Mead's new experience as a grandmother or like Anaïs Nin's experience of the Sophia archetype. Anne Sexton too in *The Death Notebooks* finds her most affirmative images through her foothold in the solid bedrock of matrilinearism. Angelou's partial affirmation of self comes from Momma, but she falls far short of the metaphysical matrilinearism of the other three authors, probably because she confronts her devouring actual mother only through her brother. Thus rootedness in matrilinearism seems to underlie a sense of meaning and connections in the cosmos. Again we return to Jung's insights on the Eleusinian rites, perhaps among the most brilliant analyses of his career:

> It is immediately clear to the psychologist what cathartic and at the same time rejuvenating effects must flow from the Demeter cult into the feminine psyche, and what a lack of psychic hygiene characterizes our culture, which no longer knows the kind of wholesome experience afforded by Eleusinian emotions. . . . Demeter and Kore, mother and daughter, extend the feminine consciousness both upwards and downwards. They add an "older and younger," "stronger and weaker" dimension to it and widen out the narrowly limited conscious mind bound in space and time, giving it intimations of a greater and more comprehensive personality which has a share in the eternal course of things.[22]

To men as well as women, participation in the Mysteries "offered a guarantee of life without fear of death, of confidence in the face of death."[23] In other words, the symbol of matrilineal ongoingness symbolizes hope for immortality, the continuity of the individual life. Men obviously stand apart in this mother/daughter duality although they clearly respond to the image. It is the privilege of women to present the image and to embody the consciousness toward which the image strives. The energy with which women autobiographers are analyzing and establishing their matrilineal roots seems the clearest and perhaps most publicly accessible demonstration of this force, now emerging, becoming articulate once more in a period of human history thirsting for spirit and meaning.

12.

Anaïs Nin's *Diary* in Context

LYNN Z. BLOOM and ORLEE HOLDER

No woman is an island, nor is any woman's autobiography or diary. Despite the fact that these forms of personal narrative are "metaphors of the self," or the unique record of a specific individual's life and life-work,[1] each autobiography or diary also has characteristics which identify it with a genre and gender.

Our concern in the following study is with Nin's *Diary* in relation to these larger contexts: how it corresponds to definitions of autobiography in general; whether or not it follows the standard conventions of autobiographical form and technique; and finally, whether or not it exhibits the characteristics of structure and theme which typify the autobiographies of other leading women writers. Our method will be first to examine these larger contexts in themselves and then to turn specifically to a consideration of Nin's work.

Autobiography as a literary genre has several distinguishing characteristics which are usually found in combination. In *Autobiographical Acts*, Elizabeth W. Bruss identifies several of these.[2] First, the autobiographer is the source of both the subject matter and the structure of the text, while the autobiographer's existence is assumed to be publicly verifiable, independent of the text itself. Second, autobiographies purport to be true, whether they treat of private experiences or publicly observable occasions; readers are expected to accept the autobiographer's truth, although they are free to try either to verify or discredit this. Third, autobiographers purport to believe what they assert, even though there may be other ways to interpret the same

206

phenomena. These characteristics also apply to those works which can be subcategorized as diaries.

In addition to these general features, autobiographies also reflect certain conventions with respect to narrative technique. With rare exceptions (notably *The Autobiography of Alice B. Toklas* by Gertrude Stein), autobiographies are written from the first person point of view, in a style more casual and informal than their author's other works. The focus of both autobiographies and diaries is intimate, their authors omniscient. But whereas autobiographers speak softly to an audience, one by one, diarists usually talk to themselves. Consequently, although both forms may be highly allusive, autobiographers usually interpret their esoteric references; diarists do not have to. Everything recounted, however, is either experienced, recollected, or interpreted[3] by the autobiographer, who rarely consults outside sources or offers external verification of the heart's truths or the intellect's perceptions. The reader is expected to take on faith that, and what, the autobiographer has written in good faith. So, too, with diaries.

Finally, autobiographies and diaries may present, among other materials, narrative incidents, vignettes of personal relationships, character sketches, accounts of travels, essays on various topics, dialogues, copies of letters sent or received. In diaries, these are likely to be included under whatever dates they occurred in the writer's life. Autobiographers have more latitude; although their organizational pattern may be chronological like that of diaries, it may also be topical or thematic.

Until recently, most theory which informed autobiographical criticism was based on analyses of works by men. Contemporary women critics, however, have pointed out that there are significant differences between men's and women's autobiographies, particularly in matters of organization. Wayne Shumaker sees "the typical [man's] autobiography as a summing up, a review of the whole life or an important segment of it—the stepping back of a painter to have a look at the finished canvas."[4] It is structured, orderly. In contrast, as Suzanne Juhasz and Estelle Jelinek have observed,[5] women's autobiographies tend to be much less clearly organized, much less synthetic. Therefore, they are more like diaries, honest records of the moment, white-hot, which do not "impose the order of the next day on the record of the previous day."[6]

Virginia Woolf's description of her *Diary* applies to many other women's autobiographies as well: "Something loose knit and yet not slovenly, so elastic that it will embrace anything, solemn, slight or beautiful that comes into my mind."[7] A randomly selected entry from Woolf's *Diary* (pp. 175–76) verifies this assertion. It has one major theme, "'Things have gone wrong, somehow,'" and contains eighteen diverse illustrations of that, edited omissions notwithstanding.

Finally, in her paper, Jelinek also convincingly argued that the themes and content of men's autobiographies "concentrate on the public goal rather than on the private experiences" which are often the focus of diaries and of autobiographies by women; women autobiographers, she observed, "usually write to clarify and affirm their identities rather than to idealize or aggrandize themselves."

An examination of these general observations, as they are explicitly or implicitly reflected in the autobiographies or diaries of Simone de Beauvoir, Hortense Calisher, Sally Carrighar, Colette, Lillian Hellman, Mary McCarthy, Gertrude Stein, and Virginia Woolf,[8] will further help to establish the appropriate context for an assessment of Nin's writing.

With respect first to the matter of diffuse organization (or structural discontinuity, should one prefer), if in quasi-random fashion one looks at the two pages closest to the middle of each of the works in question, and identifies the topics or subtopics thereon, one meets with the following results. McCarthy's *Memories* and Colette's *Earthly Paradise*, each with a two-page spread adhering closely to a single topic or two, provide the only examples of tightly organized autobiographies. The probable explanation for this situation has to do with the fact that many of the topical sections in their works were written and published as separate essays before being assembled into autobiographical format. Colette's editor, furthermore, imposed the structure on *Earthly Paradise*.

In any case, the other female authors employ a rough chronological organization, from the book's beginning to end. Within this, they pursue an infinite variety of topics, most often loosely linked by a casual thematic continuity or the accident of common occurrence in time or place. Much less often does the organization represent a logical argument or a cause and effect sequence. Thus in two pages on Russia in 1942, Hellman discusses three topics and twelve subtopics (*Unfinished Woman*, pp. 122–23). De Beauvoir's two-page analysis of social critic Garric's influence on her covers three main topics and thirteen subtopics (*Memoirs*, pp. 176–77). And Stein's catalog of her Paris friends introduces four major figures and eighteen subtopics, with the all-purpose transition, "It was about this time"—that Roger Fry . . . or Wyndham Lewis . . . or . . . (*Autobiography . . . Toklas*, p. 122). Diffuseness is indeed the common organizational mode.

As for a consideration of how the quest for identity is handled in these works, here one is led to focus upon two common concerns: how these writers see themselves as women; but especially, how these women see themselves as writers, for that is their primary interest.

With the exception of Stein, these women show occasional concern with some of the physical and biological aspects of their womanhood. McCarthy succumbs to the conventions of female biology in feigning menstrual periods to satisfy the expectations of her boarding school teachers, innocent nuns. Most of these autobiographers, especially as young women, delight in looking attractive, even seductive; Hellman amusingly recollects her stint as a "Flaming Youth" flapper (*Unfinished Woman*, pp. 34–39). Some of these women, Carrighar and Woolf, for instance, are depicted as being physically and psychologically fragile, though not because they are female but because they are human.

More pervasively, women autobiographers discuss their familial, social, and professional roles. As daughters, they tended to love and identify with whichever parent was an achiever, or with the one who was the kindest and most understanding of their temperament and aspirations. Often the father was both.[9] Carrighar's father, for instance, provided her with an emotional antidote to her paranoid mother's attempts to murder her, psychologically and literally.

Most of these women are, like achievers in general, oldest or only children. Often they assume a nurturing relationship to their own younger siblings, which generally has symbiotic benefits that may extend into adulthood. De Beauvoir loved her younger sister because "she was my accomplice, my subject, my creature" (*Memoirs*, p. 45).

All of these women have strong attachments to one or more persons who reciprocate their love, though they are usually indifferent to the conventional labels that define such relations or roles: "best friend," "lover," "wife," "mother." Their strength and self-reliance lead them to fulfill their various sex-related roles on their own terms, rather than society's, as they determine their own life-styles, friends, activities. Their independent incomes (sometimes earned from writing) keep them from the traditional female economic dependence on their partners, whom they sometimes support, as Colette, Stein, and Woolf do. And in most cases they offer their intimates substantial emotional nourishment.

Yet in their autobiographies these women consistently understate their emotional commitments to other people (they are intermittently more passionate about their writing), either during the establishment or at the dissolution of once meaningful relationships. Of her first marriage Calisher says, essentially, "My marriage was slowing down; five years later it would come to a stop" (p. 105). Stein says nothing at all about her intimate relationship with Toklas. De Beauvoir's copious volumes, devoted as much to Sartre as to herself, are the exception rather than the rule. Of these women only Calisher and Colette were mothers during the period their autobiographies cover, and even in these accounts their children are conspicuously subordinate to their writing. Colette, for instance, states that she had "a masculine pregnancy" and sees herself as "a writer who gave birth to a child" (pp. 203, 206). Yet irrespective of whatever female roles these autobiographers play, they identify first and foremost as writers, secondarily as women (except for Stein), but scarcely as "women writers," with its sometimes second-class connotations.

So the women whose autobiographies cover their adult lives (all but McCarthy's do) are understandably concerned with their growth and maturation as writers. De Beauvoir says she wrote her multiple volumes to show, through her experiences and perceptions of the world, how she acquired and realized her "vocation as a writer" (*Prime of*

Life, p. 10). Most of these autobiographers explain this process in considerable detail, in the context of the other significant aspects of their lives. As Calisher says, her lifelong fate has been "to be seized by work, and led through it to many loves" (p. 395).

Carrighar describes the long and often painful sequence of trying on several careers for size, including acting and advertising, until she finally found one that fit—nature writing—and was able to earn a living at it. The other women knew from adolescence (if not earlier) that they would write; part of their maturation depended on finding an appropriate medium and ultimately on gaining recognition. As Stein's ventriloquistic persona, Alice B. Toklas, says in *The Autobiography*, "Gertrude Stein was . . . [at the age of forty-six] a little bitter, all her unpublished manuscripts, and no hope of publication or serious recognition" (p. 197).

As they continue to write, these women continue to change and grow. Their autobiographies reveal a concurrent literary and human maturation. Thus in 1919 Woolf observes of her just-completed novel *Night and Day*, "In my own opinion *N&D* is a much more mature and finished and satisfactory book than *The Voyage Out*. . . . I've never enjoyed any writing so much as I did the last half. . . . Is the time coming when I can endure to read my own writing in print without blushing—shivering and wishing to take cover" (pp. 10–11). Woolf also uses her *Diary* to explore and solve problems with her writing. As a diary rather than an autobiography, it can reflect the concerns of the moment: "I think . . . I shall enrich [*To the Lighthouse*] in all sorts of ways; thicken it; give it branches—roots which I do not perceive now" (p. 79).

When the other autobiographers analyze and criticize their own creative writings, as Stein, Calisher, and De Beauvoir do continually, they are writing after the fact of creation has been accomplished. So they look at the works more as finished products rather than as manifestations of the ongoing process which Woolf's *Diary* records, and concentrate on explaining their meaning and significance. Thus De Beauvoir says of *The Ascendancy of the Spirit*: "The construction . . . was defective, being neither a collection of individual stories nor a continuous novel. My didactic and satirical aims were labored far too heavily, and once again I had avoided real self-exposure" (*Prime of Life*, p. 181).

These autobiographers sometimes describe their methods of writing and their creative processes, usually self-generated, sometimes stimulated by other writers. In Colette's case, however, her creativity was originally imposed by the Simon Legree entrepreneur of popular fiction to whom she was married for thirteen years. Monsieur Willy would say, "'You ought to put down what you remember of your board-school days. Don't be shy of the spicy bits. I might make something of it. Money's short'" (p. 90). And Colette would write.

At other times, these authors analyze the genesis and development of particular characters (Colette's Chéri, pp. 245–50); literary techniques (Calisher's shift from the man's to the woman's central consciousness in fictional point of view, pp. 108–09); and whole works: Stein's *The Making of Americans* "had changed from being a history of everybody the family knew and then it became the history of every kind and of every individual human being" (*Autobiography . . . Toklas*, p. 113).

These women often depict with vigor (and sometimes with venom) the literary and professional contexts in which they lived and worked, as Hellman does continually: "The theatre is not a natural world for those who question whatever is meant by glamour" (*Unfinished Woman*, p. 63). Some, such as Woolf, Stein, and De Beauvoir, derive extraordinary stimulation from intellectual coteries. The extent to which the autobiographers delineate these contexts, whether human or geographical, helps to place their work in the relevant literary, cultural, and sometimes political milieux of their times. They are concerned with their literary reputations, even if they disagree with publishers or critics, as Stein did for so long. She has Alice say, somewhat defiantly, "Gertrude Stein realizes that in English literature in her time she is the only one. She has always known it and now she says it. She understands very well the basis of her creation and therefore her advice and criticism is invaluable to all her friends" (*Autobiography . . . Toklas*, p. 77). They are pleased—but not preoccupied—with the money they receive for their literary endeavors, which they interpret as a validation of their artistic vision. Woolf sums up an enviable situa-

tion: "And I have L[eonard] and there are his books; and our life together. And freedom, now, from money paring. And . . . my reviews,
my fame . . . " (p. 224).

These women are writers, quintessentially and predominantly, but
they are also friends, lovers, wives, mothers, leaders of salons. Their
personal writings affirm these multiple identities and blend their private, public, and professional selves. This intermingling contributes to
the diffuseness of their autobiographies, "deep old desks or capacious
hold-alls, in which one flings a mass of odds and ends" (Woolf, p. 13).

In respect to form, then, and in their concern with clarifying and
affirming their identities as women and as writers, the autobiographies
of these women seem more akin to diaries than to autobiographies
written by men, on which some aspects of autobiographical theory
have largely been based. Anaïs Nin's six-volume *Diary*, her lifework,
is both similar to and distinct from the genre created by these women
writers, and its peculiar qualities deserve further examination.

Though Nin's work is actually a hybrid form, alternately functioning
as diary, writer's notebook, and autobiography, in its appearance, form,
and style *The Diary of Anaïs Nin* follows the general conventions of
autobiographical writings (as outlined by Bruss). More importantly,
Nin's *Diary* also illustrates the structural discontinuity and pervasive
thematic concerns which seem to typify women's autobiography in
particular.

As is the case in other autobiographies and diaries, here the author
is the foundation for both subject matter and structure in the volumes.
Although she is often hazy about the appropriate point of view for her
fiction ("In whose consciousness does the whole appear?"), Nin herself
recognizes that "The diary was held together, was given its unity, by
my being at the center" (V, 112). Similarly, in her own *Diary* she
quotes what James Leo Herlihy had written about her in his: "Anaïs
will never be a mistress of artistic forms. This flaw is the price her
novels pay for the perfect integration of art and life achieved in the
diary. Where is the form in the diary? The life" (V, 231).

Nin also presents her material as the truth about herself, her experiences, and her perceptions. Though she often notes that memory
is faulty, she always discovers (particularly while recopying manu-

scripts) that the diary entries captured the truth about what happened or what was experienced. Several times while editing, she considers destroying rather than publishing the diary, to protect "human beings it might wound"; however, she soon realizes that to do so would be to kill "a lifegiving creation, to save a few from the truth" (V, 149).

In like manner, even when presenting apparently incredible, unbelievable events or personalities, Nin never suggests that she is being anything but accurate (if subjective) in her treatment. Frank Baldanza, in an impatient discussion of Nin's fiction, complains that "one can question the quality of sympathy evoked for straitjacket cases. Miss Nin usually presents these persons in a manner that forces the reader to participate directly and wholeheartedly in their fantasies and hallucinations. . . . "[10] The *Diary* also compels the reader to identify with the author's particular truths, opinions, and cast of acquaintances. This is usually accomplished by establishing a value system whereby the reader who is unable to see things the way she does, feels that Nin would place him/her alongside the other bourgeois critics, socialists, bureaucrats, or unimaginative suburbanites she regularly castigates. This creates a problem in the *Diary* because the "true" picture Nin presents of herself (or Henry Miller or Kenneth Patchen or various critics) is often obviously adjusted in accordance with her biases, anxieties, or periodic desires for flattering exaggeration or stylization. Without worrying about verifying the truth concerning people or events, the reader must still worry about verifying the problematic nature of Nin's diary persona.

If Nin's *Diary* exhibits the general characteristics of autobiographical works, many of its techniques are also conventional. In compiling 15,000 manuscript pages, Nin certainly used the diary as an intimate, chronological record of her life. It was her obsession with this personal, daily diary, her "opium" (I, 285), that prompted Rank, Allendy, and others to urge her to abandon it. Its highly personal nature also produced the intense fear Nin experienced even while attempting to solicit potential publishers. In Volume VI she records one of her nightmares in which it seemed that by publishing the diary she was exposing herself "to the maliciousness of the world"; however, Nin finds at the dream's conclusion that "another force, far stronger, was pushing me on—I had faith in the diary. I had put my most natural, most truthful writing in it. I was weary of secrecy, of showing only a small portion of my work" (379).

Thus, while the impulse to continue writing in the diary notebooks was essentially personal, the editing process, marked by Nin's desire to present portions first to a limited and then to an extensive audience, reflects the concerns of an autobiographer cognizant of external readers. From her early attempts to charm back her overly critical father with a diary/letter to him, to her increasing willingness to show entries to friends, associates, prospective publishers, and even potentially hostile critics (Henry Miller, James Leo Herlihy, Maxwell Perkins, and Maxwell Geismar, to name only a few), Nin expanded the focus of the diary beyond herself so as to reach a wider and wider audience. Or, rather, as she states toward the conclusion of Volume VI, the *Diary* showed that "if one goes deeply enough into the personal, one transcends it and reaches beyond the personal" (399).

The conflict between writing for oneself and writing for others, between private woman and public personality, is reflected throughout Nin's work. The autobiographical impulse triumphs, but not effortlessly: "The impulse to give and the impulse to hide fought a mighty battle. . . . I would call it a battle between the woman and the creator. The woman, protective, secretive, placing the needs of others before her own, accustomed to her mysteries which man has feared; and the creator, no longer able to contain her discoveries, her knowledge, her experiences, her lucidities, her compiling of the hidden aspects of people so ardently pursued" (VI, 381).

Like most other autobiographical works, the *Diary* is written in the first person, in marked distinction to Nin's fiction. While often treating similarly intimate material, the fiction is written in the third person (except for rare instances when characters' internal thoughts are conveyed directly within parentheses). Unlike other autobiographical writings, however, Nin's *Diary* is written in a prose style more conventionally structured and formal than that used in her other work. More effort is made to control the language and its effect in the fiction, since Nin attempts to write poetically within the context of novel or short story form. Nevertheless, the *Diary* prose seems more formal because complete sentences and fully developed ideas (coupled with more extensive descriptions) are the rule there, not the exception as they often are in the fiction. The reason for this is clear: in the fiction Nin is frequently concerned with revealing characters' dream-consciousness through intricate patterns of symbolism as well as through what she hoped was a prose equivalent to jazz. Nin felt that her writing, like jazz, could be "the only American expression or manifestation of life rhythms, emotion, the senses and surrealism" and as such could constitute "the future of American writing, its rescue from puritanism and photographic reality" (VI, 75). To do this in the fiction, she pulls out all the stops—using fragments, allusive and metaphorical references, and incantation-like repetition of phrases, clauses, and sentences. Prose in the fiction is linked through often obscure patterns of association rather than through the tenets of grammar, syntax, or the "canons of usage" Baldanza so wants to find there,[11] and to the extent that the *Diary* functions as writer's notebook, repository of honed-down set pieces and character sketches, these same techniques appear in it as well.

However, as Jean Garrigue has noted, essentially Nin's diary is "a way of getting the real thing down, immediately, almost instantaneously, before time had cooled first impressions."[12] This view is supported by Nin's wish that, instead of recalling sometimes painful past events in order to edit the diary, she "could create fiction out of the present, but the present is sacred to me, to be lived, to be passionately absorbed but not transfigured into fiction, to be preserved faithfully in the diary" (V, 33). The formal sentence structure of the *Diary* prose most often conveys ordinary details of everyday life in a conventional manner or captures "the real thing" in complete detail so that later, perhaps, Nin can use the material in the fiction and present it through the patented, lush, stylized, and often fragmented poetic prose for which she is noted.

Nin's volumes also resemble other autobiographical works in their treatment of time and event. The *Diary* is presented as a chronological record, in blocks of time (1931–34; 1934–39; 1939–44; 1944–47; 1947–55; 1955–66), but Nin makes no attempt to indicate more specific dates for entries, and the *Diary* effectively flows from year to year, decade to decade, without any obtrusive preoccupation with dating. Insertion of season and year at various places in the work was done, one assumes, by her editor, Gunther Stuhlmann, albeit with Nin's help.

The diffuse organization that characterizes women's autobiographies is evident in the lack of even topical or thematic organization in Nin's *Diary*. The fact that the same topics and themes recur at random intervals throughout the six volumes is less indicative of any exterior coordinating principle than it is of her ongoing struggle for emotional and creative maturation. Accordingly, time and time again, she announces conclusions—only to withdraw them, to the frustration of the reader not prepared for such diffuseness. For example, because there is no logical progression or the "summing up" found in the more structured autobiographies of some men and women, one gets situations like that in Volume V, where Nin writes: "My feelings have changed about America. . . . I want to help, to teach. . . . I feel reintegrated into the human family. I have overcome the neurosis at last" (253)— only to harp on the same complaints and exhibit the same psychological problems all over again in Volume VI. It is only fair, however, to observe that Nin herself expressed frustration over this aspect of the diary mode. At times she wishes she could wrest more control over the material, impose more order: "I would love to finish the 1955 diary properly. Being also a novelist, I love to wind up with some sort of climax, as in a novel. To point up a climax and make prophecies. I sometimes have the feeling that the diary is not a finished work and needs filling in" (VI, 30).

A kind of order can be imposed upon the *Diary*, however, through an identification of the basic types of material presented and the recurrent themes which appear. In particular, Nin relies upon the following: vignettes of personalities or character sketches of friends and acquaintances, from well-known people such as the Millers, Antonin Artaud, Gore Vidal, or Edmund Wilson to unknowns like the Sierra Madre firemen, Nina Primavera, or "Count Laundromat" (these sketches are often directly incorporated into the fiction, as the last two are in *Collages*); descriptions of countries visited, primarily France and Mexico (often these are also used in the fiction, as the description of Acapulco is in *Seduction of the Minotaur*, and they prefigure the series of travel articles Nin would later do for *Westways* magazine); letters sent to or received from famous people as well as lesser-knowns, with Nin making no discrimination between letters from Miller or Durrell and those from convicts or fans; brief essays or monologues on her life as a woman and an artist.

The pervasive themes Nin presents through these kinds of material closely resemble those found in the women's autobiographies we have already mentioned. Like some of those women, Nin is concerned with her "feminine physique." Indeed, many critics have admonished her for apparent vanity. The famous scene in which she bares her breasts to Dr. Allendy, who labels them "perfectly feminine" (I, 90–91), is usually cited, though others, such as her effort to make herself up even while in the hospital (VI, 181), could also be mentioned. However, at its best, Nin's desire to maintain her looks becomes part of her feminist crusade. This is reflected throughout the *Diary* (see, for instance, VI, 61) and in her 1974 letter to *Ms*. The magazine had recently printed an outdated photo of Nin, who wrote: "I never expected a magazine devoted to women to print such a distorted photograph of me (May 1974). And believe me, it is not a matter of vanity, but a vital matter to other women. I have spent much of my time seeking to help women overcome the fear of aging. I have made myself an example of how one could work, live, act and look at 70. . . ."[13] Poor health, operations, and periods of recuperation are mentioned in the *Diary*, but have significance only because they take her away from her work.

Social, psychological, and professional roles, rather than physical ailments, preoccupy Nin, as they do the other women autobiographers. Nin's father fixation, throughout most of her early and adult life, dominates the *Diary* and has been discussed extensively in most treatments of her work. Nin herself gives scant attention in the *Diary* to her brother, Joaquin (references in Volume V are the exception). She turns her one literal experience with motherhood into a graphic sketch about the stillbirth (I, 338–49; this sketch was later modified and included in the *Under a Glass Bell* collection of short stories). But we must always remember that Nin was restricted by personal requests from including in the published work original entries that she had made concerning certain close relatives and assorted friends. What would seem to have remained intact are her revealing comments about her difficult relationship to her mother, Rosa Culmell-Nin. After her mother's death, Nin remarks:

> It was not the loss of my mother which reawakened my love for her, it was because my mother's disappearance removed the stigma of her judgments, the dangers and guilt brought about by her influence, and left me a simple human being no longer concerned with my own survival, but able to recognize her qualities.
>
> During her life I fought her influence, and she fought in me the kind of women who had displaced her.
>
> When she died I could recognize our similarities. She did not recognize a form of maternity in my protection of the weak and helpless. (V, 182)

Thus, the "mothering instinct" in Nin is directed toward other people's children (Renate Druks' son, Peter, or the Champion children, for instance) or toward men: "Nature connived to keep me a man's woman, and not a mother; not a mother to children but to men" (I, 346). This latter impulse results in the sometimes destructive relationships with Gonzalo, Miller, and others which Nin describes in the *Diary*.

One of Nin's most interesting roles is as psychoanalytic patient, and her experiences, especially with Otto Rank and Inge Bogner, constitute a major part of the *Diary*. Although, as Jane Larkin Crain observes,[14] the psychoanalytic motif is often present in contemporary feminist fiction, except for Carrighar none of the other women we have mentioned exhibits in their autobiographical works Nin's dependence on psychoanalysis. Even this preoccupation, however, takes second place to Nin's most persistent concern: how to function as a writer, particularly in America.

Though Nin decided at a very early age to write, at no time during the thirty-five-year period the *Diary* covers is she able to make a decent living by her work. (Ironically, it is the publication of the *Diary* that changes that situation.) Nin's remark to Bogner, "I have worked very hard, yet I earn so little" (VI, 19), is a constant refrain in all six volumes, and this inability to make money was more than an inconvenience to Nin; it convinced her that there was no audience ready to accept or nurture her creativity.

The chronicle of related defeats in the *Diary* is amazing; publishers fail to support her efforts or botch distribution of her work (III, 259), requests for fellowships are rejected (V, 85), screen adaptations of the novels never come through (see Volume VI remarks on efforts to adapt *A Spy in the House of Love*), and, depending on how vulnerable Nin is to criticism at the time, reviews are seen as either "lukewarm" (V, 157), "scathing" (VI, 279), "malicious" (V, 163), or simply obtuse (see Nin's perception of Diana Trilling, IV, 121–22). More incredible, then, is Nin's ability to continue affirming her own creativity despite decades of neglect by and hostility from the outside world.

What distinguishes Nin's *Diary*, in fact, is that without imposing any artificial structure on the material, she still compels the reader to perceive her life and career as unified, cohesive, and of one fabric. At the conclusion of the *Diary*, one feels Nin has successfully reached a workable balance between the conflicts in her life. She has reconciled the demands on her, by strangers and friends alike, to be alternately mother, wife, lover, benefactress, companion, or advisor. She has started to come to terms with the belief she possesses in her own work and the general public's inability to recognize its significance. And she has discovered, in editing the diary itself for publication, that it rather than the fiction is to be the appropriate format through which to share herself, as woman and as writer. As she observes in the last lines of the *Diary*, it would have been "simpler, shorter, swifter not to seek this deepening perspective to my life and lose myself in the simple [and more masculine?] world of war, hunger, death" (VI, 400), but by taking the lengthier and more complicated route, she has produced instead a fascinating, highly textured work in the mode of quality autobiographical writings by women.

13.

Towards a Theory of Form in Feminist Autobiography: Kate Millett's *Flying* and *Sita*; Maxine Hong Kingston's *The Woman Warrior*

SUZANNE JUHASZ

"So many memoirs are failures," said Virginia Woolf, because "they leave out the person to whom things happened. . . . They say: 'This is what happened'; but they do not say what the person was like to whom it happened."[1]

To know and to reveal "what the person was like" is an especially imperative goal for feminist autobiographers, who seek understanding of women as they "are" and not as they have been defined by a sexist society. Those definitions, as we know, come not only from society's ideology but from its forms in which beliefs are expressed and perpetuated. Autobiography as a literary genre has traditionally been one of those masculine institutions: by and about men, it has established for us all many of our notions about what people are like, what lives are like (especially, what constitutes important and meaningful lives), and how one writes about people and their lives. Consequently, a primary element in expressing the truth of self in women's autobiography is to find verbal forms appropriate to that act. Often, traditional forms won't do. Certainly, they have to be evaluated and no longer automatically adopted. The recent autobiographical writing of Kate Millett (*Flying* and *Sita*) and of Maxine Hong Kingston (*The Woman Warrior: Memoirs of a Girlhood Among Ghosts*) exemplify two kinds of formal experimentation characteristic of recent feminist autobiography. Millett's style develops from the concept of dailiness as a structuring principle for women's lives; Kingston's from the notion that fantasy, the life of the imagination, creates female identity.

Millett's autobiographies exemplify a dominant trend in feminist thought about women's writing. It finds a source and a model in what has historically been not only the major form of autobiographical writing by women but the primary kind of writing that women have done: that private, personal, and secret writing occurring in the diary. No one would question the autobiographical nature of such writing; but its status as "autobiography," which is a formal and public literary genre, has traditionally been denied.

"A long diary will indeed reveal the development of the person of the writer but will do so in a totally different manner from an autobiography," writes a theorist of autobiography, Karl Weintraub. He continues:

> Just as it is a sin against the spirit and nature of chronicle to alter it in the light of subsequent insight, it is a sin against a diary to impose the order of the next day on the record of the previous day. Just as little as you obtain "history" by scissor-and-pasting chronicle to chronicle do you obtain autobiography by stringing up the diurnal record leaves. History and autobiography derive their value from rendering significant portions of the past as interpreted past; for both the incoherent realia of life have been sorted out and those selected have been assigned their fitting place in a fuller pattern of meaning.[2]

Significance, objectivity, distance: these are the major critical criteria for autobiography that dominate the writing of modern critics of the genre. "If autobiography is to become typically . . . a meaningful art form . . . it must accept the responsibility not only of re-imagining a life, but of discovering within the life something greater than the sum total of incidents and observations."[3]

Such criteria are appropriate for most autobiographies that men have written; they also suit most lives that men have lived. "Women are concerned with the context," wrote the psychologist David McClelland in the 1960s about gender differences: "men are forever trying to ignore it for the sake of something they can abstract from it."[4] McClelland's male students, reading Virginia Woolf's *A Room of One's Own*, complained about her "circumstantial, complex, contextual" style; "why can't she get to the point?" they exclaimed (p. 181). This "point" is made, again, in a succinct remark by the woman protagonist of Andrea Newman's novel, *The City Lover*: "He insists that I am obsessed with trivia; I insist that he is weighted down by significance."[5] Thus Estelle Jelinek, in a comparative study of female and male autobiographies, notes the generally chronological and linear style of autobiographies by men, a style that seems to reflect their primary socialization towards achieving the goal of a successful career.[6]

If these general distinctions between male and female style have some foundation in truth, and I think that they do, other generalizations prove applicable and useful in beginning to describe patterns in women's lives and writings.

When you ask a woman, "what happened?", you often get an answer in the style that McClelland has labeled circumstantial, complex, and contextual. You hear a series of "he saids" and "she saids"; you are told what they were wearing, where they were sitting, what they were eating; and slowly the story unrolls. The woman is omitting no detail that she can remember, because all details have to do with her sense of the nature of "what happened." A man, on the other hand, will characteristically summarize: give you the gist, the result, the *point* of the event. I often find myself asking, "but how did that come about? what did you say? what did she say?" He usually hasn't remembered.

In their form, women's lives tend to be like the stories that they tell: they show less a pattern of linear development towards some clear goal than one of repetitive, cumulative, cyclical structure. One thinks of housework or childcare, of domestic life in general. Even if a woman is a professional and conducts her work life largely according to male patterns (since most professions are male dominated and/or controlled), it is generally not easy or usual, because she is a woman, for her to separate out neatly the powerful domestic and personal relationship-oriented strands in her life. Dailiness matters to most women; and dailiness is by definition never a conclusion, always a process.

The classic verbal articulation of dailiness is, of course, the diary. In form the diary moves in independent units of experience in an extended present tense. Most diaries (except those written for the express purpose of recording a specific series of public events) are about the personal life and the life of every day. Crises or climactic events may indeed occur, but they will happen in the diary, as they do in life (until or if they are restructured according to a new perspective of temporal distance, interpreted meaning, acquired objectivity) as daily events. The perspective of the diarist is immersion, not distance. The diary is finished when the pages run out, not when some denouement and conclusion are reached. Lives, too—of men as well as women—have this formal proclivity; it is one of the characteristics of living that people have often used art to try to remedy.[7]

Traditionally, the diary belongs to and stays in the private world. It is personal and thus secret: it comes with a lock and a little gold key. Traditionally, too, women and their lives have belonged to and stayed in that same private world. Hence both the logic, and the conflict, that comes when women begin to validate their kind of lives as meaningful and the diary model as an appropriate form for the expression of their lives; in the process, bringing such lives and such genre out from the private into the public world. The wall between public and private is a strong and a serious one. The threat that has been experienced when women (who belong to the private world) try to enter the public world is real enough; but even more frightening is the act of breaking down the wall itself, of making the private public. This is what is happening when feminist writers like Kate Millett write books like *Flying* and *Sita*, autobiographical writing for which the diary serves as model.

"It had occurred to me," writes Millett in *Flying*, "to treat my own existence as documentary." She continues:

There are many reasons why I shouldn't have. Among them some credit is due to common sense. I did realize my scheme was in bad taste, a divulgence superfluous even before one considers its impropriety. I have a powerful respect for the pleasing, reasonable dishonesty of civilized discretion. One reason I thought it worth doing is because I'm fairly sure had someone once tried to tell me all this I would have been interested. Especially if I had heard it while there was still time. One's impressions during such an experience, the bits of what an observer sees and thinks then—recording them, even if they were my own, might, I hoped, just conceivably have some marginal value. I'm still not sure.[8]

The diary format, the "bit of what an observer sees and thinks then," "one's impressions during an experience," is appropriate to the purpose behind this writing: to offer the personal self, the personal experience to the world in the hopes that it will make a difference to oneself and to others. Later in *Flying*, Millett describes a conversation with Doris Lessing about women's writing. Lessing tells her:

But the most curious thing is that the very passages that once caused me the most anxiety, the moments when I thought no, I cannot put this on paper—are now the passages I'm proud of. That comforts me most out of all I've written. Because through letters and readers I discovered these were the moments when I spoke for other people. So paradoxical. Because at the time they seemed so hopelessly private. . . . (p. 444)

Asked, in one passage of the book, to explain the book that she is writing, Millett answers: "It's myself. It's a record as I go along doing my thing. Like a documentary. . . . It demands I remember everything and be honest" (p. 244). In form, *Flying* is huge and long, crammed with detail, moving forwards and backwards in seeming random through time and space, repeating itself, going over and over the events of Millett's life. "Such writing insists that we abandon the illusion that experience is discrete and isolate or that time is linear, with neatly separated points of reference," writes Annette Kolodny about *Flying*, contrasting its structure to the "formal, distilled narrative we usually get from men."[9] *Flying*, in other words, displays many of the formal characteristics that are associated with private writing; yet it is a published, hence public, document.

Its major thematic concern parallels its structural problem. For in *Flying*, Millett, feminist leader, political activist, author, sculptor, filmmaker, is struggling to establish a relationship between her private and her public selves. Her sense of genuine discrepancy between the two is the force that propels her writing.

> I can't be Kate Millett anymore. It's an object, a thing. A joke at cocktail parties. It's no one. I'm only the fear in my gut. Just let me watch it from the sidelines. Like other women can. Enjoy the luxury of looking on while someone else does it for us. (p. 15)

She is uneasy with a self that excludes the personal from its parameters. "Kate Millett" doesn't seem real to her, because "she" has no meaning other than what is granted to her by the public world. On the other hand, however, Millett worries to her friend, Nell: "My book's got no politics; can't be serious, merely personal. Sniffs of the confessional" (p. 371). The norms of society, well-learned, are difficult to dispel.

The book that Millett writes moves back and forth between public and private spaces, feminist confrontations, and the struggles between lovers, attempting to weave them together by focusing on the personal dimensions of public acts, by affirming the human significance of the private moment. Millett uses *Flying* to create for her reader (who is in the public world) a Kate Millett who is more than object by relentlessly insisting that her personal self be known and taken into account. She is also performing this service for herself, to exorcise her own fears about self-meaning, self-worth. When *Flying* is over, all 678 pages of it, I think that it has succeeded at this task. The sheer accumulation of detail—detail that is sometimes profound, sometimes trivial, sometimes thrilling, sometimes dull, sometimes insightful, sometimes redundant—establishes a world characterized by its dailiness, and a person living in that world. Immersed entirely in that life, the reader finishes with a sense of knowing who Kate Millett is.

Sita, the next installment of Millett's autobiography, published two years after *Flying*, becomes a total rejection of the public self. It records, with the same painstaking (and painful) attention to the detail of the daily that characterized the first volume, Millett's addiction to a dying love affair. The major symptom of her disease—or proof of her love (in *Sita* these are one and the same)—is the fact that she cannot define herself in any way by her public self, "Kate Millett"; nor does she want to do so.

> Do I cling and pursue this love because I have really nothing else to do—or am I unable to write because my slavery to this infatuation makes work impossible? The former. No, the latter. The former because you have not finished a book in three years. The latter, because that is the period of time you have known her. [10]

Reviewers literally hate this book. They hate it because it is so personal. "What bothers me is that Millett has been so overcome by self-seriousness that she thinks her personal doings are important to the rest of us," says Sara Sandborn in the *New York Times Book Review*. [11] The underlying assumption here seems to be that "Kate Millett" is interesting or worthy of attention only when she is that public person, that celebrity who does things in the public world. Reviewers hate as well the style that creates this personal quality, that style which we have come to identify with private writing and the private world.

> She conveys absolutely everything, including her (well-founded) doubts about how good a job she's doing. Breakfast, lunch, dinner; it seems that Kate can't bear to leave out a single meaningful detail. After you've been reading for a while, say a week or so, the book starts to take on a certain interest, the kind I remember once finding in a soap opera when I was sick in bed with fever. Will Pia speak to Kate in the kitchen today? Will Sita come home to dinner? (Much hangs on this.) [12]

The sarcastic comparison to the soap opera is a telling one, because it is the dailiness (both literally and figuratively) of that particular "woman's genre," as much as its melodrama, that has exempted it from consideration as art. In the daytime, a female audience takes it seriously; at night, it can only be subject for satire.

Yet another reviewer likens *Sita*'s style to yet another amateur, domestic, and personal form—the home movie. "*Sita* is like an endless home movie, one that repeatedly loops back on itself, showing the same scenes over and over again, never going anywhere."[13] These responses in their very hostility indicate how accurately that style does articulate the world from which it comes: the personal, private world of women.

The major effect of that style is, once again, a sense of immersion. The world of *Sita* is painful, humiliating, anxious, obsessive, also tedious, repetitive, cumulative; it is genuinely depressing, a total downer. One is glad, when the book is over, to be freed from that state and from that state of mind. Yet one has indeed been there in experiencing the book; and "there" is exactly where Millett, too, has been. There is no doubt that she has shared her experience.

Hers it most certainly is. We never get the other side, as one reviewer points out. By why should we? Nor is Millett, in the grip of obsessive love, blessed simultaneously with a high degree of distance, objectivity, and interpretative powers vis-à-vis her situation. So? Our own reading of her text can give us, perhaps, such insight. Again, it is a characteristic of traditional autobiography that the writer possess such perspective on her or his experience; the form of the diary, on the other hand, explicitly denies such distance.

What Millett is self-conscious about in writing *Sita* is the act of writing *Sita*. She begins keeping a notebook about her experience with Sita to "study it, even record, possess it" (p. 60). As she keeps the notebook, she begins to recognize its various and varying functions, and even the ways in which they contradict one another: "just to survive, to fight off panic" (p. 60); "magical transformation of pain into substance, meaning . . . the notebook then, like a shield against all that happens" (p. 137); "the notebook assumes its real aspect, an untidy scribble without meaning or body or direction" (p. 137); "so imperfect. Holes everywhere. Whole passages unwritten, key events never set down. Laziness, inability to record accurately, well, completely" (p. 253); "If you record a day of your life, does the decision to do so change the shape of that day? . . . What do you leave out, what do you falsify? What do you mar by the imposition of a pattern?" (p. 273); "and the more she returns to you, the less you need it [the

notebook]. The notebook was only useful in her absence, a poor substitute" (p. 275). She posits "the disguise of fiction, the defense of it"
(p. 252), the temptation of moving "out of the suspect waters of the
personal, the autobiographical, the experimental—into the safe harbor
of fiction. High art." Her answer: "Not wanting to. Wanting to just go
on and on writing as it happens, keeping a record of time and experience, perception—however imperfect" (p. 253).

Millett recognizes the simultaneous power of words to alter experience and to reveal, release it. Ideally, she is seeking a form for her
words that will as little as possible impose a pattern upon experience
from outside (i.e., her own consciousness of her own consciousness);
seeking a form that will permit whatever pattern is within her experiences, albeit obscured by them, to emerge, to float to the surface that
her book creates. Hence her insistence on documentation, on honesty,
on sheer quantity. Yet she is also aware that her ideal book is forever
unobtainable, since words must always select and shape. So that the
form she chooses gives the *effect* of verisimilitude; that is its fiction.
And to create such an effect, this kind of writing seems to need the
length, the looseness, even the carelessness that we have been taught
are certain signs of bad writing. "It's too long, it's too much, it's too
repetitious," cry the reviewers. Yet try to imagine these books cut and
crafted to some spare design. Would they work, as they do now, to
immerse the reader thoroughly in a daily life?

Finally, there is the companion question of significance; or, was it
worth the telling? "For personal writing to work," says Karen Durbin
in her review, "it must become, finally, impersonal" (p. 81). Earlier,
Durbin says that "for the writing to work, it must transcend." Yet the
two sentences are not automatically parallel: transcendence need not
equal impersonality. We need to remember Lessing's remarks to Millett, that the moments when she spoke most for others were the moments that seemed most hopelessly private. In the Millett of *Sita*, for
example, I recognize myself, and it is an uncomfortable lesson, for it
is a self whom I would prefer not to be. Watching Millett, I understand something of the needlessness of that sort of pain which I, too,
court, and even begin to contemplate some ways in which I might
avoid encountering it. Certainly, Millett's telling transcends self-in-

dulgence, as her personal experience confronts and illuminates my personal experience. There are no doubt many more readers who also share that particular "personal." In the process, the process of sharing the personal by means of a book, she is altering our definitions of the personal by giving it a public dimension.

Through a prose form modeled upon the diary, Millett brings the private life into the public world. Yet there is in recent feminist writing another way: another style, another voice, another attitude towards the nature of the self and the form of its creation. Maxine Hong Kingston's *The Woman Warrior: Memoirs of a Girlhood Among Ghosts*[14] is a collection of short prose pieces—stories, fictions, fantasies—which make an autobiography. This writing believes in the creative, rather than imitative, power of the imagination to construct a self.

"The cliché that women, more consistently than men, turn inward for sustenance seems to mean, in practice, that women have richly defined the ways in which imagination creates possibility: possibility that society denies," writes Patricia Meyer Spacks in her study of prose by women, *The Female Imagination*.[15] Because there is usually a profound discrepancy between the options that society offers to women and the potential that they find within themselves, women frequently have complex inner lives, worlds of fantasy: "her sex entitles her to the indulgence of an inner life" (p. 241). Spacks describes the important relationship between fantasy and society in the characters that women writers have created, as in this analysis of *Middlemarch*:

> Society as a fact of experience and society as a fact of the imagination, then, may play opposite parts in a woman's life. As an imaginative fact, it becomes an enlarging force, drawing the woman to understand grand and hidden possibilities of her traditional activities, making her richly conscious of ways she can affect others. As an experimental fact, it limits women, restricting their possibilities of action. For men, in *Middlemarch*, different patterns shape themselves. "Society," in their experience, limits them relatively little, in comparison with women (even foolish Mr. Brooke can present himself as a political candidate—though his personal limitations eventuate in his harsh rejection by the community), permits them much. But a curi-

ous constriction of the imagination seems to result. Men—Fred, Causabon, Lydgate—imagine personal accomplishment, public recognition, their fantasized contributions to the world important mainly as means to recognition. Encouraged in simple forms of egotism, they do not develop beyond them. Women, required to make heroic efforts to surmount the temptation to indulge in passive compliance with the power it offers (the power of Rosamond and, in more benign form, Celia), grow more surely than men; but society, finally, cuts them off from full expression of the meaning of their growth. (p. 239)

She also discusses that relationship between the women writers and their own lives, concluding that writing, for women, seems to have represented the only viable possibility for freedom: "women dominate their own experience by imagining it, giving it form, writing about it" (p. 322).

Spacks is pointing to another form of the private that constitutes the reality which women experience; not the domestic life, the world that Millett tries to validate, but the inner life of the imagination, which is also "real." It is the urge to legitimize the truth of the imagination, especially because it is so often in conflict with the truth of society, that informs Kingston's book. For her, as Spacks suggests, writing—words—emerges as the only means of freedom; here is a particularly severe and complex fight. *The Woman Warrior* is about trying to be an American, when you are the child of Chinese emigrants; trying to be a woman, when you have been taught that men are all that matter; trying to be a writer, when you have been afraid to speak out loud at all.

Because *The Woman Warrior* asserts the power of the imagination, it is a book of stories. In Chinese culture the crucial phrase is a verb, "to talk-story," for the stories that Kingston's mother constantly told to her were her own primary means of piecing together a sense of reality.

> Whenever she had to warn us about life, my mother told stories that ran like this one, a story to grow up on. She tested our strength to establish realities. Those in the emigrant generations who could not reassert brute survival died young and far from home. Those of us in the first American generations had to figure out how the invisible world the emigrants built around our childhoods fit in solid America.

> The emigrants confused the gods by diverting their curses, misleading them with crooked streets and false names. They must try to confuse their offspring as well, who, I suppose, threaten them in similar ways—always trying to get things straight, always trying to name the unspeakable. The Chinese I know hide their names; sojourners take new names when their lives change and guard their real names with silence. (p. 5)

The stories that she herself tells are not about "characters" with herself as "author": Kingston and her heroes share identities. As she defines them—an aunt in China who could never be spoken of because she had committed adultery, borne an illegitimate child, and killed herself and the baby; her mother, who was a doctor and a wise shaman in China, and a laundress in America; even a fabulous woman warrior who conquers all of China to avenge her village—they define her, the shy, bright little girl, who learned early that "there's no profit in raising girls. Better to raise geese than girls" (p. 46) and also that "the ideographs for *revenge* are 'report a crime' and 'report to five families'"; that "the reporting is the vengeance" (p. 53).

For example, in the first story, "No Name Woman," Kingston brings into being her aunt, dead and hitherto unacknowledged. "'You must not tell anyone,' my mother said, 'what I am about to tell you. In China your father had a sister who killed herself. She jumped into the family well. We say that your father has all brothers because it is as if she had never been born'" (p. 3).

Kingston postulates how her aunt might have become a prodigal, trying various possibilities.

> My aunt could not have been the lone romantic who gave up everything for sex. Women in the old China did not choose. Some man had commanded her to lie with him and be his secret evil. I wonder whether he masked himself when he joined the raid on her family. (p. 5)

> But perhaps my aunt, my forerunner, caught in a slow life, let dreams grow and fade and after some months or years went towards what persisted. Fear at the enormities of the forbidden kept her desires delicate, wire and bone. She looked at a man because she liked the question-mark line of a long torso curving at the shoulder and

straight at the hip. For warm eyes or a soft voice or a slow walk—
that's all—a few hairs, a line, a brightness, a sound, a pace, she gave
up family. (p. 8)

In exquisite prose—such care taken with words because they carry the
responsibility to probe and provide contours of the truth—a portrait
of her aunt emerges. "Imagining her free with sex doesn't fit, though.
I don't know any women like that, or men either. Unless I see her life
branching into mine, she gives me no ancestral help" (p. 8).

The perspective is both contemporary and feminist, and still Kingston keeps taut the threads between the two women—lines of family,
race, gender—so that she might come to know herself. The fact of
being at once Chinese and not-Chinese is the center around which all
other issues of identity cluster. Chinese in America, struggling to
maintain their sense of self, call Americans "ghosts," seeing America
as a spirit-world, not real, in which they exist. But for the child of
Chinese parents, born in America, the Chinese and China are equally
ghost-like: both a dead presence yet alive and a heritage from the
dead.

My aunt haunts me—her ghost drawn to me because now, after fifty
years of neglect, I alone devote pages of prose to her, though not
origamied into houses and clothes. . . . The Chinese are always very
frightened of the drowned one, whose weeping ghost, wet hair hanging and skin bloated, waits silently by the water to pull down a substitute. (p. 16)

The book's most powerful story supplies its title: in "White Tigers"
Kingston imagines herself as a hero, a swordswoman, a woman warrior. From her mother she had learned the chant of Fa Mu Lan, who
fought gloriously and returned alive from war to settle in the village.
"I had forgotten this chant that was once mine, given to me by my
mother, who may not have known its power to remind. She said I
would grow up a wife and a slave, but she taught me the song of the
warrior woman, Fa Mu Lan. I would have to grow up a warrior
woman" (p. 20).

"White Tigers" moves from the subjunctive ("The call would come from a bird that flew over our roof" [p. 20]) into the indicative ("The door opened, and an old man and an old woman came out carrying bowls of rice and soap and a leafy branch of peaches" [p. 21]), from "as if" to "is," to develop a myth of the woman warrior, whose identity negates either of those words, "woman" and "warrior," in favor of the other, even as it does not find them mutually exclusive. A contemporary American feminist perspective unites with a traditional Chinese story to define the possible and potential connection between power and femaleness.

Kingston tells of herself as a little girl in China, leaving her village to be raised in the mountains by an old couple, who teach a magic that means control of mind, spirit, and, consequently, body. When she is ready, "when I could point at the sky and make a sword appear, a silver bolt in the sunlight, and control its slashing with my mind" (p. 33), she returns to her village to lead an army out and avenge the wrongs that have been perpetrated against her people. Her parents "carve revenge" on her back: burning words into her skin, a list of their quarrels, oaths, and names. (Her back is a story.) Her army conquers everywhere, to the emperor himself, and she inaugurates a peasant to begin the new order.

During her years as leader, she marries (a childhood friend now grown, who had searched to find her again) and conceives a child.

> Now when I was naked, I was a strange human being indeed—words carved on my back and the baby large in front.
> I hid from battle only once, when I gave birth to our baby. In dark and silver dreams I had seen him falling from the sky, each night closer to the earth, his soul a star. Just before labor began, the last star rays sank into my belly. My husband would talk to me and not go, though I said for him to return to the battlefield. He caught the baby, a boy, and put it on my breast. (p. 40)

At last she encounters the baron who had drafted her brother. She tells him that she is a female avenger, who wants his life in payment for his crimes against her village. When he denies them, she rips off her shirt to show him her back. "'You are responsible for this.' When

I saw his startled eyes at my breasts, I slashed him across the face and on the second stroke cut off his head" (p. 44).

The telling of the myth is juxtaposed against a second story, that of her childhood in America (society's self as against her imagination's self), in which Kingston describes her desire to be a woman warrior.

> My American life has been such a disappointment. "I got straight A's Mama." "Let me tell you a true story about a girl who saved her village." I could not figure out what was my village. (p. 45)

> "Bad girl," my mother yelled, and sometimes that made me gloat rather than cry. Isn't a bad girl almost a boy? (p. 47)

The complex ambiguity involved in trying to bring the two selves into accord becomes poignantly apparent.

> Once I got outside the house, what bird might call me; on what horse could I ride away? Marriage and childbirth strengthen the swordsman, who is not a maid like Joan of Arc. Do the women's work; then do more work, which will become ours too. No husband of mine will say, "I could have been a drummer, but I had to think about the wife and kids. You know how it is." Nobody supports me at the expense of his own adventure. Then I get bitter: no one supports me; I am not loved enough to be supported. That I am not a burden has to compensate for the sad envy where I look at women loved enough to be supported. Even now China wraps double binds around my feet. (p. 48)

But the book arrives at an answer: it proposes the writer as woman warrior, and in doing so defines both the specific autobiographer of this memoir and, I think, the task of the woman autobiographer in our time.

> The swordswoman and I are not so dissimilar. May my people understand the resemblance soon so that I can return to them. What we have in common are the words at our backs. The ideographs for *revenge* are "report a crime" and "report to five families." The reporting is the vengeance—not the beheading, not the gutting, but

the words. And I have so many words—"chink" words and "gook" words too—that they do not fit on my skin. (p. 53)

It is through words—through finding them, forming them, saying them aloud, *in public*—that Kingston reaches selfhood. In "A Song for a Barbarian Reed Pipe" she describes the "dumbness—a shame—" that "still cracks my voice in two, even when I want to say hello casually, or ask an easy question in front of the check-out counter, or ask directions of a bus driver" (p. 165). The movement into public song has been literal as well as symbolic. Hence, I believe, the formal perfection of her work: its precise lyricism, its control, its sheer poetry. That the stories achieve this, in English, makes a formal statement equivalent to her theme. Unlike Millett, who equates a traditional literary style with the patriarchy and with sexism, she does not seek a form that sabotages the tradition. Kingston is the daughter of Chinese emigrants. Writing in English and doing it well is for her an issue related to self-identity, an issue, of course, not relevant to Millett's life and work. Unlike Millett's autobiographies, Kingston's book has been applauded by reviewers; it received the National Book Critics' Circle Award in 1976. Its style, as correct as it is exquisite, seems to make acceptable to literary people the sophisticated criticism in its themes. Or perhaps its acceptance comes from the fact that the source of strength for Kingston's creation of self is the mind, a place which most people find neither powerful nor threatening because they think it unreal. The private world that Millett exposes, on the other hand, with her ragged prose, is obviously very threatening. It does represent "reality."

Both Millett and Kingston depend upon the power of language to effect their common goal, that of making the self public—of defining it and creating it through and in this process—but they find the spaces in which that self resides and grows to be different. For Millett, it is from a private but external world, the world of daily and domestic objects and actions, that authenticity derives. She seeks forms that will corner this truth: trying to name enough of the daily world to bring it into linguistic being. Into the book. She is continually frustrated. "I haven't shown enough, said enough," she cries, but goes on trying, aware, as well, that this very stance is the artifice of her form—that she stylizes the look of no style. Kingston, on the other hand, creates a careful, highly polished stylistic surface in order to give form to a world that is invisible, the imagination, wherein dwells the reality that shapes existence. Kingston's approach makes creating, rather than recording, the significant autobiographical act.

Both concepts of the nature of self, experience, and truth correspond to versions of reality that are characteristically, if not uniquely, female. Because women's lives are traditionally private lives, Millett uses the model of the diary, the classic form for private writing. The diary provides the sense of factualness (of the documentary, of nonfiction), the sense of the personal, the sense of process, the sense of dailiness, the sense of immersion rather than conclusion or analysis or patterning, that she requires for autobiography. Because women also live, traditionally, another kind of private life, an inner life of the imagination that has special significance for them due to the outright conflict between societal possibility and imaginative possibility, Kingston makes autobiography from fiction, from fantasy, from forms that have conventionally belonged to the novel (that form at which women writers, when they have been at all professional, have excelled). In neither of these modes of autobiography do the criteria of distance, objectivity, and significance, norms characteristic of autobiographies by men or works modeled upon them, apply. In order to say "what the person was like to whom it happened," to quote Virginia Woolf again, feminist writers are expanding the possibilities of formal autobiography.

14.

The Lady's Not for Spurning:
Kate Millett and the Critics

ANNETTE KOLODNY

Kate Millett's *Flying* was not kindly received by the reviewers when it appeared in 1974. Although one might be inclined to dismiss René Kuhn Bryant's attack, which appeared in the *National Review*, as motivated by her politics and by her overt hostility towards both Millett and Gay Liberation, nevertheless, her description of *Flying* as only "an endless outpouring of shallow, witless comment" repeated the sentiments of many a more sympathetic reviewer, as did her distaste for the way in which the book documented its subject "minute by remorseless minute, if not second by interminable second." Muriel Haynes, writing in the *New Republic*, for example, made much the same observation when she called the book "a leviathan . . . that demands of the reader an analyst's endurance." But the most surprising response was undoubtedly Elinor Langer's "Forum" article, in *Ms.*, which dismissed the book on the grounds that "confession is not disciplined autobiography."[1]

Responses like these—all by female reviewers—belie the currently fashionable notion that women will naturally be receptive or sympathetic to another woman's writing. Supporting that notion, of course, is the assumption that women share certain rather specific areas of experience which men and women do not (as a result both of biological and cultural factors), and that they will therefore automatically recognize and understand the content of another woman's work. Yet *content*

238

in these reviews never really seemed to be the issue. Bryant objected to the book's detailed all-inclusiveness as "inchoate when it is not incoherent," and Langer rejected a narrative format in which "free association has supplanted thought." For Muriel Haynes, the *form* was unfinished, representing only an "assemblage of raw materials."[2]

Typical as they are of the many other critical responses to greet *Flying*, these remarks suggest that while women may well be desirous of greeting and encouraging the recently increasing outpouring of women's writing, they are, in reality, no better able to deal with some of the new and different forms that writing is taking than is the more traditional male reviewing establishment. Nor is it difficult to understand why. Kate Millett obliquely addressed the point in her response to Langer's article. Declaring "the shame is over," and insisting that, henceforth, it would no longer be possible to constrain or constrict the kind of information incorporated into women's writing, she was suggesting, if only by implication, that women might well begin to produce books with contents we have not previously seen before and, as a result, that such contents might themselves demand forms or evolve into artifacts we are hard put to label.[3] Millett herself claimed to have written "not quite an autobiography,"[4] and responded to critics by insisting that her book "refuses and eludes any literary category, just as it was meant to."[5]

Muriel Haynes, perhaps, most clearly put her finger on the problem when she insisted that the "assemblage of raw materials" presently comprising the text "*might* have been transmuted to literature" (italics mine) had Millett only been capable "of 'that particular detachment' esteemed by Henry James."[6] It is a prescription that comes not only out of Henry James, of course, but out of the entire accepted canon of Western autobiographical writing—a canon, for the most part, of male manufacture. The three eighteenth-century Englishwomen who published their "amorous confessions" and thereby pushed formal autobiography in the direction of acknowledging and expressing "the feelings" are generally forgotten, their writings rarely enough read, let alone taught.[7] It is only with the discoveries, rediscoveries, and reprintings of the last few years, in fact, that Agnes Smedley's autobiographical novel, *Daughter of Earth,* or Anaïs Nin's diaries have been made widely available; and only now do Susannah Moody's journals begin to appear on course lists, along with Elizabeth Cady Stanton's *Eighty Years and More.*

Until just recently, then, the standard studies of autobiography have offered us a genre—spanning St. Augustine and Peter Abelard through Rousseau and Goethe in Europe, or homey Ben Franklin through Henry Adams and Lincoln Steffens in the United States—in which successive generations of male writers have been able to refine and define their lives according to variously accepted norms of importance, personal and/or cultural. Omissions and deletions have constituted the very art of the form, resulting, as William L. Howarth argues, in a highly self-conscious and intentional "self-portrait—one far different from [the] original model, resembling life but actually composed and framed as an artful invention."[8] "Life, then, thus truncated, simplified, compressed, and cleaned of distracting excrescences," according to Wayne Shumaker, another student of the form, has traditionally provided "the autobiographical subject."[9]

Since the publication of Millett's *Sexual Politics* in 1970 and, shortly thereafter, Germaine Greer's *The Female Eunuch,* women have come more and more to protest the fact that they themselves appear to be "an artful invention"—in most recent years, having been defined, framed, restricted, and simplified (for their own purposes) by everyone from Norman Mailer to Madison Avenue advertising executives. It would, then, be reasonable to expect that when a woman who had herself been a leader in this protest decided to set down her own life's story, she might well disavow, or at least alter, the male tradition. A woman who devoted her Ph.D. thesis to the study of the inadequate and inauthentic presentation of women in literature would hardly be satisfied with presenting her own life as that "literary simplification of an extremely complex reality" which Wayne Shumaker summarizes as the heritage of male autobiography.[10] Indeed, it is the very complexity of their reality that women today are trying so desperately to map. Moreover, the fine distinctions between public and private, or trivial and important, which had served as guides for the male autobiographer have never really been available to women. Traditionally taught that what was "important" for them lay wholly in the private sphere, having no public consequence, women internalized a picture of themselves that itself precluded the kind of self-attention which might generate autobiography.

With purposes very different from that of the male autobiographer, then, intent upon collecting *all* the "tidbits of thought, memory, grasshopper trivia" (p. 515), and without access to any significant countertradition of female autobiography from which to learn, Millett produced a text which in no way resembles that disengaged, self-critical, self-distanced, and self-scrutinizing brand of autobiography we have been taught to read and critics have come to expect. But then any demand that women write the same kind of formal, distilled narrative we usually get from men implies a belief that women share the same kind of reality as men; clearly, this is not the case. All of which brings into question not only the way in which most critical reviewing is practiced, but the theoretical formulae upon which that practice is based. Treated, however, as an ongoing reading experience, rather than measured against a procrustean bed of received expectations to which it was never intended to conform, *Flying* reveals its own internal organizing principles, as it explores the many-layered associative intertwinings of consciousness, memory, and image.

Although the structuring chronology of *Flying* covers roughly the eighteen months following the publication and success of *Sexual Politics*, that time frame is stretched—through flashback, flashforward, and free association—to encompass virtually her entire life. In the first chapter, appropriately entitled "Fugue State," Millett introduces us to many of the thematic motifs and narrative threads which, as the book continues, will be repeated, expanded, and explored in a variety of contexts. In what are almost tiny film clips of association and reference, we learn that she is about to return to the United States after five weeks in London (p. 3); that she has been involved in making a film (p. 4); that she is struggling to write still another book—but that it isn't coming along, and that, partly as a result of this, partly as a result of other (as yet unnamed) things, she fears going "over the ledge before winter's out" (p. 4). There are flashbacks and anxious anticipations: memories "from the Connecticut summer days when they sold the first copies of *Sex Pol*" (p. 5), and anxiety at meeting those who will greet her at the end of the flight, at Kennedy airport (p. 7).

Through all the apparent confusion of names and places, the purposefully confused time sequences, and the jumbled chronology of events and feelings, the reader desperately searches for some kind of organizing principle or some thread of continuity by which to negotiate what Millett herself calls "a bridge between the voice talking in my head and prose as I'd known it." If it is indeed to prove what she promises—a "documentary" of her existence (p. 81)—then the book must offer the reader some cohering picture to which all the disparate images can be related. Will the narrative concentrate on love relationships, we wonder, or on the story of love's demise? Certainly, the many references to Celia in the opening pages hold out this possibility—as do those to Vita, and JayCee, and Fumio. Or will this be a documentary on movie-making, as is strongly suggested by the many references to her work on a film, and by the statement, "Already the movie has made me better. Now I have finished something" (p. 7)? Or, perhaps, these pages are to document a crack-up or derangement, as Millett shares with us her growing sense of separation from "all the normal people" (p. 6). Or, just as plausible, we might anticipate a psychological narrative of identity crisis, the rejection of fame and spotlight by a Kate Millett who wishes to "be someone else now. Not the one who wrote that goddam book" (p. 7). Each time such a possibility is held out, however, it is immediately denied, as the narrative proceeds to other concerns and other times. As a result, the reader repeatedly experiences loss, confusion, and disjunction, as all attempts at ordering are thwarted again and again; after five or six pages of this, she would quite reasonably admit to a growing nervous anxiety that she is not understanding what is before her.

By page 7, then, the reader is primed and ready for that coherent "something remembered from childhood," an episode which at once validates and explains her reading anxiety by giving thematic expression to what, until this point, had been a repeated stylistic device. Simultaneously, this episode blares forth, in the sharpest possible relief, several of the central thematic motifs whose fuguelike variations will permeate the pages to follow. For, the story remembered from childhood, the story of a little girl sexually attacked by a strange man in a strange car in the middle of a snowstorm, is a story of multiple and simultaneous experiences of loss, all of them happening over and over again in the eternal now of memory impinging upon present experience.

In what is perhaps one of the best and most vividly sustained sequences in the book, Millett shares with us the child's growing terror, her denial, and, finally, her anguished admission that, "This is real now. It's danger" (p. 9). Reliving every detail through a child's present-tense language, we, as readers, bolt with the girl running for safety, "running with the air blue in the snow," only to be shattered with the child's climactic discovery: "I have lost it." At first, pausing with the period break, the reader assumes that what has been lost is the girl's virginity—a quite natural assumption following the detailed description of attempted sexual assault. The following sentence, however, identifies the loss: "My turtle. The brace to keep my teeth straight." Instead of trivializing the situation or allowing us some momentary relief from tension, however, the sentences relentlessly insist that *all* loss, to a child, is serious: "I have lost twenty-five dollars. . . . Mother said they could never afford to buy another" (p. 9). In quick succession, then, the loss of the brace is compounded by a loss of health (as she gets pneumonia), the loss of a father (the parents separate), the threatened loss of family ties ("Will I still get to see Aunt Christina now?"), and the even more threatening loss of Nancy, "my best friend": "If I have to drop out of Derham [private parochial school] 'cause it costs money I can't ever see Nancy again" (p. 10).

Only in the final paragraph of the sequence is the worst admitted: the loss of innocence that we'd feared all along. But even here, as she lies in bed thinking, recovering from pneumonia, multiple experiences get compounded—the memory of the man in the car, the strange responses of others to her love for Nancy, the pubescent sexual awakening, and all the weighty baggage of a Catholic upbringing:

> Lying in bed sick I think about the man. The blue car. I touch myself and my head gets hot. It's a sin. A sin to have gotten in his car. I

have been touched by him. Did I lose my virginity? What does it mean really? Not a sin if I escaped. Even if I ran away, was it a sin? But a sin to lose the turtle. Sometimes I want him back. He could put the thing in me. Then I would know what it is. If he put it in me I would stop itching. . . . Think about the basketball game at St. Thomas. Be one tonight, it's Friday. . . . Nancy'll be there too. Ashamed again, thinking that. 'Cause people act funny about us when we say we're in love. Before Thanksgiving vacation we told the seniors and they laughed, kind of scary, like when you've made a mistake. The nun heard and she got mad. Sally's boyfriend heard us talking on the phone and said a magic word to Mother. Lesbian. It takes so long to get well. Already it's eight weeks. Doctor Flannigan says six more. There's nothing to do but remember. Over and over. This secret. The blue Mercury. His face sort of blurry. The terrible purple thing. Then running. It keeps happening. If I yell no one hears me, the house is empty. Will he find out where I live, get me, tell on me? Face hot, sweating, is it the fever? I wonder. It's a sin and thinking is a sin. How do I stop it from happening? (pp. 10–11)

Such writing insists that we abandon the illusion that experience is discrete and isolate or that time is linear, with neatly separated points of reference. The linear chronology we had been trying to piece together since the opening pages, and our consequent anxiety over our inability to find order in all that apparent chaos of narrative, now all coheres around a recognition that experience is itself chaotic; and that, through every page that follows as through every one we have so far read, Millett will explore (among other things) the recurrent confusions and consequent flights from danger, as well as that continuing sense of loss, which is at once one loss and all losses, that makes up the daily reality of vulnerable little girls in our society.

So, in spite of the fact that her text makes no pretense to artistic purpose or to conscious artistic structure, the opening "Fugue State" actually functions as such, by introducing not only the first major example of the flying imagery (the flight from danger) and some of the major stylistic devices to be employed throughout, but, more important, by delineating, if only in piecemeal fashion, the many-layered and interrelated thematic motifs which will flesh out and adumbrate the book's action or story line. These include the concern for personal and cultural change—the seeking of a *vita nuova*, as it were; the difficulty of understanding or making sense of personal experience; the involvement with various love-partners; the need to find more suitable parent figures and to make peace with an unaccepting, and even rejecting, personal mother and father; and, finally, that which seems to have been the book's motivation as well as its most compelling theme, "a quietly desperate search for self" (p. 83). For, if this book is *about* anything, it is about that. Following the publication of *Sexual Politics*, she explains, "I suddenly acquired significance for others just as I ceased to hold any for myself. Filed and catalogued as a phenomenon, whatever purpose I might hold for myself now evaded me. As it was no longer mine, my life grew loathsome." Determined that "steps had to be taken," she embarked on this combination confession, memoir, and autobiography, hopeful that it would move her closer "towards recovering my being" (pp. 82–83).

What we might call the "story" of that recovery involves the various activities of the year and a half following *Sexual Politics'* success: her various speaking engagements and love affairs, the trip to London to edit her film, the film's debut in New York, and repeated shuttles between the Bowery, Connecticut, her farm, and, finally, Provincetown. But while a reader may feel compelled to sift some kind of sequential ordering out of the myriad trips and relationships, the narrative itself is not organized either by chronology or sequence; episodes from the past are recalled with similar frequency in each of the book's first four parts. If there is any underlying structural or organizational principle, then, it lies in the repeated elaboration and adumbration of certain key thematic motifs—many of them linked to the "flying" imagery. The overall synchronic effect of this kind of structure further reinforces our sense of what it means to be "wondering . . . always if I am going forward or backward" (p. 299). It is, in short, a structural device by which to project and examine her fear that "inch by inch growing older we become what we came from and left" (p. 523).

By wrenching events out of their original causal or chronological order, relating them by memory and free association to other events that have only private, or even idiosyncratic, associational continuities, Millett allows them to take on new shapes and to suggest significances they might not otherwise have held. Thus, the private iconography of her emotional symbology is revealed, while, at the same time, the otherwise everyday and familiar no longer evades notice by virtue of its very familiarity.[11] To demonstrate this, however, I will be forced to treat some of these thematic motifs as separate and individual; still, it should be remembered from my earlier comments on the childhood memory episode that nothing in this text is presented as isolate or discrete.

The book is divided into five parts: "Vertigo," "The New Life," "Blick. The English Notebook," "Trajectory," and "Landfall"—in that order. Part 1, "Vertigo," moves from the opening "Fugue State" to a whirling presentation of people and events, jumping back and forth between present and various pasts. It incorporates many more shorter sections—vignettes, brief character sketches, memory fragments, etc.—than do any of the following parts, and gives us, also, the impetus for the book's beginning, and provides an appropriate context for the "flying" imagery frame. Opening with Millett en route to the airport, as she leaves London, this section offers us a dizzying recitation of other flights to other places, until they all meld into a confused blur of meaningless motion: "Flying now is flying then, another trip to Podunk, another speech" (p. 21). In contrast, the urge to write the book appears to be, at least in part, an attempt to get at meaningful beginnings and to order what follows. "Starting in the spring last year, just a year ago in New Haven, I slept with a woman for the first time in eight years," she explains. "Starting in the spring. . . . Naomi suggested I begin the book there starting when it all started again" (p. 20). The precision of this one, single, isolate event stands in sharp contrast to her confused memory of "the dark of those speechifying days, arriving in airports, met by some little knot of greeters," and her consequent resort to the, by now, most familiar use of the flying imagery—flight as escape from danger or entrapment: "I escape their anxious attention . . . for the ladies' room and a quick fantasy of jumping through the window to freedom" (p. 93).

The title of Part 2, "The New Life" (an intentional reference to

Dante's *Vita Nuova*), is both serious and ironic, for it invokes the "new life" promised by the women's movement at the same time as it details her frantic attempts to make another kind of "new life" for herself through her love for Celia—a woman who, in a later chapter, will reject her. If any single attitude may be said to pervade this part, it is ambivalence: ambivalence as to her proper role in the making of the film, ambivalence about her own complicated sexuality and its implications, ambivalence about consciousness-raising groups and the problems of individualism and elitism in the women's movement as a whole, and ambivalence about the value or meaning of the Columbia University demonstrations of 1968 (itself another isolated example of stunningly effective writing). What we also see, in this part, is how much the writing of the book is itself another kind of flying, a verbal *rite de passage* into that "new life" she envisions both for herself and for society at large. Forcing her to come to grips with her own ghosts and deepest fears, the very process of writing seems to promise both a way of laying those ghosts to rest forever while, at the same time, initiating her into at least the precarious possibility of being able to "trust paradise. Daedalus never melted," she reminds herself at the end (p. 243).

Thematically and psychologically, Part 3 coheres around the ordered imprinting of meaningful images. Her attempt to help "pattern" Winnie, the brain-damaged child of the friends with whom she stays while in London, and her concern to make a good print of her film, both stand as external projections of her private attempts to discover her own authentic images and "be who I am" (p. 240). Looking at Winnie, she says, "He is art, too, we are creating him" (p. 282); and, later, thinking about herself, she concludes, "And now I must renovate my interior. Winnie helps. And Nell" (p. 346). Nell, Winnie's mother, is teaching Millett how to print and edit her film, acting as a kind of guru and Mother Confessor to her throughout this section.

In order to facilitate the various processes of renovation and "transformation" (p. 293) which she envisions in this section, however, there is the obligatory and almost archetypal descent to the underworld. For the initial fact of arriving at Nell's home in London has meant, not liberation, but entrapment—as the use of the flying imagery makes clear. Winnie's presence is that of "a tyrannical force in the basement. Dominating every moment." As a result, Millett initially sees herself, and Winnie's parents, as a threesome "all . . . caged in this house. I flew in, arriving solitary, free as a bird on my wings. And they talked to me, said they were trapped. And now it's all three of us, the rescuer too is stuck" (p. 303). To get unstuck, the rescuer seeks aid from the powers of the underworld: in this case, a meeting of gay activist groups in a sleazy London basement. Full of literary allusions to all such previous mythic descents, this sequence shows her successfully gathering volunteers to help pattern Winnie, and then concluding: "I have gone to the underworld, through its labyrinths and waiting, its uncertainty. Asked. And received. From my own people" (p. 320).

The arduous journey successfully negotiated, with its final victory of *self*-confirmation, she is now able to liberate the flying imagery from its previous cage and describe herself and Nell ecstatically "taking wing into a scatter shot of movie notions, ways to capture the living present. Preserve the life we know, reinterpret, present in our own terms as women" (p. 310). With the descent to the underworld, change and transformation become associated with the tapping of yet unused sources of power, while, through the flying imagery, they become synonymous with the experience of liberation and unfettered freedom. The previous uses of that imagery—as flight from the present, flight from the past, and flight from danger—are now transformed so as to include flight *towards* something and the idea of flight as freedom.

To what end such flight might direct itself, or what, in specific terms, that newfound sense of freedom might encompass, however, she cannot formulate, explaining to Paul (Winnie's father), "I just care about change. . . . I'm not quite sure what it is or what I can do" (p. 277). But, for all her admitted vagueness, there is a tantalizing playing, in these conversations with Paul, with the idea of several simultaneous interrelated orders of change: "Political and economic structure of course, socialism of course. But more. Change in personal dynamics, in group life and community, in sex roles, in the self released." And, again, as she explains it to Paul, for her, "'the revolution . . . is not necessarily an uprising in the streets or the old business of

seizing power. . . . The revolution is change. Not merely rearrange-
ment, but a deep emotional type of transformation that must also take
place inside us. It's a better way to live'" (p. 330).

Interesting, though perhaps insubstantial, political theory, this concentrated concern for the nature of change and the imprinting of acceptable images leads, almost inevitably, to a far more important explication of related literary theory, exploring just what such thematic
concerns demand of women, particularly, when they are attempted in
narrative form. Purposefully reminding us of Doris Lessing's *Golden
Notebook* in its title—"Blick. The English Notebook"—Part 3 is high-
lighted by a luncheon conversation with Lessing. A telling and central
portion of the book, Lessing's remarks validate precisely what Millett
is attempting in her narrative: that is, the revelation and exposure of
the private, normally unacknowledged portions of women's existence;
and, as such, a profound transformation of the old rules of narrative
discourse.

"'Let me tell you what it [*The Golden Notebook*] meant to me,'"
Millett says to Lessing:

> "In a detail you may find ridiculous. It's the moment your heroine
> shall we say," we smile, "finds herself in a toilet at the outset of her
> period. In St. Paul we call it the curse." We smile again. "And the
> blood is running down her legs while she struggles with toilet paper.
> Kleenex. That sort of thing. In a book! Happens every month of adult
> life to half the population of the globe and no one had ever men-
> tioned it in a book." (p. 357)

Confirming Millett's reading response in her own reply, Lessing both
validates the experiment Millett is attempting in the narrative we are
engaged in reading and, also, reinforces our sense that for women to
explore their private worlds demands of them a willful—and often anxious—breaking of previous codes of silence and a determination to
push aside the accepted boundaries of narrative content. For, as Lessing explains, "'The very passages that once caused me the most
anxiety, the moments when I thought, no, I cannot put this on paper—are now the passages I'm proud of. . . . Through letters and
readers I discovered these were the moments when I spoke for other

people. So paradoxical. Because at the time they seemed so hopelessly private . . . '" (p. 357).

To the literary critic, this is a significant exchange, not simply because change and the nature of self-transformation are what *Flying* is all about, but because it is what *Flying* is doing. It is a point most reviewers, however, seem either to have missed or ignored, assuming that Millett's problem was a neurotic compulsion for public confession, rather than the more serious one of finding an appropriate language by which to describe certain kinds of previously unacknowledged experience. Certainly Millett posed the problem clearly enough when she admitted to Lessing "'feeling so vulnerable, my god, a Lesbian. Sure, an experience of human beings. But not described. Not permitted. It has no traditions. No language. No history of agreed values.' 'But of course people wish to know,'" Lessing countered, "'And you cannot be intimidated into silence. Or the silence is prolonged forever'" (p. 358).

With Part 4, titled "Trajectory," Millett has returned to New York, her film now edited and ready for screening. She pictures herself in this section as a continuously moving body, navigating both emotional and geographic pathways. As the flying imagery is explored and expanded, so, too, is the vocabulary of filmmaking. Driving to the hospital to visit Celia after surgery, for example, she images her present moment and its past associations as movie footage: "My magic side fiddling with the mind's old footage of Celia and New Haven. Cut it in here or use it earlier?" (p. 390). Subdivided into two parts, "Ascent" and "Descent," Part 4 is at least figuratively plotted (and I use that word in both its literary and navigational meanings) by her ebullient anticipation at seeing Celia Tyburn again, followed by the pain and guilt of Celia's abrupt rejection. "Ascent" and "Descent" here, then, mark a flight of the emotions.

While the emotional and sexual involvement with the *person* of Celia may be concluded in this section, however, Millett's involvement with what Celia had represented—that is, the possibility for a "new life"—is not. Continuing the thematic explorations of all the earlier sections, Part 4 includes a series of self-searching questions, a new kind of personal catechism, which ends with the following: "What is your life about? About change, I think lately" (p. 403). The entire section closes with a reversion to moviemaking, to an acknowledgment of the difficulty of becoming "what we want to be. But we are not yet," to a discussion of "the sexual revolution" (p. 461), and, finally, to a summary of Nell (briefly flown in from London) advising Millett on the complexly fragile nature of friendship and love (pp. 463–64). In short, this section is a compilation of the many and varied persons and thematic units we have met before, with nothing lost or abandoned. The point of such inclusions, of course, is that the path of a trajectory is usually plotted as occurring in several simultaneous dimensions at once. The title of Part 4, thereby, connotes its theme, its style, its content, and its structure.

Similarly with the title of Part 5, "Landfall," suggesting a goal sighted, or a journey completed. The shortest of the book's five parts, "Landfall" follows the action of a single summer in Provincetown; in fact, "Provincetown" stands as the subtitle for Part 5, suggesting that town's geographic and symbolic significance as a kind of resting place. In the course of Part 5, Millett flies from Provincetown in order to attend a panel on nonviolence in New York, and then returns to spend an idyllic time with her new lover, Claire. There is a continuing concern, throughout these activities, to accurately record everything for the book now before us. Notebooks and tape recorders intrude upon the days and hours of original living and are then consulted again, during the winter, when Millett has returned to Provincetown, in order to complete the writing, "now remembering then" (p. 524). Throughout, there is an almost novelistic tying-up of loose ends, a recapitulation if not an ending, as Millett muses on almost all the major "characters"—"thinking softly of Celia, whom I will always love," and Fumio, "and Vita," and so on (p. 544). Carefully orchestrated sequences of flying imagery give this section its structural coherence by relating each successive action and activity to its appropriate iconographic representation; theme and story are thus united in and by the imagery.

With the last airplane trip depicted in the book—to attend the conference on nonviolence—the act of flying ceases to represent only the dizzying transportation of her personal frenzy from one place to another; and even though it appears to start out that way, the initial flight from Provincetown, via Boston, to New York actually involves the discovery of a helpful and generous father and a consequent experience of rebirth. Having missed her scheduled flight out of Provincetown, she is aided in securing a private flight by a friendly businessman, a Mr. Van Arsdale, "this new father of mine" (p. 500). She can "rest now," she reassures herself, "Van Arsdale has saved you" (p. 501). At the conference itself she will find Flo Kennedy, "the real mother of us all" (p. 503). This discovery of appropriate parent surrogates nicely coincides with her experience of being "reborn in an airplane"; a new life, she boasts, has been "breached in an aisle over Boston Airport" (p. 501).

By the time she goes back to Provincetown, flying is no longer either escape or escapade; finally, it represents a return—both to Claire and to the book which we are reading. Taking off, out of New York, she exclaims, "The plane lifts with the same uncertainty that lovers know. Yet I knew this morning. . . . Because I know I am going back. Now it is only time until I am with her [Claire]" (p. 515). As the plane's takeoff had served as an appropriate metaphor for the uncertainties of the emotions, so, too, its altitude marks a quality of experience she has enjoyed commanding for herself: "Fly, stay high, living it" (p. 516). The mere "living it" obviously isn't enough, however. With "the plane in air now" (p. 515), its flying (if not her own) assured, she meditates upon the meaning of the book she is trying to write about the life she is trying to live. Just as the flying is a progress from one place to another, so, too, she realizes, the book in her head is an analogous process, striving towards another kind of landfall, "a way of inventing the self. Striving toward one you can live with" (p. 516). With the termination of this particular journey, then, she has reached an unprecedented triumph of acceptance, both of herself and of flying, with all its multivalent associations: "'The flight back was beautiful,'" she announces, "'I love to fly'" (p. 520).

The next important and sustained use of flying imagery again follows a statement of concern over her book—her fear that she "will fail," that she "will not get anyone right in the book" (p. 524). The associative connections of memory provide the perfect correlative for such creative flights and depressions, as she proceeds to recall an afternoon spent flying kites with Claire and Molly. The first two kites don't fly, but "the last kite," "the black one," does indeed take off. And, as it does, Millett appropriates its flight as an emblem of "all my hopes, my self, my future." Almost fearfully, she asks, "Will it fly?" It does—so successfully, in fact, that it snaps its own string, to "go like a meteor for heaven." Like her own erratic fits and starts, however, the kite is one moment headed for "eternity, the wonder of it free," and in the next, "helpless unhooked . . . fall[ing], plung[ing] into the sea, a star broken" (p. 526). Reminiscent of the image of a bird with a broken wing, which anticipates Edna Pontellier's last swim out to sea in Kate Chopin's 1899 novel, *The Awakening*, the kite plunges, clause by clause, inflection dropping (exactly as in the Chopin passage), "into the sea." But, again as in the Chopin novel, the descent is not here experienced as either defeat or loss. As Edna Pontellier felt herself reborn—in some of the most beautiful imagery of that novel—as she swam beyond her power to return, so, too, Millett experiences a kind of death-and-renewal: "For an instant my heart too was with it, my self, until almost by surprise I accept its death" (p. 526).

Alternatively marking and structuring the events of this last section are the image sequences suggestive of death and rebirth. We are asked to picture Saint Joan "in her flames calling out"; and, in the last sentences of the kite-flying episode, we are treated to a description of the corpses of dead squid floating on the water, through which the three women steer their boat. "Landing the boat," Millett continues, "we walk through the dead. The corpse of each squid makes us more alive" (p. 527). The overall effect of this kind of alternation is to make us reconsider and reconstruct much of our earlier reading experience of the book in such a way that we seem to see Millett as a type of the perennial phoenix, forever rising out of the ashes of her own previous deaths and anxieties.

In a halo of light imagery, the exploration of the evocative and expansive qualities of flying continues, culminating in "a crisis of beating wings." She compares "the cries" of her lovemaking with Claire to the sound of "birds filling the room." But the expansiveness of this imagery cannot be contained; it moves out to include the world and joy itself, as Millett sings a brief paean to the world's "beauty, flying as it does" (p. 536). In Provincetown, then, secure in Claire's love, the emotional landfall is reached: "I am sure of her at last" (p. 537). With that comes another kind of renewal, as the old nemesis of Celia is dispelled, and "the new spirit enters" (p. 538).

It goes without saying, of course, that there are many such symbolic "landfalls" in Part 5. The book itself, for example, both literally and figuratively reaches its end. As it does so, the various thematic concerns move toward resolution, while, accompanying these, the flying images undergo their most dramatic and final transformations. Flashbacks occur with decreasing frequency, as Millett attempts a reconciliation with her past, not by reliving it, but by redeeming it—in and through the present.

An episode on the last two pages makes the point clear. It records a moment between a father and another little Katie who, miraculously, lives next door on the beach.

> There is a child next door, a little girl squatting in the dirt, playing alone. Incredible but her name is Katie. She is me then when I look at her. When I was eight Mallory was three and broke my sand castle. I punched her in the stomach. Hard. For a moment she turned blue. My dear little sister bellowing because I had hurt her. Dad spanked me. A violent man then. I screamed. We never broke the circuit. This Katie has a brother and a father who walks out of this house down below me, gray haired, looking like an intellectual on vacation, not very physical fellow. . . . The father takes his son's toy and spins it. A launching rocket. But the thing is unpredictable, the plastic suddenly vicious in the air, explodes, hurling a jagged part at his eye. He is hit. Blood of the cut. He goes into the house and comes out with a handkerchief. It is hard to keep your manly dignity when a child's toy has nearly blinded you while some female in blue glasses is observing you from a balcony. But he has not lost it. Nor his temper. Gentle as his little girl rushes to him, comforting him. (pp. 545–46)

Emotionally participating in the scene, Millett completes her apparently endless search for parent figures, declaring: "Now I have overwhelmed my childhood. Free of its patterns finally" (p. 546). Some internal balance has been restored, as the mind, through the imagination, allows the personal father to be replaced by the felt, albeit vicarious, experience of this gentle, almost archetypally benign and loving father.

But the breaking of the personal pattern, and the subsequent recording of it in these pages, however, has larger resonances for the student of American literature. Self-consciously disengaging herself from the traditional view that women who experiment with their lives are either damned or doomed, Millett rejects both the tradition and its imagery and declares herself done, once and for all, with "this last broken-wing story" (p. 545). Replacing it, instead, as this book closes, is the buoyant imagery of birds in flight:

> Gulls so many of them I try to count them but they split and break
> I cannot place and order them in the sky. Flying in a haze of wings
> noises cries. Chaos and serenity together. (p. 546)

As a closing statement, it is also an apt description of the mind we have come to know so intimately in these pages and an apt imagistic rendering of our experience of coming to grips with that mind. In other words, Millett's sense of what her life feels like to her, and our sense of what it has meant to participate in that life through this narrative, are both, like the gulls splitting and breaking, an experience of "order forming itself and then [being] lost again" (p. 339). In pursuit of order, Millett has lived her life and composed this text; but because her experience could or would not easily accommodate itself to ordering, so, too, her story of that experience, like the failed counting and placing of the gulls, similarly resists order, placement, organization— in short, resists narrative form as we have come to expect it in autobiography. Hence, this narrative ends, not with the serenity of a "chair tilted against a sunny wall,"[12] but with an insistence that, in some lives, if truth be told, chaos is not always reduced to order, but may exist simultaneously with it: "Chaos and serenity together."

Most good critical book reviewing nowadays is practiced on the assumed knowledge of a literary history which itself tacitly accepts a commonly agreed-upon "traditional canon." It is this canon, or tradition, against which anything novel or experimental is distinguished and measured as an innovation. More recently, under the influence of the structuralists, this has been refined into the virtually formulaic dictum that "the essence of every new work of art" demonstrates the "simultaneous preservation of tradition and [a] breaking away from tradition."[13] Unfortunately, this unquestioned assumption of the usefulness of a coherent line of influence leaves critics and reviewers alike at a loss to deal with works that, of necessity, make use of several different cultural backgrounds at once.

As a scholar trained in both the European and American literary inheritances, Millett was obviously able to take advantage of previous epic journeys to the underworld, Dante's *Vita Nuova*, and the narrative experiments of Joyce and Woolf. Such piecemeal pickings from works of other genres, however, hardly constitute the kind of coherent background from the vantage point of which most critics like to view a work, or out of which most male authors are privileged to write. Important in the Millett text, and germane to any full understanding of it, are the recurrent references to women writers and their work, the application of film techniques to language, and the comic-book heroics of Wonder Woman and Mary Marvel. Again, however, this is hardly a coherent tradition specifically relevant to the autobiographical genre itself nor, some would argue, a coherent or satisfying tradition in any sense of the word.

The result is a text which, out of necessity, resorted to daring experimentation and sheer invention—attempting to build a "bridge," as it were, "between the voice talking in [her] head and prose as [she'd previously] known it" (p. 81). Not that the experiment was an unqualified success. In her unwillingness to leave anything out, based on her observation that too much had already been excluded from what has been written by and about women, she gives us not always "the full shape and continuity of experience,"[14] but instead the uncomfortable sense of wading through a "collection of the clutter in [her] mind" (p. 225). The writing is often self-indulgent, the narrative associations too abstruse or too idiosyncratic to be meaningful, and some of the people do indeed come across as only "tin echoes . . . feeble sketches." Little wonder Millett agonized over the book's composition, feared she would never complete it to her satisfaction, and, reluctantly, ended up in "bitter disappointment," admitting "This is not literature" (p. 338).

Not literature in the sense of something that will speak beyond its own time and place, perhaps. But it *was* a necessary literary experiment. In attempting to tell the story of a life in a way it hadn't been told before, and, especially, the story of so unconventional a life as her own, Millett broke many long-standing codes of silence and omission. By "telling certain truths, truths about the media and politics, about psychological and social change as they are lived, about unconventional loves and the struggle for a new ethic," Millett herself realized, "something in the fabric, the old fabric of things, was threatened, was ripped and torn."[15] To deal with such assaults upon "the old fabric of things," our professional reviewing establishment is too little prepared.

To counter that ineptitude, the feminist critic/reviewer must ask her colleagues to accept the various ways in which the moment-to-moment content of a life may shape the form of its narrative, and, further, she must insist upon a serious examination of the resulting text—however odd its form may at first appear, and in spite of any personal misgivings one might have about the details of the life depicted. Moreover, as long as women continue to produce texts which cannot easily be accommodated to our previous notions of form and structure, it will be the special duty of the feminist critic, additionally, to insist upon restoring to the language of critical analysis its sense of reading as an ongoing process. That is, we must restore and reiterate the fact that our experience of a text is not an experience of any kind of whole or totality, as a genre definition would imply, but, instead, a series of feelings, emotions, expectations, responses, questions, revelations— in all, discrete events which, in aggregate, make up not our experience of the book, but the *history* of that experience.[16]

Looking back over our various experiences of reading *Flying*, for example, we see that our involvement in the abbreviated phrasings, present participles, and omitted grammatical subjects of stylistically choppy sentences has been *our* way into sharing the narrator's own broken and discontinuous experience. The narrative's refusal to obey normal rules of sequence and chronology reminds us how all past experience participates in the present. And the sometimes annoying use of flashbacks, together with an idiosyncratic manipulation of free association, articulates her and initiates our awareness of those "eternal patterns we only repeat," while, at the same time, provoking us to share her determination upon "breaking through, insisting we can transcend the welts and scars of youth . . . beat them, escape" (p. 490). The apparently loose or disjointed sentence style, coupled with an analogous associational structure, we see, constitutes not only our recurrent reading experiences of the book, but its major themes, as well.

The constant search for an authentic and appropriate *vita nuova* in these pages, then, is at once a personal and anxiety-filled pursuit of a more satisfying life-style and a difficult search for a narrative form through which to delineate the urgency of that pursuit. In expanding the *content* of autobiographical narrative, revealing things that have not previously found their way into women's prose, Millett was not only a self-styled political revolutionary intent upon "a transvaluation of values," but a conscious artist attempting an alteration "of the very *forms of apprehension*" (p. 360; italics mine). The great male lives, distilled and apprehended through patterns of order and hierarchy, and the popular notions of women, apprehended through images of frail birdlike creatures and comic-book caricatures like Mary Marvel, both demanded rejection. Careening, in these pages, "full tilt from broken wing to superwoman" (p. 356), in the end rejecting and transcending both, Millett at once tries to set up alternate images of flight to depict female experience and, also, holds firm to her perception that an appropriately meaningful pattern by which to order her experience, in fact, is not available to her. What her life did convey, and what we shared with her, was precisely that "assemblage of raw materials" which Muriel Haynes, quoting Henry James, had so deplored.

What is being revealed here, among other things, is the lack of appropriate cultural definitions for women in our contemporary society. The implications of addressing that lack are at once literary and political: for, in altering the images and narrative structures through which we compose the stories of our lives, we may hope to alter the very experience of those lives as well.[17] By so oddly rearranging and representing the events of her own life, Millett essentially defamiliarized a great deal of quite ordinary experience—in addition to incorporating the previously unacknowledged and the unusual—and thereby opened both to new perception.[18] To discover or invent alternate images through which to express our sense of ourselves is one way out of the broken wing/Mary Marvel syndrome; while to see in a new way what we have not seen before presents at least the possibility of a liberating vision.

In terms of literary history, it is a situation not unlike that of the eighteenth century, the first great age of autobiographical outpourings, when, as James Cox put it, "the modern self was being liberated as well as defined."[19] As more and more women today seek precisely those goals—that is, liberation and self-definition—we may expect even more startling autobiographical narratives to come. Because, as Wayne Shumaker points out, "literature cannot have exploited all the varieties of human experience, [the autobiographer] is likely to explore milieux and vicissitudes concerning which there is no literary tradition."[20] Millett's text, I am certain, is only one of the first to assert the truth of that statement and its unique application to women's narratives in particular.

ABOUT THE AUTHORS

Marcus K. Billson, Assistant Professor of English at the University of Arizona, completed his doctorate in Comparative Literature in Germany on a grant from the Deutscher Akademischer Austauschdienst. His publications include studies on Emily Dickinson, Jean de Joinville, and Albert Speer. He is presently writing a book on the memoir genre.

Regina Blackburn is Assistant Professor of American Studies and Director of Ethnic and Minority Studies at Simpson College (Iowa). She is a locator for Iowa and Minnesota in the project Contributions of Black Women to America: 1776–1977 and midwestern representative for the Association of Black Female Historians.

Lynn Z. Bloom, Associate Professor of English at the College of William and Mary, is the author of *Doctor Spock: Biography of a Conservative Radical* (1972), co-author (with M. L. Briscoe) of *A Bibliography of American Autobiography 1945–80* (forthcoming), and editor of *Natalie Crouter: A Diary of Internment* (1979). She has also published numerous articles on biography, autobiography, and composition.

James E. Breslin is Professor of English at the University of California, Berkeley. He is the author of *William Carlos Williams: An American Artist*. His essays have appeared in *PMLA*, *Journal of Modern Literature*, *The Georgia Review*, and *The Iowa Review*. He is now completing a book on contemporary American poetry.

Stephanie A. Demetrakopoulos is Associate Professor of English at Western Michigan University. She has published extensively in seventeenth-century literature and the area of feminine archetypes. Presently, she is working on two books: one on the figure of Eve in Milton's work, the other on images of older women.

Carol Edkins is a former graduate student in American literature and women's studies in the English department at the University of Texas at Austin. She currently resides in Austin, Texas.

Orlee Holder is Assistant Professor at Northeast Missouri State University, where she teaches a Women and Writing course and a variety of literature and composition classes. Although her special interest is Anaïs Nin's fiction, she has also participated in panels on feminist pedagogy and on issues in contemporary American literature.

Estelle Cohen Jelinek obtained her doctorate from the State University of New York at Buffalo. She has published a number of articles in the areas of American literature, women's literature, and autobiography in such journals as *College English* and *Off Our Backs*. She is now writing a book on the tradition of women's autobiography.

Suzanne Juhasz is Assistant Professor of English at the University of Colorado, Boulder. Her books of criticism are *Naked and Fiery Forms: Modern American Poetry by Women, a New Tradition* and *Metaphor and the Poetry of Williams, Pound, and Stevens.* Her poetry and fiction appear in anthologies and journals.

Annette Kolodny has published extensively in the fields of feminist literary criticism and early American literature and culture. *The Lay of the Land,* a feminist psychohistorical analysis of American pastoral, will be followed by *Westering Women: Pioneers on the New World Languagescape,* being completed under grants from the Rockefeller and Guggenheim foundations.

Mitzi Myers received her degree from Rice University and has taught at several universities in California. She is especially interested in women novelists and autobiographers of the eighteenth and nineteenth centuries and has published essays on William Godwin, Wollstonecraft, Martineau, and Mary McCarthy.

Cynthia S. Pomerleau received her Ph.D. in English literature from the University of Pennsylvania in 1974. Since then, she has worked as a free-lance writer and researcher and as director/editor of an oral history project on women physicians at the Medical College of Pennsylvania.

Sidonie A. Smith, Associate Professor of English at the University of Arizona, teaches courses in Images of Women and Women Authors. Her publications include a book on Afro-American autobiography and articles on Fanny Burney, Jean Rhys, and feminist utopian fiction.

Patricia Meyer Spacks, Professor of English at Yale University, is the author of *Imagining a Self,* a study of eighteenth-century English autobiographies and novels, and of *The Female Imagination.* She is currently writing a book on the social mythology of adolescence.

Elizabeth Winston received her B.A. from Vanderbilt University and her M.A. and Ph.D. from the University of Wisconsin, Madison. She taught at State University College, Fredonia, N.Y., and Mary Washington College, Fredericksburg, Va., before joining the faculty at Pennsylvania State University in Middletown in 1978.

NOTES

1. Introduction

1. Edgar Johnson, *One Mighty Torrent: The Drama of Biography* (New York: Stackpole Sons, 1937), p. 27. Others in this tradition include Donald A. Stauffer's *English Biography Before 1700* (Cambridge: Harvard University Press, 1930), Edward H. O'Neill's *History of American Biography, 1800–1935* (Philadelphia: University of Pennsylvania Press, 1935), Arthur Melville Clark's *Autobiography: Its Genesis and Phases* (Edinburgh: Folcroft Press, 1935), and E. Stuart Bates's *Inside Out: An Introduction to Autobiography* (New York: Sheridan House, 1937).

2. Stephen Spender, "Confessional Autobiography," *The Making of a Poem* (London: Hamish Hamilton, 1955); Georges Gusdorf, "Conditions et limites de l'autobiographies," in *Formen der Selbstdarstellung*, ed. G. Reichenkron and E. Haase (Berlin: Duncker & Humblot, 1956); Stephen A. Shapiro, "The Dark Continent of Literature: Autobiography," *Comparative Literature Studies*, 5 (Dec. 1968), 421–52; Barrett John Mandel, "The Autobiographers' Art," *Journal of Aesthetics and Art Criticism*, 27 (1968), 215–26; James M. Cox, "Autobiography and America," *Virginia Quarterly Review*, 47 (Spring 1971), 252–77; Francis R. Hart, "Notes for an Anatomy of Modern Autobiography," *New Literary History*, 1 (Spring 1970), 485–511.

3. O. B. Hardison, Jr., *New York Times Book Review*, 29 June 1975.

4. Louise Montague Athearn, *San Francisco Chronicle*, 21 July 1974.

5. Unsigned communication from a reader of this article.

6. William Matthews, *British Autobiographies: An Annotated Bibliography* (Berkeley: University of California Press, 1955), p. viii.

7. Of course, there are exceptions to this tendency. The unremitting success autobiographies by Isadora Duncan (*My Life*, 1927), Margaret Sanger (*Autobiography*, 1938), and Elizabeth Gurley Flynn (*The Rebel Girl*, 1955) immediately come to mind.

8. Ellen Moers, *Literary Women* (New York: Doubleday, 1975), p. 107.

2. The Emergence of Women's Autobiography in England

1. Lucy Hutchinson, "The Life of Mrs. Lucy Hutchinson," in *Memoirs of the Life of Colonel Hutchinson* (London: Henry G. Bohn, 1854), p. 30.

2. Margaret Cavendish, Duchess of Newcastle, "The True Relation of my Birth and Breeding," in *The Life of William Cavendish, Duke of Newcastle*, ed. C. H. Firth (London: George Routledge & Sons Ltd., n.d.), p. 156.

3. Alice Thornton, *The Autobiography of Mrs. Alice Thornton of East Newton, Co. York*, ed. Charles Jackson (Edinburgh: Surtees Society, 1895), p. 98; p. 126.

4. Hutchinson, p. 63.

5. Anne Fanshawe, *Memoirs of Lady Fanshawe* (London: Henry Colburn & Richard Bentley, 1830), p. 46.

6. Mary Penington, *Some Experiences in the Life of Mary Penington*, ed. Norman Penney (London: Headley Bros., 1911), p. 10.

7. Fanshawe, p. 36.

8. Anne Halkett, *The Autobiography of Anne Lady Halkett*, ed. John Gough Nichols (London: Camden Society, 1895), pp. 20–22; Mary Rich, Countess of Warwick, *Some Specialities in the Life of M. Warwicke*, ed. T. C. Croker (London: Percy Society, 1848, vol. 22), p. 19; Fanshawe, pp. 98–99.

9. Cavendish, p. 162.

10. Rich, p. 4; Thornton, p. 75.

11. Rich, p. 11.

12. Thomas Raymond, *Autobiography*, in *The Autobiography of Thomas Raymond and Memoirs of the Family of Guise of Elmore, Gloucestershire*, ed. G. Davies (London: Camden Society, 1917), p. 31; pp. 44–45.

13. Edward Hyde, *The Life of Edward Earl of Clarendon* (Oxford: University Press, 1857), I, 15.

14. John Bramston, *The Autobiography of Sir John Bramston, K. B., of Skreens, in the Hundred of Chelmsford* (London: Camden Society, 1845), p. 103.

15. John Reresby, *The Travels and Memoirs of Sir John Reresby, Bart.* (London: B. McMillan, 1813), p. 168.

16. Joan Vokins, *God's Mighty Power Magnified* (London: Northcott, 1691), pp. 18–19.

17. Teresia Constantia Phillips, *An Apology for the Conduct of Mrs. T. C. Phillips* (London: G. Smith, 1761), III, 49–50.

18. Edward Gibbon, *Gibbon's Autobiography*, ed. M. M. Reese (London: Routledge & Kegan Paul, 1970), p. 55.

19. Samuel Richardson, *The Works of Samuel Richardson*, ed. E. Mangin (London, 1811), VII, 313.

20. George Anne Bellamy, *An Apology for the Life of George Anne Bellamy, Late of Covent-Garden Theatre. Written by Herself* (London: J. Bell, 1785), I, 59.

21. Ibid., IV, 118.

22. Delariviere Manley, *The History of Rivella*, in *The Novels of Mary Delariviere Manley*, ed. Patricia Köster (Gainesville, Florida: Scholars Facsimiles and Reprints, 1971; facsimile reproduction of the 1714 edition), p. 748.

23. Catherine Yeo Jemmat, *The Memoirs of Mrs. Catherine Jemmat, Daughter Of the late Admiral YEO of Plymouth. Written by Herself* (London, 1771), I, 124–26.

24. Jonathan Swift, "Letter to a Very Young Lady on her Marriage," *The Prose Works of Jonathan Swift*, ed. Herbert Davis (Oxford: Shakespeare Head Press, 1948), IX, 88.

25. Jemmat, II, 56.

26. Bellamy, I, 192.

27. Ibid., II, 203.

28. Fanny Burney's diary, quoted in Donald A. Stauffer, *The Art of Biography in Eighteenth-Century England* (Princeton: Princeton University Press, 1941), p. 128.

3. Quest for Community

1. Kenneth H. Baldwin and David K. Kirby, eds., *Individual and Community: Variations on a Theme in American Fiction* (Durham, N.C.: Duke University Press, 1975), p. viii.

2. This is especially true for the Quakers since the Quaker community only really began to establish itself in America during the eighteenth century.

3. See the bibliography in Anna Robeson Burr's *Religious Confessions and Confessants* (Boston: Houghton Mifflin, 1914), although Burr does not distinguish between American and British Quaker autobiographers. Luella Wright's bibliography (see below) is almost exclusively devoted to British Quakers.

4. Lyle Koehler, "The Case of the American Jezebels: Anne Hutchinson and Female

Agitation During Years of Antinomian Turmoil, 1636–1640," *William and Mary Quarterly*, 31, no. 1 (Jan. 1974), 58.

5. See Charles Evans, *American Bibliography*, 12 vols. (Chicago and Worcester: Blakely Press, 1904).

6. Nathaniel Hawthorne in *The Scarlet Letter* gives this function to the aged Hester Prynne.

7. Koehler, "American Jezebels," 59.

8. See Daniel B. Shea, Jr., *Spiritual Autobiography in Early America* (Princeton: Princeton University Press, 1968).

9. Ibid., p. 100.

10. See Edmund S. Morgan, *Visible Saints: The History of a Puritan Idea* (New York: New York University Press, 1963), pp. 66–73, for a complete description of the conversion process. The quote is from p. 68.

11. Elizabeth White, *The Experiences of God's Gracious Dealings with Mrs. Elizabeth White* (Boston: S. Kneeland and T., 1741), p. 1. All further quotations are parenthetically cited.

12. Elizabeth Mixer, *An Account of Some Spiritual Experiences of Elizabeth Mixer* (New London, Conn.: Green, 1736), p. 3.

13. Alan Simpson, *Puritanism in Old and New England* (Chicago: University of Chicago Press, 1955), p. 24.

14. Luella Wright, *The Literary Life of the Early Friends* (New York: Columbia University Press, 1932), p. 199.

15. Ibid., p. 201.

16. Jane Fenn Hoskens, *The Life and Spiritual Sufferings of That Faithful Servant of Christ* (Philadelphia: Evitt, 1771), p. 3. All further quotations are parenthetically cited.

17. Elizabeth Ashbridge, *Some Account of the Life of Elizabeth Ashbridge* (Philadelphia: Friends' Book Store, n.d.), p. 10. All further quotations are parenthetically cited. See Shea for a brief history of this manuscript, p. 30n.

18. Shea, p. 250.

19. Ibid., p. 15.

20. Wright, p. 155.

21. Mrs. Chloe Willey, *A Short Account of the Life of Mrs. Chloe Willey* (Amherst, N.H.: Cushing, 1807), p. 5.

22. Catherine Phillips, *Memoirs of the Life of Catherine Phillips* (Philadelphia: Budd and Bartram for Johnson, 1798), p. 74.

23. Simpson, p. 44.

4. *Harriet Martineau's Autobiography*

1. *Harriet Martineau's Autobiography*, ed. Maria Weston Chapman, 2 vols. (Boston: James R. Osgood, 1877). Volume 2 includes both the last section of the *Autobiography* and the *Memorials*, which consist of various personal material from the whole life span, including the twenty-one years between completion of the *Autobiography* and Martineau's death. Page references incorporated in the text refer to this edition and differentiate between the *Autobiography* proper and autobiographical matter from the *Memorials*.

2. Martineau's symptoms were actually due to a massive cyst—ten by twelve inches and ovarian in origin—which was displacing internal organs. Theodora Bosanquet, *Harriet Martineau: An Essay in Comprehension* (London: Frederick Etchells & Hugh Macdonald, 1927), pp. 245–49, cites and discusses the relevant medical reports.

3. Richard Garnett, *The Life of W. J. Fox* (London: John Lane, 1910), p. 82. Garnett summarizes the contents of many revealing early letters, now destroyed.

4. "Doddridge's Correspondence and Diary," *Miscellanies*, 2 vols. (Boston: Hilliard, Gray, 1836), II, 343–75. The most important of Martineau's early essays are reprinted in these two volumes.

5. "Emancipation of Woman," in *Ideas and Beliefs of the Victorians: An Historic Revaluation of the Victorian Age* (1949; rpt. New York: E. P. Dutton, 1966), p. 255. For such a supposedly "objective" writer, Martineau made adept use of personal experience throughout her career. "On most subjects, the best we have to tell is our own experience," she says in *Household Education* (London: Edward Moxon, 1849), p. 59.

6. *Society in America* (London: Saunders and Otley, 1837; rpt. New York: AMS Press, 1966), III, 174.

7. Eliot to Mrs. Charles Bray, 20 March 1877, *The George Eliot Letters*, ed. Gordon S. Haight (New Haven: Yale University Press, 1955), VI, 354.

8. *Society in America*, III, 169.

9. *Life in the Sick-Room: Essays by an Invalid*, 3rd ed. (1844; rpt. London: Edward Moxon, 1849), pp. 168–69.

10. See Priscilla Robertson, "Home as a Nest: Middle-Class Childhood in Nineteenth-Century Europe," in *The History of Childhood*, ed. Lloyd deMause (1974; rpt. New York: Harper & Row, 1975), pp. 407–31, for similar accounts of the conditions of childhood; I have discussed Martineau's relations with her mother and their subsequent influence more fully in "Unmothered Daughter and Radical Reformer: Reconstructing Some Interconnections in Harriet Martineau's Career," in *The Last Tradition: Mothers and Daughters in Literature*, ed. Cathy N. Davidson and E. M. Broner (New York: Frederick Ungar, 1979).

11. Quoted in R. K. Webb, *Harriet Martineau: A Radical Victorian* (New York: Columbia University Press, 1960), pp. 206–07.

12. [W. J. Fox], "Poor Laws and Paupers," *Monthly Repository*, n.s. 7 (June 1833), 377.

13. Stephen A. Shapiro, "The Dark Continent of Literature: Autobiography," *Comparative Literature Studies*, 5 (1968), 422.

14. "Essays on the Art of Thinking," *Miscellanies*, I, 57–121. Early and late examples of Martineau's concern with necessity are "Essays on the Pursuit of Truth," *Miscellanies*, II, 174–96; Henry George Atkinson and Harriet Martineau, *Letters on the Laws of Man's Nature and Development* (London: John Chapman, 1851), pp. 100, 125, 194, 291. George Levine, "Determinism and Responsibility in the Works of George Eliot," *PMLA*, 77 (June 1962), 268–79, is a good analysis of necessity and its implications.

15. *Household Education*, p. 262. "Of good influences," she says, "the most powerful and continuous is the presence in the mind of a lofty ideal," p. 260.

16. "Female Writers on Practical Divinity, No. I, Mrs. More," *Monthly Repository*, 17 (October 1822), 593–96; "Female Writers on Practical Divinity, No. II, Mrs. More and Mrs. Barbauld," *Monthly Repository*, 17 (December 1822), 746–50; "Female Education," *Monthly Repository*, 18 (February 1823), 77–81. She used the masculine pseudonym "Discipulus."

17. Thomas Carlyle to Ralph Waldo Emerson, 1 June 1837, *Correspondence of Thomas Carlyle and Ralph Waldo Emerson*, ed. C. E. Norton (Boston, 1883), I, 126, quoted in Francis E. Mineka, *The Dissidence of Dissent: The Monthly Repository, 1806–1838* (Chapel Hill: University of North Carolina Press, 1944), pp. 234–35.

18. Quoted in Webb, p. 204.

19. *Eastern Life, Present and Past* (1848; rpt. Boston: Roberts Brothers, 1876), p. 407.

20. On the fictional ordering of confessional autobiography, see Northrop Frye,

Anatomy of Criticism: Four Essays (Princeton: Princeton University Press, 1957), p. 307. Martineau's philosophical confessions may be usefully compared with those discussed in Kathleen Dehler, "The Need to Tell All: A Comparison of Historical and Modern Feminist 'Confessional' Writing," in *Feminist Criticism: Essays on Theory, Poetry and Prose*, ed. Cheryl L. Brown and Karen Olson (Metuchen, N.J. and London: Scarecrow Press, 1978), pp. 339–52.

5. The Paradox and Success of Elizabeth Cady Stanton

1. *Eighty Years and More: Reminiscences, 1815–1897* (New York: Schocken Books, 1971), p. 8. Subsequent page references, given in the text, are from this edition.
2. *Notable American Women, 1607–1950*, ed. Edward T. James et al. (Cambridge: Harvard University Press, 1971).
3. Ellen DuBois (*Feminism and Suffrage*, Cornell University Press, 1978), an authority on Stanton, notes that nothing among Stanton's papers indicates her feelings about her mother.
4. Catharine Stimpson, "'Thy Neighbor's Wife, Thy Neighbor's Servants': Women's Liberation and Black Civil Rights," in *Woman in Sexist Society*, ed. Vivian Gornick and Barbara K. Moran (New York: Basic Books, 1971), p. 625.
5. *Notable American Women.*

6. The Autobiographer and Her Readers

1. Patricia Meyer Spacks, *The Female Imagination* (New York: Knopf, 1975), p. 194.
2. *Lady Morgan's Memoirs*, ed. W. H. Dixon, 3 vols. (London: William H. Allen, 1862), I, 230.
3. Perhaps Lady Morgan rejected motherhood partly because she had seen its negative effect on her younger sister Olivia. Olivia married four years before Lady Morgan and immediately began producing babies—too many of them in Lady Morgan's view. Olivia was "all over morbid maternity." Lady Morgan's husband, Sir Charles, playfully advised Olivia to read "three thick volumes of Malthus on Population." See Lady Morgan, *Passages from My Autobiography* (London: Richard Bentley, 1859), pp. 60, 92–93, 102–03.
4. Ibid., p. 318.
5. J. M. S. Tompkins writes that by the end of the eighteenth century, a host of young women in England had been forced by poverty to "market" their literary talents. They wrote mainly epistolary domestic novels—sentimental, didactic, occasionally satirical. See *The Popular Novel in England, 1770–1800* (1961; rpt. Westport, Conn.: Greenwood Press, 1976). For the situation in the United States, see Helen Waite Papashvily, *All the Happy Endings* (New York: Harper Brothers, 1956).
6. Ann Douglas Wood, "The 'Scribbling Women' and Fanny Fern: Why Women Wrote," *American Quarterly*, 23 (Spring 1971), 3–24. George Eliot deplored a similar lack of professional commitment and aesthetic integrity among "lady novelists" in England. See "Silly Novels by Lady Novelists," *Westminster Review*, 46 (October 1856), 442–61, reprinted in *Essays*, ed. Thomas Pinney (London: Routledge & Kegan Paul, 1968), pp. 300–24.
7. Mrs. Humphry Ward, *A Writer's Recollections* (New York and London: Harper Brothers, 1918), I, 216. See also I, 202, where Ward asks permission to repeat a compliment she received for her work for the *Dictionary of Christian Biography*, and II, 18–19, for her response to Henry James's assessment of her first novel.
8. Harriet Martineau, *Autobiography*, 3 vols. (London: Smith, Elder, 1877), I, 101. Subsequent references appear in the text.

9. Ellen Moers, *Literary Women* (Garden City, N.Y.: Doubleday, 1977), p. 47. See pp. 32–62 for a discussion of "women's literature of social action."

10. Charlotte Perkins Gilman, *The Living of Charlotte Perkins Gilman* (New York: Harper and Row, 1975), p. 311. Subsequent references appear in the text.

11. Spacks, pp. 213–14.

12. Elizabeth Haldane, *From One Century to Another* (London: Alexander Maclehose, 1937), p. vi. Subsequent references appear in the text.

13. Women in Britain did not gain full national suffrage until 1919. For a discussion of the strictures on women before that time, see Eugene A. Hecker, *A Short History of Women's Rights* (1914; rpt. Westport, Conn.: Greenwood Press, 1971), pp. 146–47.

14. Ella R. Christie, "Haldane, Elizabeth Sanderson," *DNB: 1931–1949* (1940).

15. Edith Wharton, *A Backward Glance* (New York and London: Appleton, 1934), pp. 293–94. Subsequent references appear in the text.

16. Ellen Glasgow, *The Woman Within* (New York: Harcourt Brace, 1954), p. v. Subsequent references appear in the text.

17. Edna Ferber, *A Peculiar Treasure* (1938; rpt. Garden City, N.Y.: Doubleday, 1960), p. 21. Subsequent references to *APT* appear in the text.

18. The Elsie Dinsmore books by Martha Farquharson Finley (1828–1909) were published between 1867 and 1905. For examples of Ferber's ironic references to Dinsmore, see *APT*, p. 157, and *A Kind of Magic* (Garden City, N.Y.: Doubleday, 1963), p. 110.

19. Harriet Monroe, *A Poet's Life* (New York: Macmillan, 1938), p. 249.

20. Mary Austin, *Earth Horizon* (New York: Literary Guild, 1932), p. 217. Austin is known for her evocation of the Southwest and of American Indian culture. Probably her most famous books are *The Land of Little Rain* (1903) and *The Land of Journey's Ending* (1924).

21. In a letter recommending the traditional female careers of marriage and maternity, Stein's sister-in-law, Sally, refers to Leo's dissenting view on the matter. See James R. Mellow, *The Charmed Circle: Gertrude Stein & Company* (New York: Praeger, 1974), p. 39.

22. Gertrude Stein, *Everybody's Autobiography* (1937; rpt. New York: Random House, 1973), p. 114. Subsequent references appear in the text.

23. Edith Sitwell, *Taken Care Of* (New York: Atheneum, 1965), p. 20. Subsequent references appear in the text.

Evelyn T. Beck, Estelle C. Jelinek, and Kevin Sweeney have helped me greatly in clarifying my ideas on women's autobiographies. I wish to thank them for their criticism and advice.

7. Selves in Hiding

1. Hannah Arendt, *The Human Condition* (New York: Doubleday, 1959), p. 68.

2. *The Autobiography of Eleanor Roosevelt* (New York: Harper and Brothers, n.d. [1958?]), p. 60. Subsequent references are incorporated in the text.

3. Dorothy Day, *The Long Loneliness* (New York: Harper and Brothers, 1932), p. 25. Subsequent references are incorporated in the text.

4. Golda Meir, *My Life* (New York: G. P. Putnam's Sons, 1975), p. 98. Subsequent references are incorporated in the text.

5. Emma Goldman, *Living My Life*, 2 vols. (New York: Alfred A. Knopf, 1931), I, 10. Subsequent references are incorporated in the text.

6. Emmeline Pankhurst, *My Own Story* (London: Eveleigh Nash, 1914), p. 26. Subsequent references are incorporated in the text.

7. Barbara Hardy, "An Approach Through Narrative," *Towards a Poetics of Fiction*, ed. Mark Spilka (Bloomington: Indiana University Press, 1977), p. 31.

8. *In/Sights*, compiled by Joyce Tenneson Cohen (Boston: David R. Godine, 1978).

8. In Search of the Black Female Self

1. Stephen Butterfield, *Black Autobiography in America* (Amherst: University of Massachusetts Press, 1974), pp. 2–3.

2. All quotations from the autobiographies are taken from the following editions: Ossie Guffy, *Ossie: The Autobiography of a Black Woman* (New York: Norton, 1971); Delle Brehan, *Kicks Is Kicks* (Los Angeles: Holloway, 1970); Zora Neale Hurston, *Dust Tracks on a Road* (Philadelphia: J. B. Lippincott, 1970); Pearl Bailey, *The Raw Pearl* (New York: Pocket Books, 1978); Nikki Giovanni, *Gemini: An Extended Autobiographical Statement of My First Twenty-Five Years of Being a Black Poet* (New York: Penguin Books, 1971); Gwendolyn Brooks, *Report from Part One* (Detroit: Broadside Press, 1972); Lorraine Hansberry, *To Be Young, Gifted, and Black* (New York: Signet Books, 1971); Helen Jackson Lee, *Nigger in the Window* (Garden City, N.Y.: Doubleday, 1978); Maya Angelou, *I Know Why the Caged Bird Sings* (New York: Bantam Books, 1969); Anne Moody, *Coming of Age in Mississippi* (New York: Dial Press, 1968); Angela Davis, *Angela Davis: An Autobiography—With My Mind on Freedom* (New York: Random House, 1974); Shirley Chisholm, *Unbought and Unbossed* (Boston: Houghton Mifflin, 1970).

3. Butterfield, p. 1.

4. Ibid., p. 6.

5. Marvin D. Wyne, Kinnard P. White, and Richard H. Coop, *The Black Self* (Englewood Cliffs, N.J.: Prentice-Hall, 1974), p. 52.

6. Ibid., p. 7.

7. From W. Somerset Maugham's *The Razor's Edge*; quoted in Wyne et al., p. 30.

8. Imamu Amiri Baraka (Leroi Jones), "An Agony. As now," in *The Black Poets*, ed. Dudley Randall (New York: Bantam Books, 1971), p. 211.

9. William Grier and Price Cobb, in *Black Rage* (New York: Basic Books, 1968), devote an entire chapter to black womanhood. The quote is from p. 41.

9. Gertrude Stein and the Problems of Autobiography

1. Richard Bridgman, *Gertrude Stein in Pieces* (New York: Oxford University Press, 1970), pp. 209–37.

2. B. L. Reid, *Art by Subtraction* (Norman: University of Oklahoma, 1958), p. 186.

3. *Everybody's Autobiography* (New York: Random House, 1973), p. 303. Subsequent references are made in the text to *EA*.

4. "What Are Master-pieces and Why Are There So Few of Them," in *Writings and Lectures, 1909–1945*, ed. Patricia Meyerowitz (Baltimore: Penguin, 1967), p. 152. Subsequent references are made in the text.

5. *The Autobiography of Alice B. Toklas* (New York: Vintage, 1960), p. 251. Subsequent references are made in the text.

6. *Gertrude Stein in Pieces*, pp. 209–17.

7. Ibid., pp. 213–17.

8. *Narration* (Chicago: University of Chicago Press, 1935), p. 19.

10. Lillian Hellman and the Strategy of the "Other"

1. Roy Pascal, *Design and Truth in Autobiography* (London: Routledge & Kegan Paul, 1960), pp. 5–6; and Robert F. Sayre, *The Examined Self: Benjamin Franklin, Henry Adams, Henry James* (Princeton: Princeton University Press, 1964), p. 7.

2. Although this terminology is borrowed from Sigmund Freud's *Interpretation of*

Dreams, it would be misleading to designate our methodology in this study as psychoanalytical. Nevertheless, as will become apparent to our reader, we have been influenced by the English version of Jacques Lacan's *Ecrits: A Selection*, tr. Allan Sheridan (New York: W. W. Norton, 1977). Freud and Lacan have repeatedly observed that the "self" only becomes a meaningful and therefore viable concept when viewed through the provision of the "other." Our reading of Hellman is based on the implications of this observation as we see them from time to time in her work.

3. That Hellman deliberately attempted to avoid concentrating on herself much of the time in her memoirs was stated very precisely to an interviewer from *Rolling Stone*: "Well, I don't always like writing about myself or talking about myself. . . . I don't ordinarily talk about myself very much. That's why I try to write memoirs without being a central part of them." Christine Doudna, "A Conversation with Lillian Hellman," *Rolling Stone*, 24 February 1977, p. 55.

4. Lillian Hellman, *An Unfinished Woman: A Memoir* (New York: Bantam, 1969), p. 7. All future references to this edition are cited as *UW* in the body of the text. Both in the case of this work and *Pentimento*, we have chosen to employ the paperback editions because of their ready accessibility.

5. Hellman opts for the drama as the medium best suited for her art despite her explicit comments about her inability to feel at home in the theater (*UW*, p. 63), because the drama is informed by the objectifying process so natural to Hellman's creative temperament. The word of the playwright becomes the voice of the actor on stage. The characters in a play become "others," outside the author and audience, people to watch, interpret, enjoy, learn from. Yet they are also clear mirrors in which to observe the reflection of the self. A character's ability to reveal its mirroring function is dependent on the play of identity and difference (that is, in other words, the audience's empathy) we see structuring Hellman's strategy of the "other" in her memoirs.

6. Friedrich Nietzsche writes in "The Birth of Tragedy," *The Birth of Tragedy and the Genealogy of Morals*, tr. Francis Golfing (Garden City, N.Y.: Doubleday, 1956), p. 50, "The metaphysical solace (with which, I wish to say at once, all true tragedy sends us away) [is] that, despite every phenomenal change, life is at bottom indestructibly joyful and powerful. . . ."

7. Lillian Hellman, *Pentimento: A Book of Portraits* (New York: New American Library, 1974), p. 1. All future references are cited as *P* in the body of the text.

8. Our discussion of the "Bethe" chapter illustrates very clearly the process of Hellman's narrative strategy present in all the portraits. Space limitations dictate the exploration of only this one portrait.

11. The Metaphysics of Matrilinearism in Women's Autobiography

1. C. G. Jung and C. Kerényi, *Essays on a Science of Mythology: The Myth of the Divine Child and the Mysteries of Eleusis* (Princeton: Princeton University Press, 1949), p. 162. See also C. Kerényi, *Eleusis: Archetypal Image of Mother and Daughter* (New York: Schocken Books, 1967).

2. Albert E. Stone, "Autobiography and American Culture," *American Studies: An International Newsletter*, 12 (Winter 1972), 26.

3. Stephen A. Shapiro, "The Dark Continent of Literature: Autobiography," *Comparative Literature Studies*, 5 (1968), 447–48.

4. Ibid., 436.

5. Stone, 25.

6. The best treatment of the difference between male and female gender consciousness is by Nancy Chodorow, "Family Structure and Feminine Personality," in *Woman*,

Culture and Society, ed. Michelle Zimbalist Rosaldo and Louise Lamphere (Stanford: Stanford University Press, 1974), pp. 43–67.

7. Joseph E. Illick, "John Quincy Adams: The Maternal Influence," *Journal of Childhood and Psychohistory*, 4 (Fall 1969), 185–97.

8. James M. Cox, "Autobiography and America," *Virginia Quarterly Review*, 47 (Spring 1971), 169.

9. I have already treated at length the matriarchate in Anaïs Nin's journals: "Archetypal Constellations of Feminine Consciousness in Nin's First Diary," *Mosaic*, 11 (Fall 1978), 121–37; and "Anaïs Nin and the Feminine Quest for Consciousness: The Quelling of the Devouring Mother and the Ascension of the Sophia," in a forthcoming anthology published by *Bucknell Review*, ed. Harry Garvin.

10. All references to the four autobiographies analyzed herein will appear within the text; it is self-evident which text is referred to. I use Margaret Mead, *Blackberry Winter* (New York: William Morrow, 1972); Lillian Hellman, *Pentimento* (New York: New American Library, 1973); Maya Angelou, *I Know Why the Caged Bird Sings* (New York: Bantam, 1973); Maxine Hong Kingston, *The Woman Warrior* (New York: Vintage, 1977). I also refer to Lillian Hellman, *An Unfinished Woman* (New York: Bantam, 1969).

11. Mead's grandmother, Angelou's grandmother, and the black women in Hellman's works all embody the Primordial Goddess in her Positive Elementary Character as developed in Erich Neumann's *The Great Mother*, trans. Ralph Manheim (Princeton: Princeton University Press, 1963). In this archetype he says that "the symbolism of the rounded vessel predominates" (p. 95), the gigantic torso represents the "sheltering, protecting, and nourishing elementary character" (p. 96), and that her "very unwieldiness and bulk" give her a "sedentary" character that contributes to her "enthroned" centrality (p. 99). Some of the statuettes of this goddess are a "human form of the maternally receptive chair" (p. 100). He also says that we are justified in applying the term "sensuous" to this archetype because of its "corporeity, the exuberant fullness and massive warmth, that emanate from such a figure" (p. 105).

12. C. G. Jung, "Approaching the Unconscious," *Man and His Symbols*, ed. Carl G. Jung (New York: Dell, 1964), p. 67.

13. See Neumann's chapter on the Lady of the Plants in *The Great Mother*, pp. 240–68.

14. Helpful here is Erich Neumann's *Amor and Psyche: The Psychic Development of the Feminine*, trans. Ralph Manheim (Princeton: Princeton University Press, 1956).

15. Neumann best describes this archetype in *The Great Mother*, devoting a full chapter to it as the highest embodiment of feminine consciousness. Here are two helpful quotations from his description: "The spiritual power of Sophia is living and saving; her overflowing heart is wisdom and food at once. The nourishing life that she communicates is a life of the spirit and of transformation, not one of earthbound materiality" (p. 331). "Sophia, who achieves her supreme visible form as a flower, does not vanish in the nirvanalike abstraction of masculine spirit; like the scent of a blossom, her spirit always remains attached to the earthly foundation of reality" (p. 325).

As shown in my article on Nin for *Bucknell Review*, this "feminine" way of relating to metaphysical reality is being fully developed and introduced into traditional Christianity by the new school of Process Theology, a sort of underground theology that is attempting to establish and define the sacrality of process, relatedness, and the limited powers of godhead.

16. I treat this image more fully in my "Iconography of Heroic Womanhood: An Interdisciplinary Illustration of the Great Mother and Sophia Archetypes in Renaissance Art and Drama," *Anima*, 4 (Fall 1977), 1–17.

17. Francis R. Hart views this as essential to creating an autobiography that is truly

a wrought, organic work of art in "Notes for an Anatomy of Modern Autobiography," *New Literary History*, 1 (Spring 1970), 485–511.

18. A good explication of the Greek goddesses as different embodiments of the feminine principle is by Philip T. Zabriskie, "Goddesses in Our Midst," *Quadrant*, 17 (Fall 1974), 34–46.

19. This is at first like a psychic rape of the matriarchate, but later she can join in this violent rejection of it too. The father becomes here a Pluto figure, inflicting depression on the Kore/daughter. For a splendid explication of this image, see Patricia Berry, "The Rape of Demeter/Persephone and Neurosis," *Spring*, 1975, pp. 186–98.

20. She projects all negative effects of this betrayal onto Bailey, a literary trick that does not behoove autobiography. It does not even work in a fictional piece; for example, Sylvia Plath projects the death urge of Esther onto Joan in *The Bell Jar* and attempts to validate this by her constant allusions to the theme of doubles. But Esther's insanity/death wish is her own and must be personally worked through—and Angelou's betrayal by her mother cannot be paid off by the destruction of the brother. Angelou seems lacking in self-awareness in that she experiences no anger or hatred toward her mother (and not much toward her father); her mother seems fixated in what James Hillman calls the "unconscious brutality" of the betrayer who never admits her sins; see his "Betrayal," *Loose Ends: Primary Papers in Archetypal Psychology* (Zurich: Spring Publications, 1975), pp. 63–82.

21. See especially June Singer, *Androgyny* (New York: Anchor Press, 1976), pp. 20–21.

22. Jung, *Essays on a Science of Mythology*, pp. 162–63.

23. Kerényi, *Eleusis*, p. 15.

12. Anaïs Nin's *Diary* in Context

1. James Olney, *Metaphors of Self: The Meaning of Autobiography* (Princeton: Princeton University Press, 1972), Chapter 1.

2. *Autobiographical Acts: The Changing Situation of a Literary Genre* (Baltimore: Johns Hopkins University Press, 1976), pp. 10–11.

3. Autobiographies "derive their value from rendering significant portions of the past as *interpreted past. . . .*" See Karl Weintraub, "Autobiography and Historical Consciousness," *Critical Inquiry*, 1 (June 1975), 827; emphasis ours.

4. *English Autobiography: Its Emergence, Materials, and Form* (Berkeley: University of California Press, 1954), p. 103.

5. Suzanne Juhasz, "'Some Deep Old Desk or Capacious Hold-All': Form and Women's Autobiography"; Estelle C. Jelinek, "Discontinuity and Order: A Comparison of Women's and Men's Autobiographies": papers read at the "Feminist Biography and Autobiography" seminar at the Modern Language Association meeting, 1976.

6. Weintraub, 827.

7. *A Writer's Diary: Being Extracts from the Diary of Virginia Woolf*, ed. Leonard Woolf (New York: Harcourt Brace Jovanovich, 1954), p. 13.

8. De Beauvoir, *Force of Circumstance*, trans. Richard Howard (New York: Putnam, 1965); *Memoirs of a Dutiful Daughter*, trans. James Kirkup (1959; rpt. New York: Harper & Row, 1963); *The Prime of Life*, trans. Peter Green (New York: Harper & Row, 1962). Calisher, *Herself* (1972; New York: Dell, 1974). Carrighar, *Home to the Wilderness* (1973; rpt. Baltimore: Penguin, 1974). Colette, *Earthly Paradise: An Autobiography*, "drawn from her lifetime writings" by Robert Phelps (New York: Farrar, Straus & Giroux, 1966). Hellman, *Pentimento: A Book of Portraits* (1973; rpt. New York: Signet, 1974); *An Unfinished Woman: A Memoir* (1969; rpt. New York: Bantam, 1970). McCarthy, *Memories of a Catholic Girlhood* (New York: Harcourt Brace Jovanovich, 1957). Stein, *The Auto-*

biography of Alice B. Toklas (1933; rpt. New York: Vintage, 1960); *Everybody's Autobiography* (New York: Vintage, 1937); *Wars I Have Seen* (New York: Random House, 1945). Woolf, see n. 7. Henceforth references to these works are identified within the text: by the name of the author, where a single work is in question, and by an abbreviated title, where two or more works by an author are involved.

9. A somewhat different set of autobiographies from those Jelinek analyzes might dispute her contention that women "hold their mother in high regard and affection" and view their father as an impersonal authority figure.

10. Frank Baldanza, "Anaïs Nin," *Minnesota Review*, 2 (1961–62), 269.

11. Ibid., 266.

12. Jean Garrigue, "The Self Behind the Selves: The Diary of Anaïs Nin, 1931–34," *New York Times Book Review*, 24 April 1966, p. 1.

13. See *Ms.*, 3 (July 1974), 7.

14. Jane Larkin Crain, "Feminist Fiction," *Commentary*, 58 (Dec. 1974), 58–62.

13. Towards a Theory of Form in Feminist Autobiography

1. Virginia Woolf, "A Sketch of the Past," *Moments of Being*, ed. Jeanne Schulkind (New York: Harcourt Brace Jovanovich, 1976), p. 65.

2. Karl Weintraub, "Autobiography and Historical Consciousness," *Critical Inquiry*, 1, no. 4 (June 1975), 827.

3. Wayne Shumaker, *English Autobiography: Its Emergence, Materials, and Form* (Berkeley: University of California Press, 1954), p. 120.

4. David McClelland, "Wanted: A New Self-Image for Women," *The Woman in America*, ed. Robert Jay Lifton (Boston: Beacon Press, 1967), p. 181.

5. Andrea Newman, *The City Lover* (New York: Doubleday, 1969).

6. "Discontinuity and Order: A Comparison of Women's and Men's Autobiography," a paper presented at the Modern Language Association national convention, December 1976 [and substantially expanded as the introduction to this anthology, *Ed.*].

7. For an earlier discussion of the diary as model for women's autobiography, see my essay, "'Some Deep Old Desk or Capacious Hold-All': Form and Women's Autobiography," a paper presented at the Modern Language Association national convention, December 1976.

8. Kate Millett, *Flying* (New York: Ballantine Books, 1974), p. 102.

9. Annette Kolodny, "The Lady's Not for Spurning: Kate Millett and the Critics," *Contemporary Literature*, 18, no. 4 (Autumn 1976), 547, 544 [reprinted in this anthology, *Ed.*]

10. Kate Millett, *Sita* (New York: Farrar, Straus & Giroux, 1977), p. 131.

11. Sara Sandborn, *New York Times Book Review*, 29 May 1977, p. 20.

12. Ibid.

13. Karen Durbin, "The Dangerous Fun of Special Pleading," *The Village Voice*, 30 May 1977, p. 80.

14. Maxine Hong Kingston, *The Woman Warrior* (New York: Alfred A. Knopf, 1976).

15. Patricia Meyer Spacks, *The Female Imagination* (New York: Alfred A. Knopf, 1975).

14. The Lady's Not for Spurning

1. René Kuhn Bryant, "Drowning in Claustrophobia," *National Review*, 30 (Aug. 1974), 990; Muriel Haynes, "Sexual Energy," *New Republic*, 6 and 13 (July 1974), 28; Elinor Langer, "Confessing," *Ms.*, 3 (Dec. 1974), 71.

2. Bryant, 990; Langer, 70; Haynes, 29.

3. Kate Millett, "The Shame Is Over," *Ms.*, 3 (Jan. 1975), 26–29.

4. Kate Millett, *Flying* (New York: Alfred A. Knopf, 1974), p. 433. Subsequent references are to this edition and are indicated parenthetically in the text.

5. Millett, "Shame," 27–28.

6. Haynes, 29.

7. A notable exception to this appears in Wayne Shumaker, *English Autobiography: Its Emergence, Materials, and Form* (Berkeley: University of California Press, 1954), p. 24.

8. William L. Howarth, "Some Principles of Autobiography," *NLH*, 5, no. 2 (Winter 1974), 365.

9. Shumaker, p. 50.

10. Ibid., p. 40.

11. See Robert Scholes, "The Contributions of Formalism and Structuralism to the Theory of Fiction," *Novel*, 6, no. 2 (Winter 1973), 140–41.

12. Shumaker's full statement reads: "Autobiography characteristically opens with the cry of an infant and closes with the chair tilted against a sunny wall" (p. 130).

13. Scholes, 146. Scholes is himself quoting from an earlier essay by Roman Jakobson, "The Dominant," rpt. in Ladislav Matejka and Krystyna Pomorska, eds., *Reading in Russian Poetics: Formalist and Structuralist Views* (Cambridge: M.I.T. Press, 1971), p. 87.

14. Howarth, 365.

15. Millett, "Shame," 28.

16. This is a kind of reading which, under a number of different descriptive labels, several critics have recently espoused. Stanley E. Fish's "affective stylistics," to which I am particularly in debt, is both demonstrated and explained in *Self-Consuming Artifacts* (Berkeley: University of California Press, 1972), esp. pp. 383–427, and in his earlier book, *Surprised by Sin: The Reader in "Paradise Lost"* (New York: St. Martin's Press, 1967). Utilizing an analogy from physics, Jerry H. Bryant describes basically the same process in *The Open Decision: The Contemporary American Novel and Its Intellectual Background* (New York: Free Press, 1970), pp. 20–21. The reading of the text offered here, then, is a selected recapitulation of the history of my own experience of reading *Flying*, and it is intended to demonstrate the special rewards such an approach offers the feminist critic: not only does it help illuminate the unique organizing patterns of image and structure in otherwise inexplicable or undefinable texts, but it also allows for an analysis generally free of the received expectations and inherently sexist preconceptions informing most generic or structuralist studies, based as they are on centuries of exclusively male data.

17. In criticizing "Millett's refusal to analyze the political structure in which the personal events she narrates took place," Langer (70) missed the larger political implications of altering perception through altering the images and narrative structures by which we encode the world.

18. Again, see Scholes's brilliant discussion of defamiliarization, 141.

19. James Cox, "Autobiography and America," in *Aspects of Narrative*, ed. J. Hillis Miller (New York: Columbia University Press, 1971), pp. 147–48.

20. Shumaker, pp. 135–36.